Philosophy of Mind
A Beginner's Guide

T0058405

ONEWORLD BEGINNER'S GUIDES combine an original, inventive, and engaging approach with expert analysis on subjects ranging from art and history to religion and politics, and everything in-between. Innovative and affordable, books in the series are perfect for anyone curious about the way the world works and the big ideas of our time.

aesthetics
africa
american politics
anarchism
ancient philosophy
animal behaviour
anthropology
anti-capitalism
aquinas
archaeology
art
artificial intelligence
the baha'i faith
the beat generation
the bible
biodiversity
bioterror & biowarfare
the brain
british politics
the Buddha
cancer
censorship
christianity
civil liberties
classical music
climate change
cloning
the cold war
conservation
crimes against humanity
criminal psychology
critical thinking
the crusades
daoism
democracy
descartes
dewey
dyslexia
economics
energy
engineering

the english civil wars
the enlightenment
epistemology
ethics
the european union
evolution
evolutionary psychology
existentialism
fair trade
feminism
forensic science
french literature
the french revolution
genetics
global terrorism
hinduism
history
the history of medicine
history of science
homer
humanism
huxley
international relations
iran
islamic philosophy
the islamic veil
jazz
journalism
judaism
justice
lacan
life in the universe
literary theory
machiavelli
mafia & organized crime
magic
marx
medieval philosophy
the middle east
modern slavery
NATO

the new testament
nietzsche
nineteenth-century art
the northern ireland conflict
nutrition
oil
opera
the palestine–israeli conflict
parapsychology
particle physics
paul
philosophy
philosophy of mind
philosophy of religion
philosophy of science
planet earth
postmodernism
psychology
quantum physics
the qur'an
racism
rawls
reductionism
religion
renaissance art
the roman empire
the russian revolution
shakespeare
shi'i islam
the small arms trade
stalin
sufism
the torah
the united nations
the victorians
volcanoes
the world trade organization
war
world war II

Philosophy of Mind

A Beginner's Guide

Edward Feser

ONEWORLD

A Oneworld Book

Published by Oneworld Publications 2005
Reissued 2006
Reprinted 2008, 2010, 2013, 2015, 2018, 2020

ISBN 978–1–85168–478–6
eISBN 978–1–78074–041–6

Typeset by Jayvee, Trivandrum, India
Cover design by Two Associates
Printed and bound in Great Britain by Clays Ltd, Elcograf S.p.A.

Oneworld Publications
10 Bloomsbury Street
London WC1B 3SR
England

MIX
Paper from
responsible sources
FSC
www.fsc.org
FSC® C018072

Contents

Preface and acknowledgments

Can science explain consciousness? Is the mind nothing but the brain? Do you have an immaterial and immortal soul, inaccessible to science and knowable only via metaphysical inquiry? Is there an ultimate and absolute difference between man and machine? Can computers think? Could there be conscious robots? These are some of the questions we will be dealing with in this book. They are among the central issues in the philosophy of mind, a field that has in recent years become perhaps the most active of the various sub-disciplines within philosophy.

It is difficult to say anything in philosophy without saying everything. Philosophical issues and arguments are so deep and complex that when you begin to examine any one of them, you will soon find that it is near impossible to come to a settled conclusion without also examining many others. This is perhaps even truer of the philosophy of mind than it is of other branches of philosophy: to inquire into the nature of the mind and its relationship to the body is to set out on a course of study that leads almost immediately to general questions in metaphysics and epistemology, and eventually even to topics in the philosophy of language, the philosophy of science, and the philosophy of religion. This, as the reader will soon discover, is one of the themes of this book. An introduction to the philosophy of mind cannot fail to be to some extent an introduction to philosophy in general. The book *is*, nevertheless, an *introduction*: no prior knowledge of the subject is needed in order to understand it; and though we will occasionally address certain technical issues, these have been kept to a minimum, and been made as reader-friendly as possible.

Another theme of the book is the continuing relevance and power of non-materialistic approaches to the philosophy of mind. To be sure, materialism – the view that the mind can be fully accounted for in terms of purely physical processes of the sort studied by the natural sciences – is today the dominant tendency in the field. But this is, perhaps surprisingly, a very recent development. Until the 1960s, materialism was a minority view among philosophers interested in the nature of the mind, even among philosophers – like C. D. Broad, Karl Popper, and Bertrand Russell – who understood and greatly admired modern science and who were irreligious, or even anti-religious, in outlook. While there are important and challenging philosophical arguments in favor of materialism, there are also equally important and challenging arguments against that view; and in fact, arguments of the latter sort are the ones that most philosophers, for most of the history of philosophy, have found the most convincing. It is possible, of course, that the majority view in the history of the subject was erroneous, and that the currently orthodox approach is the right one; but it is also possible that the historically dominant view was correct, and that contemporary philosophers have made a mistake in departing from it. Philosophy, in any case, is not about believing what is fashionable, but about discovering what is true. It is crucial, then, if one is properly to understand the philosophy of mind, that one be as familiar with the chief arguments of the anti-materialist side as one is with the arguments for materialism. This book aims, accordingly, to provide a solid introduction both to the traditional arguments against materialism and to the contemporary arguments in favor of it. This is all the more important given that even today, critics of materialism constitute a large and influential minority position within the field. It is time an introduction to the subject reflected this fact, and avoided the excessive materialist bias that has become all too common in introductory volumes. I have tried to be fair to both sides, and I hope the reader will find that I have succeeded.

It is hard to see how anyone could write an introduction to the philosophy of mind without first having taught the subject. There is no better way to find out how best to make difficult ideas as clear as possible than to try out different approaches on students and see what works. I thank the many students to whom I've taught the subject over the years for their feedback and enthusiasm, and especially the students in the undergraduate and graduate courses in philosophy of mind that I taught at Loyola Marymount University during the 2003–2004 academic year, who got an early sample, in lecture format, of some of the material in this book.

Thanks are due also to Mel Thompson, who was very helpful in hammering out the original book proposal, and to the anonymous referees at Oneworld Publications, who provided invaluable feedback that allowed me greatly to improve the manuscript. Special thanks are owed to Victoria Roddam, who has been a terrific editor and a pleasure to work with.

My beloved wife Rachel has been patient and supportive throughout the entire time-consuming project. So too (no doubt without realizing it) have our children Benedict and Gemma, to whom this book is dedicated.

1
Perception

You've just started reading this book. Or so you think. But are you certain that you're really reading it? How do you know you're not merely dreaming that you're reading a book, or having a vivid hallucination? How do you know that you're not in fact trapped in an extremely sophisticated virtual reality computer program, like the characters in the film *The Matrix*?

Perhaps you're tempted at this point to *stop* reading, convinced that such questions are frivolous, suitable maybe for late night sessions over a few beers but not for a book of serious philosophy, which is what you had hoped you'd bought. Yet there was no more serious a philosopher than René Descartes (1596–1650) – the very father of modern philosophy, as he is widely known – and he took these questions (minus the *Matrix* reference, obviously) to be of profound significance, for they formed, in his view, the starting point of a line of inquiry that not only lays the foundation for scientific knowledge, but also reveals the true nature of the human mind and its relationship to the material world, culminating in nothing less than the establishment of the immortality of the soul. As we will see, philosophers disagree over whether Descartes was right to think these things. But few would deny that his arguments are powerful and as worthy of consideration today as they were when he first put them down on paper. Nor can it be denied that, whatever one ultimately thinks of Descartes's views, they have set the agenda for modern philosophy in general and philosophy of mind in particular. For these and other reasons, we will do well to have made his starting point in the study of the mind our own.

So, your curiosity now piqued, let's return to this question that Descartes thought has such deep implications: How do you know you're really reading this book?

Dreams, demons, and brains in vats

No doubt your first inclination is to say that it's just *obvious* that you're reading it, since, after all, you can *see* it in your hands, *feel* its pages, *smell* the ink and *hear* your fingers slide across the paper. Were you so inclined, you would also be able to *taste* the chemicals in the paper and ink. In any case, your reason for believing that you're reading the book is that you're having just the sorts of *experiences* you'd expect to have while reading. Your senses tell you you're reading the book; therefore, you must be reading it.

There is a problem with this answer which can be seen by comparison with the following example. Suppose Fred tells you that there will be a party at Ethel's house this Saturday, and that you know Fred to be a frequent and very convincing liar. Sometimes he tells the truth, but very often, even when the subject matter is trivial, he does not; in either case, his demeanor is exactly the same, and it always appears very sincere. Given that Fred is your only source for this information, do you have strong grounds for believing that there will indeed be a party at Ethel's this Saturday? Surely not. You just don't know for certain, because your only evidence for this belief – Fred's word, with all its evident sincerity – would be exactly the same whether there really will be a party or not.

We are, it seems, in exactly this sort of situation with regard to our senses. They "tell" us things all the time, and their way of telling us is very convincing – "seeing is believing," as the saying goes, for it is hardest to doubt something precisely when it seems to be there right before your eyes. Yet for all that, there are well-known cases where what our experiences tell us is real is not real at all. You may have had the experience of being chased by a knife-wielding murderer, your heart pounding and a scream welling up in your throat. Terrified, you reflected on how much it all seemed like a nightmare, but being so vivid, it *couldn't* be; and then, just as the knife was set to plunge into you ... you woke up. You thought your senses were telling you that your life was in imminent danger, but you were wrong. In fact, you couldn't have been more safe, snug as you were in bed, asleep and dreaming.

But if your experiences could, in dreams, deceive you in a matter so momentous, why not in a matter as trivial as reading a book? Indeed, you know that they very often *do* deceive you in trivial matters – in every humdrum, murderer-free dream you have. So how can you be sure you're not dreaming *right now*? "But this is too vivid to be a dream!" you might reply. Yet, as I've already hinted, a dream can sometimes be so vivid that the person having it explicitly thinks, during the dream, that it *isn't* a dream. Perhaps this is one of those dreams. Besides, how do you *know* reality is always more vivid than a dream? On the basis of your memory of past dreams? But how do you know you aren't just dreaming that you're remembering those past dreams correctly? A similar problem afflicts *any* appeal to how one's dreams normally are – in black and white, say. For how can you be sure those memories are accurate? (And why couldn't this just be your first dream in color? There's a first time for everything, after all.) Nor will an appeal to evidence on the nature of dreams from psychology textbooks and the like help – maybe you're just having false dream "memories" that you ever read such books. In fact, it seems *any* evidence you could appeal to, or any test you could perform to prove you're not dreaming (for example, pinching yourself) is evidence or a test you might just be *dreaming* you're appealing to.

The bottom line is this: there is nothing in the nature of your experiences themselves that can tell you one way or the other whether they are waking or dreaming – in which case, experience, by itself, cannot tell you whether what you're experiencing right now (and at any time you consult it) is real. Nor are dreams the only basis for this disquieting conclusion. It is widely known that our experiences, in all their varieties – visual, auditory, tactile, gustatory, and olfactory – depend on processes within our brains. When, for example, you see a lemon, that is a result of light reflected from the lemon striking your retinas, which causes signals to be sent, via your optic nerves, to more central processing centers in the brain; which neural activity ultimately gives rise to your visual experience of the lemon. But if that is the natural way in which the experience of a lemon is produced, it is easy to see how such an experience might, in principle, be produced artificially – a neurosurgeon could simply stimulate directly the portion of your brain that causes the experience, bypassing the processes in the optic nerve, etc. that would normally trigger events there. Indeed, neuroscientists are even now capable of producing very simple sensations – a flash of red in one's visual field, say, or the smell of lilacs – by such stimulation.

If that is possible, it would also seem to be possible for the entire stream of one's conscious life to be produced artificially. We can imagine that neuroscientists might hook someone's brain up to a massive virtual reality supercomputer which stimulates the brain to have just the sorts of experiences that characterize normal everyday existence. But then, how can you know that *you yourself* aren't at this very moment hooked up to such a computer? You feel sure that you are reading a book, but maybe you're really just a disembodied brain, floating in a vat of nutrients in a laboratory somewhere, the subject of a bizarre experiment by some mad neuroscientists who are causing you to have the experience of reading a book – along with all the other experiences you are now having or have ever had. Perhaps they are chuckling at this very moment at how amusing it is to have just given you the experience of reading about *them*!

It was Descartes who introduced the "dream argument" into modern philosophical discussion, and though he did not discuss the "brain-in-a-vat" scenario he did also present another, perhaps even more chilling, possibility. You might find it reassuring to think that even if you are really dreaming at this moment or are a disembodied brain hooked up to a virtual reality machine, this would still all occur in the context of a physical environment that exists independently. Perhaps you can't know what exactly is going on in it at any given moment, but at least it is there – at least, that is, there is a bed you're sleeping in right now, or a laboratory somewhere with chuckling mad scientists. But what if not even all of *that* were real? What if you were nothing but a disembodied soul, with no physical body or brain at all, and the only other thing that exists is an extremely powerful evil spirit, a demon, who spends its time putting into your mind all the experiences and thoughts you've ever had? Every place you think you've ever been, every person you think you've ever met, the physical universe itself – none of it is real, just a massive, ongoing hallucination. How could you prove this isn't what is happening to you? As with the dream scenario, it seems you could have no evidence that it isn't – for any evidence you appeal to could be evidence the demon itself has manufactured.

Descartes took arguments of this sort to tell us something important about the nature of perception, namely that there is a gap – potentially, at least – between the appearance of the world that it presents to us, and the reality outside. In perception we know that appearance immediately and intimately; what we know of the reality is another, and more problematic matter. The first and most obvious consequence of this is *epistemological*, that is, it concerns the nature of human knowledge. That consequence is, in Descartes's view, not (as it might at first seem to be) that we can't know anything for certain, but rather that what we do know for certain, indeed, whatever it is we know at all, can't ultimately come directly from perceptual experience alone. In this Descartes is opposed to *empiricism* – the view that all knowledge does ultimately rest on the senses – and also, perhaps, to common sense, which holds that whether or not the senses form the basis of all knowledge, they do at least give us all by themselves some indubitable knowledge. Descartes held that the sorts of arguments just considered prove that this can't be right. The senses by themselves are in fact so feeble that they can't even tell us whether we're awake. If we do have knowledge, then (and Descartes thought we surely did) it must come from somewhere else, namely from pure reason operating independently of the senses, a view about the basis of knowledge known as *rationalism*.

The first thing you know on this basis, according to Descartes, is that at least *you* exist. How? Well, even if you really are dreaming right now, are a brain in a vat, or the victim of a deceiving evil spirit, you still must exist in the first place in order to do the dreaming or to be deceived. Indeed, if you're worrying about whether or not you're dreaming, whether there's such a demon, or whether you even exist at all, *you must exist in order to do the worrying.* If you didn't exist at all, obviously you wouldn't be around to worry about the fact. So just to *think* about whether you exist is enough to prove that you do. "*Cogito, ergo sum,*" as Descartes put it – "I think, therefore I am." This famous argument, knowable without having to rely on the trustworthiness of the senses, is in Descartes's view the starting point of all knowledge and the absolute stopping point of all doubt: if you can know nothing else, you can at least know for certain that you are real.

So far so good; but is anything else real? In particular, is the physical universe you've always assumed existed outside your mind – the mundane world of tables, chairs, rocks, trees, other human beings, dogs, cats and other animals, planets, stars and galaxies – is all that real too? It might seem that if all your perceptual experiences could be false, then there just is and can be no way to know that anything else exists. Perhaps nothing else does in fact exist – not even an evil spirit or mad scientists. Perhaps *you are the sole reality*, your perceptual experiences constituting nothing more than an indefinitely long hallucination and the entire universe a figment of your imagination. This is *solipsism*: the view that "I alone exist."

Indirect realism

Descartes himself was no solipsist. He was a staunch *realist*, who firmly believed that the world of external, objective, physical objects exists and that, even given arguments of the "dreaming" and "evil spirit" sort, we really can, through our senses, know that world. But he also thought that these arguments show that we don't know it *directly*. What we do know directly are the contents of our own minds, the rich stream of experiences that constitutes everyday conscious life. The physical world that is represented by those experiences, not mad scientists or demons, is indeed what normally causes us to have them, but the experiences themselves are all we have immediate access to. It is as if we are watching images on a television screen, without being able directly to observe the ultimate source of the images. We might suppose that what we're seeing is a live broadcast of astronauts inside a space shuttle orbiting the earth, and we may well be right – but it's at least possible that what we're really seeing is a recording of events that occurred earlier, actors on a sound stage in Hollywood and some clever special effects, or even an entirely computer-generated image. No doubt we can find out through some independent source whether it really is a live broadcast, but the fact that we can't know this just from observing the images shows that we do *need* such a source and that what we do see directly cannot be the astronauts themselves, but only a representation of them. Similarly in perception, on Descartes's view: when a book really is out there and is what's causing you to have a "bookish" experience, then you really are seeing it, though indirectly; when it's a dream or virtual reality device or demon causing the experience, you're not seeing it at all. Either way, what you "see" directly is never the book itself but only a perceptual representation of the book.

This view, that all we are ever immediately aware of is the "veil of perceptions" that constitutes our conscious experiences, is known variously as *indirect realism*, *representative realism*, or *causal realism* – "realism" because it holds that there really is a physical world existing outside our minds, "indirect," "representative," or "causal" because it holds that we know that world only indirectly, through our direct awareness of the perceptual representations that world causes us to have, via its impact on our sensory organs. A long line of famous philosophers, including empiricists like John Locke (1632–1704) and Bertrand Russell (1872–1970) – otherwise in disagreement with Descartes over the latter's rationalism – have held this view, usually on the basis of examples less bizarre than the ones we've considered thus far.

One such example would be hallucinations, which can seem indistinguishable from the normal perceptual experiences which present us with a reliable picture of the external world (that is, experiences which are, as philosophers say, *veridical*). The hallucination of a dagger in one's hand could be as vivid as really seeing and feeling it there. There might be nothing in the experiences themselves that tells you whether they are trustworthy, and this supports the notion that whatever one is directly aware of in the one case must be the same sort of thing as what one is directly aware of in the other, since otherwise there would plausibly be some difference in the intrinsic character of the experiences. But in the case of hallucinations, it obviously can't be an external physical object that one is directly aware of. So neither can an external physical object be what one is directly aware of in the case of a veridical perceptual experience. But then what one is directly aware of must be something else – a perceptual representation in the mind.

There is also the matter of the causal relations existing between perceptual experiences of physical objects and the objects themselves. There is, as implied above, a surprisingly long chain of causes involved in even so simple an experience as the seeing of a lemon. Certain wavelengths of light are reflected off the surface of the lemon, photons travel to your retinas, rods and cones are stimulated and send signals along the optic nerve, these activate neural pathways in the brain that make their way to the occipital lobe, and after a further flurry of activity the experience finally happens. So how can your awareness of the lemon fail to be indirect, with all these intermediate steps existing between that awareness and the lemon itself? Moreover, such a sequence of causes occurs over time. In the lemon case, the light reaches your eyes virtually instantaneously, but in the case of looking at the sun, the light takes a full eight minutes to reach your eyes, meaning that what you're seeing now is the sun as it appeared eight minutes ago. The light from the star Alpha Centauri takes over four years to reach us, and light from other celestial objects takes much longer – in many cases, so long that some of the objects we see in the night sky no longer exist! So, again, how could your awareness of these objects fail to be indirect? How could you be *directly* aware of something that might not even exist?

These considerations regarding hallucination and causation arguably supply, all by themselves – with no need for an appeal to bizarre suggestions about mad scientists or evil spirits – powerful support for the indirect realist view of perception. As the philosopher Howard Robinson has suggested, they are best combined into a single simple and powerful argument, which we can summarize thus:

1. By stimulating the brain so as artificially to produce a neural process that is normally associated with a certain veridical perceptual experience, it is possible in principle to bring about a hallucination that is subjectively indistinguishable from that experience.

2. But if the immediate causes of veridical perceptual experiences and their hallucinatory counterparts are of the same sort, then these effects must be of the same sort as well.

3. In the case of hallucinations, the effect is obviously direct awareness not of any external physical object, but rather of a subjective mental, perceptual representation of an external object.

4. So in the case of veridical perceptual experiences too, what one is directly aware of must be a subjective perceptual representation.

Again, this is not to deny that in veridical perceptions you really do perceive external, objective, independently existing physical objects. It's just that you perceive them only *indirectly*, through your direct awareness of something subjective and mental. You do indeed *really see* the lemon, but only on the private television screen of your mind, just as you really see the astronauts, but only on the literal television set in your living room.

Skepticism

Even if this argument is correct – and it is very controversial – it would show at most only that we *could* be right in thinking that the external, physical world of tables, chairs, other people, etc. exists, not that we *are* right. That we don't directly experience that world doesn't entail that we don't experience it at all, much less that it isn't real; but that doesn't prove that we do experience it, even indirectly, either. So we still haven't really answered the question of how anyone who starts from where Descartes did can get beyond there, to a genuine knowledge of the existence of a world outside the mind. This brings us to a motivation that many philosophers have had for trying to avoid indirect realism, opting instead for a "*direct* realist" view, on which we have unmediated perceptual contact with physical reality. Indirect realism, it is widely thought, threatens us with *skepticism* about the external world. If *all* we are ever directly aware of are our own perceptual representations, it seems that we can never have any grounds for believing that there is a real world of physical objects beyond those representations. The indirect realist view, say its critics, so cuts us off from external reality that it seems we can never again get back in touch with it; it opens a door to skepticism that it cannot shut. That provides us with a good reason to try to find an alternative analysis of perception, one which doesn't have such skeptical implications.

But it may be that there *is* no such alternative analysis. For, as Michael Lockwood has pointed out, it is simply false to suggest that the threat of skepticism is unique to indirect realism. What gives rise to the skeptical problem is the fact that it is logically possible that your experiences could be just as they are now, when you take yourself to be reading a book, and yet you aren't really reading it at all, but only dreaming, or hallucinating, or being deceived by an evil spirit or mad scientists into thinking that you're reading it. And this fact holds regardless of whether indirect realism or direct realism is true. Let our awareness of physical objects in veridical perception be as direct as you wish: it is still an open question whether, in any particular case where you think you're having a veridical perception, you really are, or can be justified in believing that you are. The facts about hallucination, the causal mediation between our experiences and the world, the dependence of perceptual experiences on events in the brain, facts that no one denies – these are what make skepticism possible, whether or not they also support indirect realism. So, the suggestion that indirect realism must be rejected because it would lead us into a skeptical problem seems to cut little ice. That problem is with us *whatever* position we take. It poses no difficulty for the indirect realist that it doesn't also pose for everyone else.

Indeed, it might even be argued that an advantage indirect realism has over direct realism, *vis-à-vis* skepticism, is that it better accounts for why there is a skeptical problem in the first place. If we're never directly aware of anything but our own perceptual representations, it is perfectly understandable that there should be occasions when we think there are external objects corresponding to those representations when there are not. The fact, and nature of, hallucination and the like becomes intelligible. But if we are usually directly aware of external objects, it is puzzling why we should sometimes have experiences that are just like the veridical ones but in which we are not aware of any external objects at all, and why those non-veridical experiences should be so much like the veridical ones. For these reasons, indirect realism might have greater explanatory power than direct realism.

Defending indirect realism against the charge that it uniquely threatens us with skepticism still leaves unanswered the key question, which is, once again, whether there is any way to *answer* skepticism and *justify* the belief that there really is an external physical world beyond one's experiences. Descartes answered skepticism by appealing to the idea of *God*, an idea that one finds within one's own mind whether or not that mind has any contact with an external physical reality. Descartes took the view that the existence of God could be proved via several of the traditional theistic arguments. But to prove God exists is to prove that an all-good being exists; and such a being, though he might allow one to make a mistake from time to time (so as to learn from it) would not allow one to be mistaken in general, for that would be contrary to his goodness. But then it follows that he would not allow one always to be dreaming, or deceived by an evil spirit, or whatever. Therefore, if one's senses lead one to believe in the reality of an external, physical world, there must really be such a world.

To do Descartes's argument justice would demand, among other things, a careful evaluation of the case for God's existence. But that would require a book of its own. Moreover, it would clearly be philosophically more satisfying if one could answer skepticism without having to appeal to the existence of God, if only because it would enable us to side-step an issue which may be as controversial as skepticism and indirect realism themselves. But, in the view of many philosophers we can indeed do so, by arguing that the commonsense belief that there are external objects corresponding to our perceptual experiences is a kind of *quasi-scientific hypothesis* that forms the best explanation of those experiences, an explanation that is constantly confirmed by the successful predictions we make on its basis. As Lockwood has argued, this sort of defense is exactly parallel to the scientist's justification of hypotheses about such unobservable entities as electrons. If our belief in electrons can be rationally justified by virtue of their being posited by a well-confirmed scientific theory, then so too can our belief in external physical objects, despite the fact that they are not directly observable.

A well-known principle of scientific explanation is *Occam's razor*, which holds that simpler and more economical hypotheses are to be preferred to needlessly complex ones, because they raise fewer further mysteries and thereby allow us to stay as close as possible to the evidence. If, for example, we can explain the slight wobble observed in a distant star by postulating the existence of one medium sized planet orbiting it, then we ought not to postulate instead the existence of seven small planets whose orbits are very close to each other. (For what reason is there to suppose seven, rather than six or eight? How exactly are the orbits of such planets related to each other? How can they have avoided colliding to form a larger body? Perhaps there are ways to answer such questions, but given that we don't *need* such a hypothesis to explain the star's wobble and that the seven-planet theory raises questions of its own and goes far beyond the available evidence, why bother with it?) One response to Lockwood's suggestion might be that it violates Occam's razor, for a skeptic could argue that the "evil spirit" hypothesis is simpler and more economical than the commonsense view, and is thus to be preferred. After all, unlike the commonsense view, which posits an enormous number and variety of external physical objects governed by complicated laws, the demon hypothesis postulates the existence of only one object, the demon itself, operating according to the simple principle of wanting to deceive.

However, as the physicist David Deutsch has argued, skeptical hypotheses like the brain in a vat and evil spirit scenarios are actually *more* complicated than the commonsense belief in an external physical world, not less; for they are *parasitic* on the latter belief. Even to form the hypothesis of a deceiving evil spirit, we first have to form the hypothesis of the existence of the commonsense world of external physical objects governed by scientific laws, and then imagine that the demon is deceiving us into believing that this hypothesis is true. That requires that the demon be complex enough to do this successfully, which means supposing that it is complex enough to interact with us in a way that exactly parallels the way a world really consisting of external physical objects would. But that means that this evil spirit would itself have to be at least as complex as a world of physical objects; indeed, it means that such a spirit must be *more* complex, for it would not only have to mimic that sort of world, but also be (as such a world would not) *consciously aware* that that is what it is doing, thus being a thinking thing, which raises further questions about why it has the motives it does, etc., questions that wouldn't arise on the commonsense view. So the evil spirit hypothesis really isn't as simple or economical as the commonsense view after all and Occam's razor should lead us to reject it in favor of the latter.

Appearance and reality, mind and matter

If all this is right, then it is indeed possible to know that the physical world outside one's mind really exists, despite arguments about dreams, evil spirits, brains in vats, and hallucinations. As we've seen, consideration of such arguments nevertheless implies that there is a gap between our experience of the physical universe and that universe itself; between appearance and reality, mind and world.

That gap can be bridged, but that it exists at all has important philosophical implications. Having explored some of the episte-mological implications, we want now to move on to the possible *metaphysical* implications of this gap, implications which are of even greater relevance to the philosophy of mind. Is the mind-world gap a gap only in the knowledge the mind has of the physical world, where the mind is nevertheless a part of that broader world, namely that part of it we call the brain? Or is it rather that the mind and the material world are fundamentally *different kinds of thing*, with the mind itself being *im*material or *non*-physical, a soul or spirit existing over and above the brain?

The discussion thus far leads naturally to such musings. Consider some of the features of your mind as it contemplates the very questions we've been asking about it in this chapter. As you wonder whether this book you take yourself to be reading is real, you note that it certainly seems to be, precisely because of the experiences you have of it – the visual look of the colors on its cover and the ink on its pages, the feel of the paper, the smell of the chemicals in the ink and paper, and so on. These aspects of your sensations – the way things look, feel, smell, taste, and sound – are referred to by philosophers as *qualia*, and appear to be features unique to the mind. A thermostat may register the information that the room has gotten cold and signal the heating system to come on; but surely, being just an assemblage of metal, plastic and wires, it doesn't feel cold the way you do. Furthermore, these qualia – the constellation of visual images, sounds, tastes, feels, smells and the like you are experiencing right now – form, not a chaotic jumble cascading through your mind without rhyme or reason, but a coherent and unified picture of the world, of which you are consciously aware *as* such a picture of the world. Moreover, you can think rationally about this picture and wonder whether it corresponds to any reality outside; and these thoughts, as well as the picture itself, have meaning or significance, representing the world as being a certain way. They have what philosophers call *intentionality*, the property of being *directed at* or *about* something, in the way that, say, pictures of cats or the word "cat" are about, mean or represent cats, rather than being mere meaningless squiggles of ink or paint.

These features of the mind – qualia, and the unified conscious awareness of which they are a part, rational thought and the intentionality it exhibits – together comprise the domain of the thinking subject whose situation Descartes vividly presents us with in the strange thought experiments with which we began this chapter. That subject is presented with a certain appearance of a reality outside itself, an appearance that reflects a certain point of view on that reality: the first-person or subjective point of view of the "I" or self who wonders about the outside world – whether it exists at all, what it's like, what relation the self bears to it. This domain of the subject seems very different from that external reality itself: the physical world revealed to us by modern science, a reality which is objective, mind-independent, devoid of any particular point of view and thus "third-person" rather than first-person – an *it* rather than an "I." It is a world we know from science to be composed ultimately of fundamental particles which have none of the features presented to us in experience, but are colorless, odorless, tasteless, and best described in the abstract mathematical language of physics. And this is no less true of our bodies and brains than of any other part of the physical world. So how could *they* in any way be the seat of the rich domain of conscious, rational thought through which we know that physical world? How could any material thing – including the grey, squishy lump of matter that constitutes your brain, which seems as brutely physical as a thermostat – have feelings, smells, tastes, and qualia in general? How could it be conscious and aware of itself and its surroundings? And how could it think rationally about itself and those surroundings, or have intentionality? After all, a thermostat's existence surely involves nothing more than the passage of electrical current through wires, the motion of a needle across a surface, and so forth;

there is no consciousness there, no meaningful and rational thought, only crude mechanical processes. But how different, really, are the electrochemical signals sent between the neurons of the brain? How are these any less intrinsically meaningless and unconscious than the electricity passing through the wiring of a thermostat?

Yet though it is difficult to see *how* the mind could be anything purely physical, modern science is often taken to imply that it nevertheless somehow *is*, that every aspect of our mental lives can be accounted for in terms of electrochemical processes in the brain and central nervous system. How to resolve this tension between what the mind seems to be and what science says it is – or what some people *claim* science says it is – constitutes the famous mind-body problem, and sets the agenda for the philosophy of mind, all the issues of which tend, in one way or another, to trace back to this basic one. It is, like the problem of this chapter which has led us to it, a matter of deciding whether appearance corresponds to reality – in this case of determining whether the mind is, as it seems to be, something immaterial or non-physical, or whether this appearance is as misleading as a hallucination produced by Descartes's evil spirit. But if Descartes's revelation of the gap between appearance and reality has led us to the mind-body problem, he also presented a possible solution to it, which is the subject of the next chapter.

Further reading

The nature of perception is a large topic belonging as much to epistemology as to the philosophy of mind. We have merely scratched the surface in this chapter, and have focused only on those aspects of the problem relevant to the issues to be discussed in the chapters that follow. Those interested in a deeper investigation will find D. L. C. Maclachlan, *Philosophy of Perception*

(Englewood Cliffs, NJ: Prentice Hall, 1989) to be a useful short introduction to the field. R. J. Hirst, ed. *Perception and the External World* (New York: Macmillan, 1965) is a good source for classical readings. Jonathan Dancy, ed. *Perceptual Knowledge* (New York: Oxford University Press, 1988) is a collection of contemporary articles. Descartes's *Meditations on First Philosophy* contains his reflections on dreams, the demon, the *cogito*, and on God as the guarantor of the trustworthiness of our senses. It is available in many editions, as is Locke's *An Essay Concerning Human Understanding*. Bertrand Russell defends indirect or causal realism in *The Analysis of Matter* (London: Kegan Paul, 1927), and his views are lucidly explained by Grover Maxwell in "Russell on Perception" in D. F. Pears, ed. *Bertrand Russell: A Collection of Critical Essays* (New York: Anchor Books, 1972). Howard Robinson defends indirect realism in *Perception* (New York: Routledge, 1994), Michael Lockwood in chapter 9 of *Mind, Brain, and the Quantum* (Oxford: Basil Blackwell, 1989), and David Deutsch in *The Fabric of Reality* (New York: Penguin Books, 1997). One influential critic of indirect realism is J. L. Austin, whose views are presented in his classic *Sense and Sensibilia* (New York: Oxford University Press, 1962). Another is John McDowell, whose "Criteria, Defeasibility, and Knowledge" can be found in the Dancy anthology.

2
Dualism

Common sense may regard as unusual and eccentric Descartes's dreaming and evil spirit scenarios, but it is not unfamiliar with the distinction between appearance and reality – or, more to the present point, with the distinction between mind and matter. Indeed, if his indirect realist account of perception goes against the grain of everyday thinking, Descartes's dualism – his claim that there is a "real distinction" between the mind and the body, that they are fundamentally different kinds of thing – is quite in line with it. We reflexively distinguish between mind and body in ordinary contexts as often as in philosophical ones, and in a way that implies that the difference between them goes deeper than a mere difference between part and whole: we do not, after all, distinguish equally naturally between "hand and body" or even "brain and body." Moreover, the metaphysical content of most religions has historically included some version of the idea that a human being has a *soul*, regarded as the seat of our mental lives, as spiritual rather than physical, and as surviving the death of the body.

Descartes's position is intended rationally to systematize and justify this commonsense view of human nature. It is, naturally enough, referred to as *Cartesian dualism* ("Cartesian" meaning "pertaining to the thought of Descartes"), though some version of it goes back in philosophy at least to Plato. In Descartes's view, the reason mind and body *seem* different in the ways sketched in the last chapter is that they *are* different, and radically so. The body is, in its intrinsic nature, exactly like every other material object, being an essentially *extended* thing (in Latin, *res extensa*): extended in space, that is to say, and defined by such properties as length, depth, height, mass, motion, and spatial location. Together with other material or extended objects, it is composed of purely physical parts – molecules, atoms, and subatomic particles – and governed entirely by the causal processes enshrined in the laws of physics. The body, and the vast physical universe of which it is a part, are best thought of through the model of a machine, their operations being as mechanically automatic as those of a watch and their elements as brute and unthinking as a watch's gears and mainspring. The mind, by contrast, is essentially a *thinking* thing (or *res cogitans*), devoid of shape, mass, location in space, or any other physical property, and governed by reason rather than mechanical causation. It is as utterly distinct from its associated human body as it is from the material world in general, though it does interact with it: changes in the body bringing about changes in the mind (as when the body's sensory organs detect a cheeseburger in the vicinity and produce, in the mind, hunger and an intention to eat) and changes in the mind bringing about changes in the body (as when the mind's intention to eat the burger causes the body to salivate and proceed to eat it).

Since there is a clear sense in which Descartes took mind and body to be distinct *substances* – a "substance" being something that exists on its own, as opposed to an "attribute" or "property" (like redness, tallness, or heaviness) which cannot exist apart from the substance which has it – his view is often described as *substance dualism*, and he is widely interpreted as regarding the non-physical substance of the mind to be what a *person* essentially is, the body being a mere excrescence, no more necessary to a human being *per se* than the clothes he or she wears. On this understanding of Descartes's view, the *real* you is something outside the material world altogether, an immaterial substance or soul temporarily inhabiting your body like a "ghost in the machine," as Gilbert Ryle (1900–1976) famously and derisively put it. But this interpretation, however common, is at best a caricature. In fact, Descartes took the interaction between mind and body to be so close that the two together constituted a third, unique substance, with its own distinctive properties: while shape, mass, and the like are confined to the body, and pure intellectual activity confined to the mind, *sensation* – pains, itches, feelings of thirst or hunger – is a feature strictly attributable only to the substance comprised of mind and body interacting together. Moreover, it is this composite substance, rather than the mind alone, with which a person or human being is to be identified.

Nevertheless, however close its connection to the body, the mind is still, in Descartes's view, distinct from it – and that means distinct from the brain, which is no less physical or extended an object than the rest of the human body. But doesn't Descartes thereby contradict common sense after all? Don't we normally use the terms "mind" and "brain" interchangeably, so that they must be regarded as the same thing – in which case the mind really is just part of the body?

Minds and brains, apples and oranges

No doubt people these days often do use these words interchangeably, but this by itself doesn't prove anything. Certainly the two words don't *mean* the same thing. In Aristotle's day, people knew about the brain, but did not take it to have anything to do with thinking, intelligence, or the mind in general – they thought its function was to cool the body. It is only because we now know that the brain has an intimate relationship to the mind that we so easily (and, from a philosophical point of view, carelessly) shift from talk about the one to talk about the other. Descartes himself was well aware of this connection, and nevertheless took mind and brain to be distinct. The brain was in his view the conduit through which the mind interacted with the body, but nevertheless as distinct from the mind as the wire that connects your television set to the cable company's local relay station is distinct from the television itself.

But *why* take them to be distinct? Why not conclude from the close connection existing between them that the mind and brain are the same?

Why do we believe that apples are different from oranges? The answer, of course, is that they just obviously are different. Oranges are orange, spherical, and have a distinct flavor very different from that of apples, which are typically red, yellow, or green and apple-ish in shape. Anyone who has observed them knows they're different; no fancy argument is needed to prove it. But the same holds true of the mind and the body, or the mind and the brain for that matter, in Descartes's view. The difference between them is "clear and distinct," as obvious as the difference between apples and oranges, and as little in need of complicated philosophical demonstration.

As we know from modern physics, a material thing is ultimately nothing more than a collection of elementary particles. That includes the cheeseburger whose appearance and aroma makes your mouth salivate and your stomach grumble in hunger, and whose flavor and texture, vividly experienced by you as you eat it, brings satisfaction. The particles comprising the cheeseburger have themselves none of these features: no color, odor, taste, or texture. Moreover, they have none of the solidity of the cheeseburger that you feel as you hold it in your hands; there is more room between the particles than is occupied by the particles themselves, so that the cheeseburger is mostly empty space. It just happens that the particles comprising the cheeseburger are so arranged that they affect your sensory organs in such a way that you experience it as a solid, textured, colorful, aromatic, and flavorful object. Intrinsically, though, it is none of these things, and neither is any other physical object – including your brain, which is constituted of physical particles just as much as the cheeseburger. Yet these features do in some sense exist in your mind, in your experiences of the cheeseburger. But then the mind, the dualist concludes, is just obviously different from the brain, for it has qualities that the brain does not have.

Consider further the nature of experiences in general, and of their qualia. When you see Fred get his hand slammed in a car door, you have no doubt that he is in pain. But this is not because you experience or observe the pain itself; you cannot peer inside the wound and see the pain the way you might see a splinter. You might observe the behavior typical of pain – screaming, crying, swearing, writhing – as well as the damage to the injured part of Fred's body – torn skin, crushed bone, blood and the like. If you happen to have the requisite equipment at hand – such as an fMRI scanner – you might even be able to observe the relevant goings-on in Fred's central nervous system. All of this is as directly accessible to you as it is to Fred. But Fred's *sensation* of pain – the *experience* of it, the *feel* of it – is something only he knows directly, from the inside. If you know it is there, it is only because you infer, from your own experience of what happens when you get your hand caught in a door, that Fred must be in pain. It is even possible that Fred doesn't really feel any pain at all: perhaps he is just an extremely eccentric prankster willing to break a hand in order to raise a laugh, and had earlier injected it with Novocain and is now only *acting* as if he feels pain. This is unlikely, but the fact that it is at least possible underlines the point that the pain itself – as distinct from its causes and effects, and the bodily damage associated with it – is not *directly* knowable to anyone but the person experiencing it.

What is true of pain is true also of other experiences. If someone flashes a camera bulb in your face, others might see you blink, wince and throw your arms up reflexively in response, but they will not, and cannot, see the after-image that subsequently occupies your visual field for a few moments. If you form a mental image of the Eiffel Tower, or think of the way your favorite song goes, others will be utterly unable to see that image or hear that song, however vivid the images are and however close they get their eyes and ears to your skull. Performing brain surgery on you won't give them access either – it's not as if they'll see a little picture of the Eiffel Tower inscribed in your grey matter or hear music coming from your hypothalamus. Nor can others directly experience what you experience as you eat a cheeseburger. Your sensations of the taste, texture, smell and look of the thing are available only to you; they can have similar experiences, should they eat their own burgers, but their experiences would then be theirs, not yours.

The feeling of pain, the look of an after-image, the taste of a cheeseburger, and so on – those aspects of experience we've labeled qualia – thus exhibit a feature that philosophers call *privacy*, a feature that seems to set them apart from physical reality. Physical objects and properties are "public," in the sense that they can, in principle, be directly accessed, via perception, by any observer. This is as true of the brain and body as of any other physical phenomenon: just as anyone is as capable of peering inside and examining the workings of your car as you are, so too is anyone capable of opening up your body or brain and examining their workings. But your qualia are directly accessible only to you, via your *introspection* of your mind's contents – you have "privileged access" to them, that no one else has or can have. Everything else in the world is objective, knowable "from the outside" or from the "third-person" point of view; qualia – indeed, mental states and processes in general – are subjective, knowable "from the inside," from the "first-person" point of view. But then it seems that these mental states and processes must be different from anything occurring in the brain, body, or any other physical thing.

Finally, physical objects and processes are not only "public" rather than "private," and intrinsically devoid of color, odor, taste, and the like, but they are also intrinsically without meaning or intentionality. Even the words you're now reading are in themselves just meaningless squiggles of ink on paper; what meaning they have is meaning we give them, by interpreting them as having meaning. The same goes for the noises made by a tape recorder or the electronic impulses generating images on a computer screen.

Intrinsically there is nothing there but sound-waves and electrical current, as devoid of significance as the sound-waves generated by a fan or the electrical current passing through the fan's motor. The reason the former have any meaning at all is, again, that we interpret them as having it – we interpret the sounds made by the recorder and the images on the screen as words rather than merely noises and shapes. So, it seems that physical objects and processes have meaning only when they derive it from minds, which have it intrinsically. This is as true of brain processes as of any other physical process – in themselves, the electrochemical signals passing between neurons surely have no more meaning or intentionality than the electrical current passing through the wires and motor of an electric fan. So, again, the mind seems just obviously different from the brain.

The indivisibility argument

A further difference between mind and matter, which Descartes took to have considerable significance, concerns the notion of *divisibility into parts.* A physical object is divisible – into halves, quarters, and so on, ultimately into its constituent molecules, atoms, and subatomic particles – and the smaller objects that remain after each division are themselves physical. As with the other features of physical objects we've noted, this is no less true of the human body and brain. But a mind is *simple*, not composed of parts and thus not divisible into further, smaller units. By this Descartes doesn't mean that we can't distinguish various aspects of the mind – its distinct capacities for reason, sensation, emotion and so forth – but rather that these aspects are, unlike the aspects of a physical object, aspects of a kind of thing that cannot be divided into further things of the same kind. You can divide a material thing into parts which are still themselves material, but you cannot divide a mind into parts which are still themselves minds. In that case, Descartes argues, the mind cannot be identified with any material thing, including the body or brain. Furthermore, it seems to follow that the immaterial substance of the mind is, unlike the body, *immortal*. Physical things can perish precisely because they are composite, and can thus be broken down into their constituent parts. The mind, being simple, has no parts to be broken down into.

Descartes's conviction that the mind is a simple substance no doubt stems in part from the *cogito* argument described in chapter 1. In knowing for certain that "I think," what I know to exist is precisely a *single* thinking thing – after all, "*I* think," not "*we* think." I do not know for certain, at least not initially, that there is any other thinking thing in the world; I can certainly coherently imagine that there isn't, that *I alone* exist, as in solipsism. But this thinking "I" just is my mind; in imagining it alone existing, I am imagining that a single mind exists, not a composite of smaller minds. Surely, then, I am imagining something simple. Consider further that when I wonder whether my body exists, I can do so in stages – I can imagine first that my torso and head are real, but my limbs a mere hallucination, and then imagine that my torso too is hallucinatory, and so forth. I can inquire into the existence of my body part by part. But the same isn't true of my mind, the "I" that thinks about its own existence. I either exist or I don't: it's all or nothing, not a matter of degree. Thus, the thing whose existence I'm concerned with seems clearly to be a simple, non-composite entity.

It is, nevertheless, sometimes suggested that modern psychological and neurological research have demonstrated that Descartes was wrong about the mind's simplicity. There are famous cases of "multiple personality disorder" (MPD), wherein a single mind seems to have fragmented into several personalities. Wouldn't this involve a mind being divided into smaller minds? There is also the odd behavior of "split-brain" patients, in whom the corpus callosum – the thick bundle of neurons connecting the two halves of the brain – has been severed. Such patients are claimed by some researchers to behave as if there were two people living in the same body, each controlling one half of it: for instance, one of a patient's hands will attempt slowly to stack blocks while the other moves in, as if impatiently, to stack them more quickly, only to be pushed aside by the first hand. Again, it would appear that what was once a single mind has divided into two.

But appearances, as we've seen, can be deceiving. In MPD, we have a phenomenon that was traditionally categorized as demonic possession. Accordingly, people exhibiting the behavior now associated with MPD described it, not as a fragmentation of a single mind into multiple ones, but as the entrance from without of a distinct and alien mind. If anything like this sort of description is correct, these cases would not count as evidence against Descartes's view at all, for they would not involve the division of a mind into smaller units, but rather the control over a single body of two distinct and otherwise unrelated minds. Of course, few philosophers these days would take seriously the suggestion that demonic possession is the best explanation of cases of so-called MPD (though this is largely because of the materialist worldview most of them presuppose, which is itself precisely what is in question in arguments for dualism). In any case, the possibility does at least show that MPD cases by themselves do not entail that the mind is divisible. Such cases need interpretation, and interpretations can reflect philosophical biases as much as philosophical conclusions.

This brings us to a more fundamental response to the MPD objection (and a more crucial one, since dualists will be much better off if they needn't resort to something as controversial as the notion of demonic possession). The reality is that it simply isn't clear that MPD cases (which are extremely rare and difficult to confirm) really are, in the first place, cases of multiple minds existing in one body. Many well-known cases of alleged MPD – such as that of "Sybil," made famous in the film of that title – have been shown to have been exaggerations or even hoaxes. "Sybil" herself has admitted that her "disorder" was more or less her own invention, that she was coaxed into believing that she had multiple personalities by therapists eager to prove that MPD was real, and that under their encouragement and in an emotionally fragile state she had manufactured and acted out various "personalities" to confirm their diagnosis. Many other MPD patients, emotionally disturbed people to start with, acknowledge that they see themselves less as literally "fragmenting" into different personalities than as fantasizing and acting out different roles – again, often under the influence of overzealous therapists.

The behavior of "split-brain" patients is no less subject to interpretation, interpretation that can reflect the enthusiastic theorizing of the researcher as much as the objective facts. To begin with, the two hemispheres of the brains of such patients are *not* completely disconnected – there are other connections between the halves that remain undisturbed, and thus there are no grounds for insisting that the halves *must* be associated with different "minds." Furthermore, under ordinary conditions, such patients behave more or less normally, or at least not in any way that suggests that more than a single mind occupies their bodies. It is only in contrived experimental contexts that they can be made to exhibit remarkable behavior, and even then that behavior is by no means obviously best interpreted as involving a "division" of the mind. Many researchers hold instead that such behavior, when examined carefully, amounts to little more than a variation on the awkwardness, failure of co-ordination, or general cognitive malfunctioning that can result from any serious injury to the brain, or an exaggeration of the absent-mindedness or incoherence that we all exhibit from time to time.

The "indivisibility" argument remains controversial, but since the evidence of the mind's divisibility is inconclusive, it seems the argument hasn't decisively been refuted.

The conceivability argument

We will return to the issue of the mind's simplicity, and the plausibility of Descartes's indivisibility argument, when we consider the
unity of conscious experience in chapter 5. Let us turn now to
what many philosophers regard as the paradigmatic argument for
dualism: the "conceivability argument." Dualism says that the
mind is *a different thing* from the body or brain and can, in principle, exist apart from them; the opponent of dualism says otherwise,
holding that the mind just *is* the brain, or at least that it necessarily
depends on it for its existence (an alternative way of formulating
the opponent's view to which we'll return in chapter 3). But to
make such a claim commits the opponent of dualism to certain
implications – implications which, the conceivability argument
tries to show, are false, so that the claim that the mind and brain are
identical must also be false.

Properly to understand the argument, we need first to understand a distinction philosophers make between different kinds of
possibility and *impossibility*. When we say that it is impossible for a
human being to run a mile in two minutes or to jump fifty feet,
what we mean is that such feats go beyond the limits set by human
physiology and the laws of physics. Such things are impossible *given
the way the world works*; they are, we might say, physically impossible
(or, what amounts to the same thing, we might say that it is a
matter of physical necessity that no one can run a two-minute
mile, etc.). But they are not impossible in the same way in which it
is impossible for a square to be circular, or for 2 + 2 to equal 5. Had
the muscles of the human body or the gravitational pull of the
earth been different, a two-minute mile or fifty-foot high jump
may well have been possible. They aren't, given the way the world
happens to work, but they would have been, had the world worked
in some other way. But no matter how different the human body,
gravity, or the laws of physics may have been, there just couldn't
have been such a thing as a circular square, and it couldn't have

been true that $2 + 2 = 5$. These things would be impossible *no matter how different* the world might have been. They are, we might say, not just physically but *metaphysically* impossible (or, in other words, it is a matter of *metaphysical necessity* that they cannot obtain). They are impossible not only in the actual, but in *any possible* world.

How do we know this? In the case of running a two-minute mile, even though we know such things to be impossible in the real world, we can give a coherent description of how things might have been different in such a way that they would be possible. We can, if we care to, describe in detail what the gravitational force of the earth, a human being's musculature and lung capacity, etc. would have to be like in order for one to run a two-minute mile. We can give a description of such a state of affairs in a way that involves no contradiction, and thus what we would be describing is, though not physically possible – not allowed by the laws of nature obtaining in the actual world – nevertheless metaphysically possible – allowed by the laws of nature in some other possible world. But we can do no such thing where circular squares and the like are concerned. A world where squares are circular and $2 + 2 = 5$ cannot be coherently described; the very attempt to describe it involves a contradiction. So there can be no such world. We might sum this up by saying that metaphysically impossible worlds, like a world with circular squares, are strictly *inconceivable* – we cannot even imagine the existence of such a world, for the attempt to do so involves a contradiction. By the same token, though, the fact that we can conceive of worlds where a two-minute mile is possible is reason to believe such worlds are not metaphysically impossible.

Suppose that we're considering a claim, not about two-minute miles or circular squares, but about identity. That is, suppose we're considering a claim of the form $A = B$, for instance, the claim that water $= H_2O$. We know that water is H_2O in the actual world, of course; it is physically impossible for something to be water without being H_2O. But is it *metaphysically* impossible too?

Couldn't there be another possible world where water is not H_2O but something else? It seems that in the nature of the case, this is not possible. Water and H_2O *are the same thing*, so how could you have the one without the other? If you could, wouldn't that show that they aren't really the same thing after all? If I could even conceivably have some water without having any H_2O, or you could have some H_2O without having any water, wouldn't this entail that water and H_2O are really just different substances?

This suggests the following principle: for any A and any B, if A = B, it is metaphysically (not just physically) impossible to have A without B (with qualifications I'll explain later on). But then, given what I've said above, it should also be impossible to give a coherent description of a world where A exists without B: A existing without B should be inconceivable. A corollary of this is that if it is metaphysically possible to have A without B, then A and B can't really be identical after all; and this means in turn that if it is conceivable for A to exist apart from B – if we can give a coherent description of A existing apart from B – then A and B just aren't identical. This gives us a way to test identity claims. If someone claims that a certain A is identical with a certain B, then we should see whether we can coherently conceive of A existing apart from B. If we cannot, this would not prove that they are identical – maybe we just haven't thought about the matter carefully enough; but if we *can* conceive of it, this would surely give us reason to believe they are not identical.

Consider the claim that the mind is identical to the brain. If this is true, then it should be, not just physically, but metaphysically impossible for the mind to exist apart from the brain. And thus, if what we've said so far is correct, it should also be inconceivable for the mind to exist apart from the brain: we should be unable to describe coherently, in manner involving no contradiction, a situation where a mind but no brain exists. Can we conceive of such a situation?

We already have, in chapter 1. Descartes argued that it was impossible for him not to exist as long as he was thinking that he did, or thinking anything at all; nevertheless, it was still at least possible that his body, including his brain, did not exist, because those things might just be part of a hallucination put into his mind by an evil spirit. That is to say, it is entirely conceivable that one could exist as a disembodied mind, with one's body and brain, and indeed the entire physical world, being nothing but a figment of one's imagination. But then it is conceivable and therefore at least metaphysically possible for the mind to exist apart from the brain. Therefore, the mind is not identical to the brain.

Lest one think that this crucially depends on the possibility of there being a Cartesian demon – which would itself be a disembodied mind, so that the argument might appear to beg the very question at issue – it should be noted that the same point could be made in terms of solipsism, the scenario in which "I alone exist" as a disembodied mind, with *nothing*, neither a demon nor a physical body, existing apart from my mind and its hallucinations. Or we can appeal to the sort of scenario vividly described by the dualist philosopher W. D. Hart. Imagine waking up one day and staggering groggily to the bathroom sink to splash some water on your face. As you gaze into the mirror, you notice, to your great horror, that where normally there would be two eyes staring back at you, you see instead two dark and vacant eye sockets – with the eyeballs completely missing! Frantic, you reach into the sockets to verify that they are empty, and, sure enough, feel nothing but the stumps of the optic nerves. This would, of course, be impossible in real life. But you can certainly *conceive* of it happening, without contradiction – you can vividly imagine having an unsettling experience of this sort, in a way that you cannot conceive of a circular square or $2 + 2$ adding up to 5. If you can conceive of this, you can also conceive that, being intrigued by your ability to see without eyeballs, and wondering if any other vision-related body parts are missing, you get out a hacksaw and carefully remove the top of your skull, only to reveal an empty cavity where your brain should be. Now you've conceived, in a nauseatingly vivid fashion, of seeing without either eyeballs or a brain. And if that's conceivable, you can take the next step and imagine that instead of seeing empty eye sockets staring back at you, what you see is your own headless body – in which case you'd be conceiving of seeing without a head. Finally, following this exercise in conception to its logical conclusion, you can imagine that what you see in the mirror is not even a headless body, but nothing more than the wall behind you and no body at all. Wondering whether someone has installed a trick mirror or if you've become a vampire, you look down at your torso, arms, and legs but find that you still can't see them, only the floor under you; nor can you feel them, as you realize that your attempt to touch them has failed – there's nothing there to touch! You would now be conceiving of seeing without a body. But seeing is a mental process, as is the frenzied thinking you'd now be engaged in; which means that what you've conceived of is your mind existing apart from a body or brain. So, again, it's conceivable that the mind exists apart from the brain – in which case they're not identical.

This argument has, as one would imagine, been subject to a lot of criticism. However, some seemingly obvious criticisms simply miss the point of the argument. It is no good, for example, to object that merely conceiving of something can't make it happen in the real world – I can't make myself fly merely by imagining that I can. That's not what the argument is saying. The claim, remember, isn't that being able to conceive of something makes it physically possible, but rather that it shows that it is metaphysically possible. It may not be, given the way the actual world works, but it could have been, had the world been different. Someone might then object that this point is trivial, since anything could have been possible in that sense. But as we've seen, this isn't so: circular squares and $2 + 2$ equalling 5 would not have been possible no matter how different the world might have been; they are *absolutely* and *metaphysically* impossible, because they involve *contradictions*, as running a two-minute mile and existing without a body do not. It might then be insisted that the claim is still trivial, for what needs to be shown is that the mind could exist without the body in the actual world, not merely in some conceivable one. But this too misses the point. For, as with water and H_2O, minds and brains, if identical at all, must be identical in every possible, and thus every conceivable, world. If it is even conceivable that a mind could exist without a brain, then mind and brain can't be the same thing – how could they be, if one could conceivably exist apart from the other? The point is related to the "apples and oranges" argument: you could have apples without oranges, so obviously apples and oranges aren't the same thing. You could also have minds without brains, so obviously they aren't the same thing either. This holds true even if, in the actual world, minds typically are associated with brains – something no dualist denies. Where there's smoke, there's fire, but obviously smoke and fire aren't the same thing. Creatures with hearts are always creatures with kidneys, but obviously hearts and kidneys aren't the same thing. Minds are typically associated with brains, but that doesn't mean they are the same thing.

There are more serious objections, however. The principle that conceivability entails metaphysical possibility, though endorsed in some form or other by philosophers of the stature of Descartes and David Hume (1711–1776), is often challenged by contemporary philosophers (though usually, it should be noted, precisely as a way of avoiding commitment to dualism, rather than for independent philosophical reasons). Take the fact that Neil Armstrong is identical to the first man to walk on the moon. Since this is a fact, it is presumably metaphysically impossible for Armstrong to exist apart from the first man to walk on the moon – they're the same person, after all. But isn't it nevertheless conceivable that Armstrong could have failed to be the first? Can't we just obviously imagine a case where the Soviets beat the Americans to the moon and Yuri Gagarin got to leave *his* boot prints there instead? Sometimes even the water/H_2O case is put forward as a counter-example. True, it is said, it is metaphysically impossible to have water without H_2O, since they are the same thing. But isn't it in fact, and contrary to my earlier suggestion, at least conceivable that water could exist apart from H_2O? Can we not coherently imagine a situation in which we have a substance that is clear, liquid, and quenches thirst, freezes and turns to gas at the same temperatures that water does, yet does not have the chemical composition of H_2O but instead turns out to have the composition X_YZ? Wouldn't this just be to conceive of water existing apart from H_2O? But if it is conceivable that water could exist apart from H_2O, or that someone other than Armstrong could have been the first to walk on the moon, even though it is metaphysically impossible for water to exist apart from H_2O or for Armstrong to exist apart from the first moonwalker, then the principle that conceivability entails metaphysical possibility must be false. It follows that the fact that we can conceive of the mind existing apart from the body does not show that this is metaphysically possible.

Formidable as these examples might seem, they do nothing to undermine the main thrust of the conceivability argument, for reasons made clear by the influential work of the philosopher and logician Saul Kripke. As Kripke has argued, strictly speaking it is identity statements involving what he calls *rigid designators* that are, if true at all, true of metaphysical necessity, that is, whose falsehood is metaphysically impossible. A rigid designator is an expression that denotes the same thing in every possible world, in every possible way that things might have been. "Water" is an example, as is any term designating a "natural kind" or naturally occurring substance such as gold or iron. "Water" in essence designates: *whatever substance it is in the actual world that has the properties of liquidity, quenching thirst, freezing and turning to gas at such and such temperatures, etc.* Thus "water" also designates whatever it is in any other possible world that fits this precise description, namely, the description of being the substance that has those properties in the actual world. "H_2O" essentially designates: *the substance having specifically such-and-such a chemical composition.* "H_2O" thus also designates whatever it is in any other possible world that has that specific chemical composition. We know empirically that *the substance in the actual world that is liquid, quenches thirst, etc.* is exactly the same as *the substance having specifically such-and-such a chemical composition.* Water, in the actual world, is H_2O. But since "water" also designates whatever the substance is in any other possible world that in the actual world is *the substance that is liquid, quenches thirst, freezes and turns to gas at such-and-such temperatures, etc.*, and that latter substance is H_2O (where "H_2O" designates whatever it is in any possible world – including the actual one – that is *the substance having specifically such-and-such a chemical composition*), it follows that "water" and "H_2O" will refer to the same substance in every possible world. That is, water and H_2O are identical in every possible world.

When we think carefully about the semantics of terms like "water" and "H_2O," then, we will see that we really can't coherently describe or conceive of a world where water isn't H_2O. When we think we're conceiving of such a world, what we're really conceiving of is a world where there is a substance that is liquid, quenches thirst, freezes and turns to gas at such-and-such temperatures, etc. that turns out to have a chemical composition of X_YZ. But precisely because this substance wouldn't thereby be the substance *in the actual world* that has these properties, it wouldn't be water, but merely a substance very similar to water. To conceive of a substance similar to water that is not H_2O is not the same thing as to conceive of water existing apart from H_2O. So the water/H_2O case just isn't at all a counter-example to the principle that conceivability entails metaphysical possibility.

What about the Neil Armstrong example? We can indeed coherently conceive of a situation where Armstrong is not identical to the first man to walk on the moon, but this would nevertheless not, on Kripke's analysis, be a counter-example to the principle that conceivability entails metaphysical possibility. For it is not metaphysically impossible for Armstrong to fail to be the first to walk on the moon, even though the identity statement

"Armstrong is identical to the first man to walk on the moon" is true. The reason is that at least one of the expressions in this statement is not a rigid designator, namely the expression "the first man to walk on the moon." This expression does not mean "the specific person who, in the actual world, first walked on the moon," but rather merely something like "whichever person turns out to be the first to walk on the moon." And of course it is metaphysically possible that someone other than Armstrong could have turned out to be that person. So we shouldn't be surprised that it is also conceivable. As long as we note carefully, along Kripkean lines, that it is only identity statements involving rigid designators which, if they are true at all, cannot possibly be false, we will see that there are no genuine counterexamples to the principle that conceivability implies metaphysical possibility.

That principle seems highly plausible in any case. Indeed, it is hard to see how even its critics could themselves regard anything as metaphysically possible in the first place, without being implicitly committed to the principle. For why does anyone accept that it is at least metaphysically possible to run a two-minute mile or high jump fifty feet if not on the basis of the fact that one can clearly conceive of this happening, or give a coherent description of it? That is not to say that anything anyone says he or she can conceive is thereby truly conceivable and therefore metaphysically possible; as we've seen, sometimes what someone thinks is conceivable turns out on reflection not to be conceivable after all. This might result not only from a failure to take note of the role of rigid designators in identity statements, but also from the commission of such fallacies as confusing a word for the object named by the word or from a failure to pay careful attention to the precise meaning of a word. (For example, someone might claim that he or she can conceive of a circular square, when in fact all the person is really conceiving of is a circle he or she is *calling* "a square," or a shape that isn't truly a square at all, but has three straight sides and one round one.) But when we've been careful to avoid such fallacies and find that we still seem capable of conceiving of a certain state of affairs, we surely have strong reason to believe that that state of affairs is metaphysically possible.

The interaction problem

The principle that conceivability entails metaphysical possibility is, then, eminently defensible. But there is another way to challenge the conceivability argument. One could simply deny that it really *is* conceivable in the first place for the mind to exist apart from the brain. That is, one could argue that, just as someone who *thinks* it is possible to conceive of water apart from H_2O is mistaken, and just hasn't really thought carefully enough about what he or she claims to be conceiving, so too is someone who thinks it is possible to conceive of the mind existing apart from the body simply mistaken, and will see, on further reflection, that this isn't really what he or she has conceived of at all.

Along these lines, one might assume that the Kripkean framework we've appealed to in defense of one premise of the conceivability argument (the premise that conceivability entails possibility) might be applied here too, in opposition to another premise of the argument (the premise that we can conceive of the mind existing apart from the body). But Kripke himself would disagree. Expressions referring to mental states and brain states are in his view both rigid designators. "The firing of C-fibers," designates: *whatever it is that in the actual world is a brain process of such-and-such a type*, and "pain," designates: *that mental state that has such-and-such a feel*. So if pain is identical to the firing of C-fibers (and, by extension, if the mind in general is identical to the brain), then they must be identical in *every* possible world, as a matter of metaphysical necessity. As what we've already said implies, it appears we can conceive of a possible world where pain exists in a disembodied mind, apart from the firing of any C-fibers or any other brain state; and thus it would follow they *can't* be identical. It might seem at first as if one could get around this argument the way we saw the dualist can get around the purported water/H_2O counterexample. In fact, there is a crucial difference between that case and this one. In the water/H_2O case, we saw that something could be liquid, thirst-quenching, liable to freeze and turn to gas at such-and-such temperatures, etc. (that is, it could have many of the properties that water does) without being water. So to conceive of such a substance apart from H_2O is not to conceive of *water* apart from H_2O. But nothing could have the feel that pain does without being pain, for pain is *nothing more than that feel itself.* So to conceive of something that feels like pain existing apart from any brain state just is to conceive of pain itself existing apart from any brain state. In the case of the conceivability argument, unlike the case of water and H_2O, what we think we're conceiving of really is what we're conceiving of. Thus, there seems no way for the critic of dualism to appeal to Kripkean semantics to respond to the conceivability argument.

There is another way for the opponent of dualism to press this sort of objection. In the previous chapter we examined the view that the mind is, in perception, only indirectly aware of the external, physical world, with this indirect awareness mediated by a causal connection between the mind and the things it perceives. But let's consider this causal element in perception more carefully. It seems clearly to be a necessary part of your perception of the book you're now reading that you have some causal connection to it, that the book itself is what is causing you to experience it. Obviously, if there were in fact no book there – if you were merely hallucinating, because someone had slipped drugs in your coffee – then you wouldn't really be seeing it at all, but only seeming to see it. But even if there were a book there, that wouldn't by itself be enough. For suppose you were right now having such a hallucination, your brain malfunctioning and your mind totally cut off from the outside world, and suppose also that, just by chance, someone has put a copy of this book down on the table in front of you. Would you really be seeing the book? Surely not, because even though you're having an experience of seeing a book, and there really is a book there, the book itself is not what's causing the experience – the drugs are causing it. So truly to see the book, not only do you have to have the experience of seeing it, and not only does the book have to be there, but the book must be what's causing the experience.

With this in mind, says the critic of the conceivability argument, examples like the "seeing without a body" scenario take on a new complexion. For if we're really to conceive that we are seeing without a body, it follows that we must also conceive that there is a *causal connection* between our mind and the things we are seeing. But it is hard to see how we can conceive of this. In normal cases of perception, we know that what occurs is something like this: light bounced off an object is reflected off the mirror, and travels in the form of photons to your eyeballs, where, the retina being stimulated, a series of complicated neural signals is initiated which results in the experience of seeing the object. But what happens in the "seeing without a body" example? Light bounced off the object is reflected off the mirror, and travels in the form of photons to … *where*, exactly? There are no eyeballs there for it to enter, indeed no body at all for it to travel to. So where does it go? It's no good to say that it goes to the mind, for on Descartes's view, remember, the mind is outside space and has no physical properties whatsoever – no shape, mass, length, width, or height at all. So how can the light, which is physical, possibly get in "contact" with it? It seems just impossible that it could. But if it can't get in contact with it, then there can be no causal connection between a non-physical mind and the physical objects outside it; which entails that the mind couldn't truly see or perceive such objects without a body. But then it turns out that we really can't conceive of seeing without a body after all. If it seems that we can, that's only because we haven't thought carefully enough about what's involved in seeing something.

Strictly speaking, this objection doesn't quite undermine the conceivability argument, for that argument requires not that we can conceive of "seeing without a body" specifically, but only that we can conceive of the mind existing apart from the body in some fashion or other. Even if we accept the criticism that the causal conditions necessary for true seeing to occur entail that one cannot genuinely conceive of "seeing without a body," we can, nevertheless, insist that it is still possible to conceive of being a disembodied mind which seems to see – that it is possible to conceive, as in Descartes's evil spirit scenario or in solipsism, of being a disembodied mind which has a stream of hallucinatory visual experiences. Obviously those experiences wouldn't truly count as literal seeing *per se*, for there would be no causal contact with the external physical world. But even hallucinatory experiences are still experiences, and to imagine having them while disembodied is still to imagine the mind existing apart from the body. So the gist of the conceivability argument still stands. The dualist could accept that the mind cannot literally see or in general perceive the world of physical objects unless it is joined to a body; cut off from a body, it becomes, as it were, trapped within itself. But that just means the mind needs the body in order to do anything other than merely hallucinate; it doesn't mean it is identical to the body or any part of it.

Even if the dualist can in this way defend the conceivability argument for dualism against the objection under consideration, that objection still raises questions about dualism itself. Perhaps we needn't claim that we can conceive of the mind and the physical world interacting in order to get the conceivability argument off the ground; it is enough to conceive of the mind existing all by itself, totally cut off from the physical world. But the dualist also wants to hold that the mind, though *distinct* from the brain and body, nevertheless does *interact* with them. And just as it is hard to see how photons could get into causal contact with a disembodied Cartesian mind, so too it is hard to see how the brain and body could either. The brain is an extended object like any other, with a mass, shape, and particular location in space, while the mind is, in Descartes's view, none of these things. So how can the mind and brain possibly interact? Of course, it seems obvious that they *do*; the problem is that dualism appears to have no way of explaining how this is possible.

The "interaction problem" has been the main difficulty facing dualism since the time of Descartes and various solutions have been suggested. One of them, known as *occasionalism*, holds that God serves as the link between mind and brain: observing that light reflected from the cheeseburger has impacted your retinas and set up a series of neural firing patterns in your brain, God causes your mind to have an experience of seeing the burger; observing that that experience has led you to decide to eat the burger, he then causes a set of neural firing patterns to occur in your brain that result in you picking up the burger, putting it in your mouth and eating it. *Parallelism* holds, alternatively, that the mind and the brain are not linked even in this indirect fashion. Rather, they are simply so constructed that the events occurring in the one are always exactly appropriate to the events occurring in the other, yet without having any mutual influence: the brain and body are so ordered that light reflected from a cheeseburger results in certain neural firing patterns, which results in the body's limbs moving it toward the burger, while the mind is so ordered that, at precisely the same time that sequence of events is occurring in the body, it undergoes a parallel series, namely, it has the experience of seeing a cheeseburger, which results in a desire for the cheese-burger, which results in an intention to go pick it up. Mind and body are like two clocks operating entirely independently, but keeping up with each other so perfectly that it *seems* that there is interaction between them. There is a "pre-established harmony" between them – pre-established by God, who is responsible for having wound up the clocks of mind and body in the first place.

It is easy to scoff at such theories if one simply takes for granted the general materialist world picture. But if one believes, as proponents of these theories do, that there is already independent evidence for the existence of God as well as for the distinction between mind and body, it is hardly unreasonable to suggest that God might have something to do with the connection (or apparent connection) between mental and material substance. As in so many other cases in philosophy, what one regards as a plausible theory is largely determined by the background assumptions entailed by one's general metaphysical commitments. Still, it is always preferable, if possible, to avoid having to defend one controversial position by appealing to another which is at least as controversial and to avoid contradicting common sense – something these theories clearly do, denying as they do that there really is a direct causal connection between mind and body.

Another, and more widely accepted theory, which only partially denies this is *epiphenomenalism*, which holds that events in the brain and body produce events in the mind, but that those mental events in turn have no causal influence on what happens in the brain and body. They are mere "epiphenomena," ineffectual by-products of the operation of the physical processes of the brain. The light striking your retinas causes you to have the experience of seeing the cheeseburger, and further brain events cause you to form the desire to eat it; but that desire itself is *not* what causes you to proceed to eat it. The experience, the desire, and everything else that goes on in your mind have no effects at all; what causes your actions are just further, purely material, unconscious brain processes. The appeal of this theory is partly that it does not, as occasionalism and parallelism do, appeal to anything as controversial as the existence of God, and partly that it is consistent with the notion that bodily behavior can be entirely explained in terms of processes occurring in the brain and nervous system – a notion that has gained widespread acceptance following the rise of modern neuroscience. Epiphenomenalists hold, as opponents of dualism do, that we can completely explain human behavior by appealing to such physical bodily processes; there is thus no need to try to explain how immaterial mental processes interact with the body, for they *don't*. They also hold, however, as dualists do, that mental processes are non-physical. Epiphenomenalism thus constitutes a kind of compromise between dualists and their opponents.

It is a notoriously unsatisfying compromise, however. Occasionalism and parallelism may deny common sense in holding that mind and body have no direct effects on one another, but at least this denial serves the purpose of solving the interaction problem, and at least they provide some explanation of why mind and body seem to interact. Epiphenomenalism, in denying at least that the mind has any effect on the body, also defies common sense, but it fails to compensate by providing any explanation in return of how the body can (as the theory claims) have an effect on the mind. Worse still, epiphenomenalism makes mysterious how we can even so much as *talk* about the mind. Presumably, for our written and spoken words to refer to the mind, they have in some sense to be the effects of what is going on in it. But the mind has no effects at all, in the epiphenomenalist view. So how are we able to talk about it? How are epiphenomenalists able to tell you anything about the mind when, in their own view, the mind cannot have any effect whatsoever on what they say?

There is more to be said about the interaction problem, and it will be said in later chapters. Suffice it for now to make two points. First, the interaction problem by itself does nothing to undermine the arguments for dualism we've considered so far. Merely to note that the Cartesian concept of the mind leads to a mystery about how mind and body interact is not to uncover any fallacy in the conceivability, indivisibility, or apples and oranges arguments. Dualists can, therefore, reasonably hold that so long as the arguments for their position have not been proved fallacious, they are in their rights in continuing to maintain that position – while also, of course, continuing to look for ways to solve the interaction problem. Dualism is in this respect really no worse off than those most fundamental theories of modern physics: relativity and quantum mechanics. Notoriously, there are respects in which these theories seem to be in conflict, and yet the evidence for each is very powerful. There are various ways of trying to reconcile them, but as yet no consensus as to which, if any, is the right one. It would be silly to insist that physicists must reject these theories, or at least one of them, until some generally accepted solution to the problem of reconciling them has been worked out. Physicists must continue the search for a scheme that will unify quantum mechanics and relativity, but there is no reason for them simply to ignore the strong considerations that favor these theories until such time as that unifying scheme has been arrived at. Similarly, it is unreasonable to expect the dualist to give up dualism *simply* because the interaction problem exists, when there are arguments in favor of dualism that are at least as powerful and worthy of consideration as any others in philosophy.

Second, contemporary philosophers have nevertheless taken the interaction problem to be, at least, a strong motivation for seeking an alternative to dualism, and they have not necessarily been unreasonable in doing so. The mere fact that interaction between a nonphysical substance and a physical one is difficult to explain does not refute dualism. But the philosophers in question take the problem to go deeper. The difficulty, in their view, is not merely that it is hard to see how a cause and effect relationship between such substances might work; it is that modern science seems to present us with a picture of the nexus of causes and effects in the physical world that leaves nothing for a non-physical substance to do. We are not in the position of failing to understand how such a substance can play the role it plays; we are rather in the position of failing to understand how it could even *have* a role to play in the first place. For the law of the conservation of energy entails that the amount of energy in the physical universe is constant. A Cartesian immaterial substance, being outside space, is outside this universe. For it to affect the physical world, and in particular the brain, it would have to introduce energy *into* the physical universe; and for the brain in turn to affect an immaterial substance, it would seemingly have to transfer energy *out of* the physical universe. Either way, the amount of energy in the physical universe would fail to be constant. So the very idea of causal interaction between Cartesian material and immaterial substances seems to violate the laws of physics.

Most contemporary philosophers have accordingly sought to develop a *materialist* conception of the mind in which it is, contrary to appearances, just another part of the physical world. More modest versions aim to show that such an alternative account will be at least as plausible as dualism, and equally capable of explaining the various aspects of our mental lives. The idea would then be that, though both dualism and materialism have strong arguments in their favor, materialism, being (allegedly) more in harmony with modern physics, ought to be preferred. More ambitious materialists would go further than this and claim that a materialist conception of the mind will, when fully worked out, show dualist arguments to be not only inconclusive, but positively fallacious or incoherent.

The case for dualism, then, cannot fully be evaluated until it is compared with the case for materialism. If the materialist can indeed show that the various features of the mind can be accounted for in purely physical terms, then dualism will, at the very least, have much of the wind taken out of its sails. But if the materialist fails to do so, that failure will itself provide some further support for dualism – indeed, many of the most influential dualist arguments in recent philosophy are precisely attempts to undermine various arguments for materialism. And if there remains a mystery of how mind and matter can possibly interact, we will see that some dualists have argued that this reflects, not a problem with the dualist's conception of the mind, but rather a problem with the materialist's conception of the physical world.

Further reading

Descartes's versions of the conceivability and indivisibility arguments for dualism are to be found in the *Meditations on First Philosophy* (in the Second and Sixth Meditations, respectively). Gilbert Ryle's famous jibe is in his *The Concept of Mind* (London: Hutchinson, 1949). As I've briefly indicated, the interpretation of Descartes's position usually presented in books on the philosophy of mind is, at best, oversimplified and a number of recent works on Descartes have set out to correct what they regard as widespread misunderstandings of what his dualism amounted to. Two examples (though with virtually the same title) are Gordon Baker and Katherine J. Morris, *Descartes' Dualism* (London: Routledge, 1996) and Marleen Rozemond, *Descartes's Dualism* (Cambridge, MA: Harvard University Press, 1998).

Dualism, though unpopular with the majority of twentieth-century philosophers of mind, has in recent years found a number of able defenders (though not always in exactly Descartes's form). See John Foster, *The Immaterial Self* (London: Routledge, 1991); W. D. Hart, *The Engines of the Soul* (Cambridge: Cambridge University Press, 1988); William Hasker, *The Emergent Self* (Ithaca, NY: Cornell University Press, 1999); E. J. Lowe, *Subjects of Experience* (Cambridge: Cambridge University Press, 1996); Karl R. Popper and John C. Eccles, *The Self and its Brain* (New York: Springer-Verlag, 1977); Howard Robinson, "Dualism" in Stephen P. Stich and Ted A. Warfield, eds. *The Blackwell Guide to Philosophy of Mind* (Oxford: Blackwell, 2003); Richard Swinburne, *The Evolution of the Soul* (Oxford: Clarendon Press, 1986); and Charles Taliaferro, *Consciousness and the Mind of God* (Cambridge: Cambridge University Press, 1994).

The issues surrounding the relationship between conceivability and possibility are enormously complex, and the philosophical literature dealing with them can be hard going. Kripke's arguments are to be found in his *Naming and Necessity* (Cambridge,

MA: Harvard University Press, 1980), which is as readable as this literature gets. More difficult, but worth the effort, is David J. Chalmers, *The Conscious Mind* (New York: Oxford University Press, 1996), which develops a semantic framework similar to Kripke's and argues that it favors the advocates of conceivability arguments and not their critics (though Chalmers' preferred brand of conceivability argument, which we'll be looking at in chapter 4, is importantly different from the Cartesian kind). Tamar Szabo Gendler and John Hawthorne, eds., *Conceivability and Possibility* (Oxford: Clarendon Press, 2002), an anthology of articles representing the various sides in the dispute over this set of topics, is not for the faint of heart.

The problematic nature of alleged cases of "multiple personality disorder" is discussed in Richard J. McNally, *Remembering Trauma* (Cambridge, MA: Harvard University Press, 2003). The philosophical significance of "split-brain" cases is the subject of Thomas Nagel's influential article "Brain Bisection and the Unity of Consciousness" in *Mortal Questions* (Cambridge: Cambridge University Press, 1979). A survey and penetrating analysis of the debate spawned by Nagel's article can be found in chapter 6 of Michael Lockwood's *Mind, Brain, and the Quantum,* cited in chapter 1.

3
Materialism

Although Cartesian dualism is today a minority view in the philosophy of mind, that should not blind us to the enormous influence Descartes has on contemporary thinking about the mind-body problem, and particularly on materialism. I say this not only because materialists are explicitly guided by an animus against Descartes's dualistic metaphysics, but also, and just as significantly, because they are at least implicitly guided by a commitment to certain other, distinctly Cartesian, assumptions. Descartes believed that the world consisted of two basic kinds of substance: thinking substance and extended substance, *res cogitans* and *res extensa*. The modern materialist rejects the former, but endorses the latter. Descartes was, it is thought, at least half right: his *res cogitans* is, by the materialist's reckoning, a fiction, but his *res extensa* most assuredly is not – indeed, it constitutes the whole of what a human being is.

To be sure, Descartes's concept of matter as essentially "extended" cannot be maintained without qualification given developments in modern physics, which hold that certain fundamental physical particles are best conceived on the model of unextended mathematical points. Nevertheless, his notion that the physical world constitutes a vast "machine," with material objects – including the human body – being but smaller machines operating within it, has come to dominate the thinking of modern philosophers and scientists alike. It has become a hallmark of intellectual life in the post-Cartesian period that *understanding* something is thought paradigmatically to involve taking it apart and seeing how it works, the way one would understand any mechanism. A physical thing, on this model, is like a clock, the operation of which can be grasped by determining how each part interacts mechanically so as to generate the behavior of the whole. Nowadays, this approach to inquiry may seem to be just obviously correct, the epitome of "thinking scientifically." Yet, as we will see later on, it constituted a dramatic departure, both scientifically and, more significantly for our purposes, metaphysically, from the assumptions that prevailed in most ancient and medieval thought – a departure that in many respects can be said to have created the mind-body problem as we know it today. That problem is thus as much an artefact of the points on which materialists and dualists agree as of those on which they do not. We will in due course be examining more carefully the nature – and the ultimate plausibility – of this approach to understanding the material world, shared by Cartesian dualists and materialists alike. The question at hand is whether, where the mind-body problem is concerned, that approach favors its materialist advocates over its dualist ones.

Tables, chairs, rocks, and trees

It is certainly no mystery *why* the approach in question has come to seem obviously correct. Modern science has, to all appearances, been one long success story, a success made possible in large part because of its commitment to the mechanistic model of the world. The behavior and properties of the ordinary middle-sized objects of everyday experience – tables, chairs, rocks, trees, water, metal, as they burn, melt, freeze, reflect light, exhibit magnetism, conduct electricity – have been explained in great detail via physical and chemical theories of extraordinary predictive power, whose application has made possible the breathtaking technologies of the modern world, technologies that would have seemed magical to earlier generations. These theories have revealed the existence of a micro-level of physical reality – a realm of molecules, atoms, electrons, protons, quarks, etc. – which our ancestors would have found equally marvelous, and they have also proved themselves applicable to, and revealed the unexpected vastness of, the macro-level of the universe – solar systems, galaxies, galaxy clusters, and the very fabric of time and space. Most relevant to our present concerns, they have proved successful in explaining the operation of the human body and its various subsystems, opening the way to the healing of diseases that have plagued humankind for millennia, the extension of longevity through medicine and the use of artificial organs, and even the assisted or artificial reproduction, through laboratory means (*in vitro* fertilization and cloning), of life itself.

It is no surprise, then, that many philosophers have taken the view that the human mind ought also to be explicable in terms of the same sort of mechanical account to which the rest of the universe has apparently yielded. This view is more or less what is meant by "materialism" – the theory that reality, or (when the term is used specifically to denote a position in the philosophy of mind) at least human reality, consists of purely material or physical objects, processes, and properties, operating according to the same basic physical laws and thereby susceptible of explanation via physical science. There is, in short, no such thing as immaterial substance, or soul, or spirit, nor any aspect of human nature which, in principle, elude explanation in purely physical terms. The mind is, paradoxical as it may sound, entirely material. (It is material, that is to say, *if* it exists at all, and there are a few radical materialists who are of a mind to deny that it does. But more on them later.)

Materialism is also sometimes referred to as *physicalism* or *naturalism*, though these terms are occasionally used by philosophers to denote views which are intended to be distinguished from materialism. This confusion in terminology is, in a way, entirely appropriate, for the materialist thesis is by no means as evident or clear-cut as it might at first appear.

Modern physical science's success in explaining the tables, chairs, rocks, and trees of everyday experience is not the only source of materialism's intuitive appeal. There is also the fact that such ordinary physical objects seem to be paradigms of what counts as *real* in the first place. If we can see, hear, taste, touch, and smell something, we know for sure (barring Cartesian evil spirits and dreams) that it exists. Conversely, our failure to provide observational evidence for something typically leads us to doubt its existence. But then, it seems that we ought to be suspicious of any claim that something other than the objects, processes, and properties of everyday experience really exists, at least if the very existence of these everyday objects, processes, and properties themselves doesn't point to the existence of some other kind of thing. Modern science has given us good reason to believe that these everyday objects, processes, and properties are constituted of the micro-phenomena described by physics and chemistry, and that they in turn constitute the macro-phenomena described by astronomy and cosmology. So we are justified in holding that such micro- and macrophenomena also exist, even though they are, in general, not directly observable. But science gives us no reason to believe that entities such as ghosts and poltergeists are real; the evidence for such things is weak, and easily explicable in more mundane terms (hallucinations, delusions, tall tales and the like). It also appears to give us no reason to believe in such things as souls or Cartesian immaterial substances. The reasonable conclusion would thus seem to be that there just are no such things. At the very least, materialists hold, we have every reason to act on the assumption that there are not, and to expect to be able to explain mental phenomena entirely in terms of the operation of physical processes and properties.

But while such considerations may give the appearance that materialism represents (as dualism claims to do) nothing more than the drawing out of the unavoidable implications of some home-spun common sense, appearances are in this case deceiving. For scientific explanations have a way of not only *explaining* what we observe in everyday experience, but also, to a very great extent, explaining it *away*. The table in front of you seems absolutely solid and impenetrable, as unlike a cloud as anything possibly could be. Yet physics tells us that a cloud, of sorts, is *exactly* what it is – a cloud of unobservable particles, each occupying less space than exists between them, so that the apparently solid and impenetrable table is mostly empty space. We take our senses to give us as much certainty as it is possible to have, and so we base our science on them. But science then informs us that our senses are largely wrong. The world revealed to us by sight, hearing, taste, touch, and smell – the world of tables, chairs, rocks, and trees – is not the touchstone of reality; that honor goes to the strange world of unobservable entities postulated by physics – the world of molecules, atoms, electrons, and quarks. What becomes, then, of the commonsensical idea that the physical objects of everyday experience are the paradigms of reality? (And if what the table *really* is is something we *don't* directly observe – a cloud of particles – then why ought we to be so suspicious of claims to the effect that certain other unobservable phenomena – souls or Cartesian immaterial substances – exist as well?)

Reduction and supervenience

As the example above illustrates, modern science also tends, in the view of many materialists, toward what is often called *reductionism*: the table is sometimes said to be "reducible to" or in reality "nothing but" a collection of particles, with the appearance of it being something other than that dismissed as an illusion. The various *properties* of the table are also reduced: what solidity it does have is said to be nothing but the state its molecules happen to be in when the field of force they generate repels those fields of force associated with other collections of particles (your hands, or the book lying on the table). Similarly, the solidity of an ice cube is nothing but the state water molecules are in when at freezing point, while the liquidity exhibited by water at higher temperatures is nothing but another state of its molecules. The temptation is to suppose that *everything* real – not just tables and ice cubes, but planets and galaxies, animals and human minds – must in some way be entirely reducible to the basic categories of physics: in some sense a planet and a mind are nothing but different kinds of configurations of molecules or atoms. The sort of materialism that makes this boldly reductionist claim is often labeled *physicalism*, the idea that basic physics reveals to us what is truly real.

The trouble is that there are things it is *very* hard to reduce down to the categories of physics in this strong sense, as most physicalists themselves will acknowledge. Cultural artefacts provide obvious examples: what makes a dollar bill the kind of currency it is seems to have little to do with the specific physical properties involved – a silver dollar is just as much a dollar as a paper one – and everything to do with social conventions, which are themselves hard to reduce to the properties of molecules in motion. Of course, all such cultural and social phenomena are ultimately mind-dependent; and the mind itself is the most notorious (and, for our purposes, relevant) example of something it seems hard to reduce to the physical, for reasons sketched in chapter 2, which we will be exploring in greater detail in the next few chapters. Moreover, physics is by no means a finished project, with the basic constituents of the material universe, and the laws governing them, all accounted for and neatly catalogued. The physics of Einstein and Heisenberg differs radically from that of Galileo and Newton, and the physics of the future may differ from both in radical ways. So in *which* physics exactly is everything real supposed to be reducible? Physicalists often reply that it is the categories of a *completed* physics – whatever body of theory future scientists will develop to solve all the problems current physics has yet to solve – that will do the job. But what if this future physics ends up having to postulate

immaterial or non-physical properties to account for mental phenomena, as some dualists have argued it will (for reasons we will be
exploring later)? In that circumstance, physicalism would turn out
to differ not at all from dualism – in which case, it would not be a
version of materialism at all.

Such problems with physicalism have led other materialistically
inclined philosophers to reject strict reduction as essential to their
position and to opt instead for the notion of *supervenience*. One
thing "supervenes" on another just in case there could not be a difference in the first without there being a difference in the second.
Materialism can accordingly be understood as the claim that all *real*
objects, properties, and processes, including those of the mind,
supervene on purely *physical* objects, properties, and processes:
nothing that happens, and in particular nothing mental, can
happen at all unless something happens at the purely physical level,
and ultimately at the level of the most fundamental entities postulated by physics. Unlike reductionism, this need not entail that the
basic entities are, in some sense, all that "really" exist: perhaps there
is a sense in which tables, chairs, rocks, trees, bodies, brains, and
even minds are every bit as real as fundamental physical particles. It
entails only that everything that happens at the level of tables,
rocks, minds, etc. ultimately happens only *because* something
happens at the level of fundamental particles. Some philosophers
who are committed to the idea of the supervenience of the
mental on the physical prefer the label *naturalism* to physicalism,
the idea being that it isn't necessarily just the basic entities postulated by physics that constitute reality, but rather the natural world
of material phenomena in general (as distinguished from purported *supernatural* phenomena, for example, Cartesian substances,
angels, or God).

Of course, as it stands, this is all pretty vague; and one of the
things that needs to be clarified is what exactly is meant by the
claim that there *could not* be a difference in the thing that supervenes without a difference in the thing supervened on. Is it that it

is metaphysically impossible for a difference in the first to occur without a difference in the second (to use the terminology introduced in the last chapter), or only that it is physically impossible? If the claim is understood in the first way, then many of the problems that afflict reductionism turn out also to afflict the suggestion that the mental supervenes on the physical (for reasons we'll be exploring later). But if the claim is understood in the second way, then it isn't clear that the position that results genuinely counts as a form of materialism. For to claim that it is physically impossible for there to be a difference at the mental level without some difference at the physical level is just to claim that there can be no such difference *given the way the actual world happens to work*; it is not to claim that it is metaphysically impossible; that is, impossible in any possible world, not just in the actual one — and thus it is not to claim anything that rules out the dualist's basic idea that it is metaphysically possible for the mind to exist apart from the brain and body.

The advocate of supervenience has, no less than the reductionist, the problem of giving a useful account of exactly *what* the basic entities and laws of physics are on which everything is claimed to supervene. The response that a "completed physics" will someday give the answer leaves open the possibility that the hypothetical physicists of the future will see fit to add non-physical or immaterial phenomena to their list. Indeed, at least one self-described naturalist, David Chalmers, has predicted that this is precisely what the physics of the future will require — which is why he counts himself not only as a naturalist, but also as a dualist, thereby explicitly rejecting any essential link between naturalism and materialism!

This last point should caution us to keep in mind that, as I indicated earlier, the terms "naturalism," "materialism," and "physicalism" — and I should now add the terms "reductionism" and "supervenience" — are used by philosophers in a bewildering variety of ways. For our purposes it will suffice to reiterate that "materialism" essentially conveys a general commitment to the idea that physical reality is all the reality there is. Attempts to spell this basic idea out in greater detail tend either to take current physics (or something like it) as the touchstone of what counts as "physical reality" (and thus frequently adopt the label "physicalism"), or instead to leave the concept of the physical somewhat open-ended (and thus sometimes opt for the label "naturalism"). Predictably, the former sort of approach, being bolder and more determinate, is harder to defend, while the latter, though easier to defend, is often less determinate, and in some cases even less clearly "materialistic" in substance. Either way, the intuitive and commonsense feel of materialism seems to last only as long as one keeps one's statement of it vague.

Cause and effect

So far it might seem that the initial plausibility of materialism is so vitiated by its indeterminacy that, while it is understandable how some might find it attractive, it is hard to see why it has become the mainstream position in the philosophy of mind. But we must not forget the interaction problem that, as we saw in the previous chapter, serves as the main objection to dualism and the chief philosophical motivation for materialism. Modern physics, as usually interpreted, teaches us that the material universe, to which dualists, no less than materialists, take the human body to belong, is causally closed. Accordingly, nothing outside it – nothing non-physical – would seem capable of having any causal influence on what happens in that universe. But then the mind, if it were a Cartesian non-physical substance, would be incapable of having any effect on the body; and yet it seems just obvious that it does. The materialist thus concludes, and surely not unreasonably, that if the mind interacts with the body, it can't be a Cartesian non-physical substance, but must be purely material or physical.

This argument appeals to general facts about the nature of cause and effect relations in the physical world. But there are also quite specific facts about mind–body interaction that give further support to the materialist thesis. We know from everyday experience that changes in the body can have drastic effects on the mind – for instance, ingesting too much alcohol or suffering head trauma can radically impair one's ability to think clearly, or even to think at all. How could this be, if the mind is as utterly distinct from the body and brain as Descartes held it to be? We also know from modern neuroscience that various specific mental functions – vision, hearing, the understanding of language, and so on – are associated with specific regions of the brain. Again, how likely would this be, if the mind and the brain were distinct things? Nor is neuroscience the only source of scientific objections to dualism. Modern biology tells us that human beings are the products of the same, purely material, process – evolution – which operates according to the same physical laws that govern the rest of the physical universe and, beginning in the purely material environment of the early history of the Earth produced cows, houseflies, and bacteria, all of which seem obviously to be purely physical entities. So how can human beings, one outcome of this material process, be anything other than purely physical entities? The theory of relativity postulates that space and time form a single continuum – space-time – so that anything existing in time must exist also in space. Yet mental processes seem clearly to exist in time, as even Descartes acknowledged, in which case they would surely have to exist in space as well. How then could they fail to be physical or material processes?

The appeal to the success of modern science in applying the mechanistic model of explanation to every other phenomenon in the universe is thus by no means the only arrow in the materialist quiver. Both the general nature of physical causality and the specific details of the causal relations between mind and body also confer considerable plausibility on materialism. Given (a) that the nature of cause and effect relations seems to require that the causes and effects of physical processes be themselves physical, (b) that application of this idea has led to a general mechanistic model of the universe that has been enormously successful in explaining every other aspect of reality, and (c) that we already know of certain specific causal links between the mind and the brain, the materialist can argue that the most reasonable conclusion is to suppose that the mind will, eventually, yield *completely* to a purely physical explanation.

None of this exhibits by itself any fallacy in the arguments for dualism – such as the conceivability argument – that we considered in the previous chapter. But some materialists have suggested that they can even present a conceivability argument of their own, to counter that of the dualist. Imagine that in the far future, teleportation devices of the sort described in science-fiction stories become possible. A person steps into a chamber here on Earth, and a supercomputer scans his or her body and brain, recording all the information gleaned, down to the last molecule. As the person's body is destroyed, this information is beamed to another chamber on Mars and an exactly similar body appears in the Martian chamber. This sort of scenario raises all sorts of interesting philosophical questions, such as whether the person who appears in the chamber on Mars is the same as the one who stepped into the chamber on Earth, or a mere duplicate. We will address such questions in chapter 8. What we want to take note of here is that it certainly seems conceivable, and thus metaphysically possible, that the person who appears in the Martian chamber will, whether or not he or she is identical to the original, exhibit exactly the same sort of behavior, and thus appear, no less than the original did, to have a *mind*. But what caused this person to exist was the storage and transmission of purely *physical* information – the information the computer scanned from the body and brain on Earth – and the use of that information to produce the person who appeared in the chamber on Mars. It would seem, then, that purely physical factors can generate a mind, in which case there is reason to believe that the mind is purely physical.

This argument is not exactly parallel to the dualist's conceivability argument. That argument was intended to prove that the mind and brain are not identical, while this one is intended to support the claim that they are or at least that the former supervenes on the latter. But conceivability arguments, if they prove anything, seem unable to prove positive claims about identity or supervenience. If you really can conceive of the mind existing apart from the body or brain, it is at least plausible that this would provide evidence that they are not identical, for if they were, how could you have one without the other? But to conceive of them existing together hardly proves that they are identical – after all, even the dualist supposes that they normally do exist together, and insists only that they nevertheless could, in principle, come apart. To imagine that all creatures with kidneys also have hearts doesn't prove that hearts and kidneys are the same type of organ; similarly, to imagine minds existing wherever brains exist hardly demonstrates that the mind and the brain are the same thing. So the materialist conceivability argument cannot, in the nature of the case, prove its conclusion. Nevertheless, it vividly illustrates, and provides intuitive support for, the conclusion the materialist draws from the other considerations we've examined: that it seems at least possible that purely material processes could entirely account for the existence and nature of the mind.

Behaviorism

Suppose we grant the strength of the materialist's case so far. As it stands, it supports at most the claim that it is possible to give a purely physical account of the mind. But how is this possibility to be made actual? Can the materialist tell us specifically how entirely material processes in the body and brain produce all the rich mental phenomena we've described in the previous two chapters – consciousness and thought, qualia and intentionality, and a robust sense of selfhood? Materialists have proposed several possible answers to this question, and the first to gain currency in the mid-twentieth century – the era in which materialism became the majority position within the philosophy of mind – was *behaviorism* (sometimes called "philosophical behaviorism" to distinguish it from the "methodological behaviorism" associated with B. F. Skinner and other psychologists, which is a different, though related, idea).

Behaviorism holds that to attribute a mind to something is to attribute to it certain *behavioral dispositions*; to have the relevant dispositions *just is* to have a mind. To experience pain, for example, is nothing more than to be disposed to exhibit such behaviors as moaning, wincing, crying, or saying "Ouch!" when one's body has been injured. To believe that it's raining outside is to be disposed to look for an umbrella, or put on galoshes whenever the weather forecast predicts rain. To feel fear is just to have a tendency to tremble and/or run away when in the presence of wild animals, or knife-wielding strangers in dark alleys. In general, to have any sort of mental state is just to have a propensity to produce certain behavioral *outputs* in response to given environmental *inputs*, and in particular in response to the effects one's surroundings typically have on one's sensory organs. If behaviorism is true, then the explanation of the mind in entirely material terms would be relatively easy, simply a matter of showing that a purely physical system is capable of exhibiting the behavior associated with having a mind – something the human body obviously *is* capable of.

Behaviorism isn't true, though. It is sometimes said that no philosophical theory has ever been decisively refuted, although probably not by anyone familiar with this account of the mind, which appears not to have a single defender today. To be fair, it is clear that behaviorism has certain advantages. It makes the mind every bit as observable and accessible to scientific study as tables, chairs, rocks, and trees, and it can seem to reflect common sense, in so far as the way we normally do have access to minds, or at least to the minds of other people, is precisely through their behavior. What you *observe* in observing someone's grief seems, strictly speaking, not to be something going on *inside* him or her, but rather just certain outward behaviors: sobbing, grimacing, and the like. Moreover, this fact, together with a certain theory of meaning prominent in mid-twentieth century philosophy – the "verifiability theory," which held that the meaning of a statement is its method of verification – seemed to make behaviorism almost unavoidable: if the only evidence you could have for verifying claims about what other people are thinking is the behavior they exhibit, then to say that they are thinking must be nothing more than to say that they tend to exhibit certain behaviors.

The verifiability theory has long since been abandoned, for a number of reasons, not the least of which is that, since it is hard to see how the theory itself could be verified, it is also hard to see how it could fail to imply its own meaninglessness; and with the verifiability theory goes the strongest argument that could possibly be given for behaviorism, in the absence of which its problems seem overwhelming. For one thing, it is notoriously difficult to see how talk about minds could ever be completely reduced to talk about behavior. To say that to believe it is raining is just to be disposed to put on galoshes or look for an umbrella is obviously not quite the whole story. Someone who believes that it is raining will do these things only if he or she desires not to get wet, and a desire is itself a kind of mental state. So the behaviorist now has to analyze *the desire not to get wet* in terms of behavior, in order to complete the analysis of *the belief that it is raining* in the same terms. But someone will desire not to get wet only if, for example, he or she also fear catching cold, and *the fear that one will catch cold* is thus yet another mental state that must be analyzed in terms of behavior – a mental state that will in turn be present only if a further mental state, *the belief that getting wet causes colds* is also present, and which will also have to be given a behaviorist analysis. And so on *ad infinitum*. There seems, accordingly, no way for the behaviorist ever to cash out all talk about mental states and processes in terms of nothing but behavior.

More fundamentally, the theory leaves out the subjectivity that, as we saw in chapter 2, seems essential to the mind. Whether or not I know about other people's minds from behavior alone, that is surely not how I know about my own: it's not as if I have to catch myself in a mirror screaming and crying before I can conclude "Hey, look at that! I must be in pain!" The subject of thoughts and experiences appears to have an access to them that others do not have, an access that does not rest on the observation of behavior. Indeed, given this subjectivity, behavior of any sort seems inessential to the mind. A good actor could convincingly exhibit all the behavior associated with the most excruciating pain, and yet not be in pain at all; an even better actor could really be suffering excruciating pain and yet, to all appearances, be feeling nothing. The mental facts – the presence or lack of the "qualia" associated with pain – would in either case consist entirely of what was going on from the "inner," subjective point of view of the actor, and be knowable only from that point of view, the behavior being irrelevant.

The issue of *causation* is also relevant here, as it was in the discussion of dualism. One of the materialist's objections to dualism is that it allegedly fails fully to account for the fact that mental states are the causes of behavior. But behaviorism also fails to take account of this. For if mental states are identical to behavior, they can't be the causes of it: your belief that it's raining doesn't *cause* you to get your umbrella, according to the behaviorist; it is your getting your umbrella. To take seriously the materialist's commitment to the causal efficacy of the mental requires the rejection of behaviorism.

The identity theory

Inspired by the fact that mental states and processes seem clearly to be inner processes of some sort, and states and processes that cause outward behavior, materialists turned away from behaviorism in the 1950s and 1960s and tended to favor instead the *identity theory*. If mental states and processes are the causes of behavior, but causes that are in some way inside the one exhibiting the behavior and thus unobservable, then there seems to be an obvious candidate from the materialist point of view for where exactly such inner causes might be found: the brain. In this view, mental states and processes are just neurological states and processes; that is, they are states and processes of the brain and central nervous system. The mind is identical to the brain.

Here again we have a claim that seems simple and obvious, but which in reality is neither. The idea is that any given mental state – your thought about your grandmother, the sensation of pain in your lower back, your memory of your last trip to London – is *the exact same thing as* the firing of such-and-such a clump of neurons in your brain. It is important to understand precisely what this means. It is *not* the claim that what happens in the mind is *affected* by what happens in the brain – that the feelings and sensations you have, your abilities to remember and think clearly, and so forth, depend on various neural structures and processes. No-one denies that – certainly not the dualist, who insists, as we've seen, that the mind and brain interact with one another (even if he has a hard time explaining how). If that were all the identity theory were saying, it wouldn't be very interesting or controversial. The theory is, rather, not that your thought is *caused* by such-and-such neurons firing, but that it *is* such-and-such neurons firing. There is *nothing more* to the thought than that. Certain electrochemical signals are sent from one part of the brain to another; and that, and only that, is what constitutes a thought, feeling, or sensation. If you were able to peer inside someone's skull and somehow see the neurons firing, you would, literally, be looking at his or her thoughts.

If that doesn't sound strange to you, you probably haven't understood the theory correctly. It is meant to sound strange; or at least, it is not meant to sound obvious. Identity theorists took themselves to be putting forward a bold scientific hypothesis, not a common sense truism. The idea was that the identification of the mind with the brain ought to be accepted as the latest in a long series of scientific reductionist explanations. As noted earlier, everyday physical things like tables and chairs, though they seem to be utterly impenetrable objects with features like color, taste, and odor, are really nothing but swarms of colorless, odorless, and tasteless microscopic particles. Physical objects have been "reduced" to collections of molecules and atoms by contemporary physics. Similarly, properties like heat, cold, liquidity, or luminance have been reduced to properties of aggregates of molecules, or atoms. So water turns out to be nothing other than a particular chemical compound, a composite of hydrogen and oxygen: H_2O. Heat, to use another typical example, is nothing but the motion of molecules – high mean molecular kinetic energy, to be slightly more precise. Such reductions reveal the true nature of everyday commonsense phenomena, and allow us to understand them and predict their behavior with greater precision than common sense makes possible.

Reductions sometimes take place *within* science: the biological concept of the gene, for instance, turns out to be reducible to the more fundamental concept of DNA. This sort of example is called an "intertheoretic reduction": the reduction, that is, of the laws and ontology of one scientific theory to those of another. The ontology of a theory is just the list of the basic entities it postulates, such as the molecules, atoms, and sub-atomic particles of modern physics; the laws of the theory are the principles it says govern the activities of the entities in its ontology, such as the principles of quantum mechanics that are said to govern the basic entities postulated by physics. In the case of an inter-theoretic reduction, the entities of the theory that gets reduced turn out to be identical to, or "nothing but," the entities spoken of by the reducing theory: genes, to over-simplify again, turn out to be reducible to, or are in reality nothing but, aspects of DNA. There is, accordingly, a law-like connection between the entities of the reduced and reducing theories: in every case where such-and-such a gene is present, such-and-such an aspect of DNA is also present.

The identity theory is sometimes formulated as a kind of inter-theoretic reduction. Our ordinary, commonsense way of talking about our minds and of explaining our behavior in terms of what is happening in our minds – speaking of beliefs and desires, for example, or of a person's behavior as being caused by certain specific beliefs and desires – is claimed to be a quasi-scientific "theory." It is, to be sure, not a sophisticated theory, stated with mathematical precision, created by an eccentric academic or graduate student, proffered in the lecture hall or tested in the laboratory. But it does, or so it is argued, have certain features of a scientific theory. It has a complex ontology – it talks not only of beliefs and desires, but also of hopes, fears, experiences, feelings, emotions, sensations – and it appeals to certain quasi-law-like generalizations: that a desire for a cheeseburger will tend to cause one to eat a cheeseburger, that the sensation of pain will tend to cause moaning and complaining, or that the belief that danger is near will tend to cause fleeing the scene. Since this "theory" is a theory about the mind, and since it is a theory that is held by the "common people" as much as by the educated, it is typically referred to by philosophers as *folk psychology*. The identity theory can thus be expressed as the hypothesis that folk psychology can be reduced to neuroscience, the science of the brain. Just as the theory that spoke of genes and the like turned out to be reducible to a theory that speaks instead in terms of DNA, so too should we reduce beliefs, desires, experiences, sensations, and emotions, to brain states and processes.

Identity theorists appeal, in defense of their theory, to the sorts of considerations adduced earlier in favor of materialism in general, and to the dependence of various specific kinds of mental functions (language, vision, etc.) on various specific regions of the brain in particular. They acknowledge that their theory might seem counter-intuitive: how, it might be asked, can subjective thoughts and sensations be nothing but electrochemical signals passing between nerve cells? But they also note that a table, for instance, does not seem much like a collection of particles, even though that is what it is. Common sense has often been challenged by the advance of science. If the identity theory too challenges common sense, that can, by itself, be no objection.

There are, however, more serious problems with the identity theory, which materialists themselves have pointed out. The first has to do with a technical distinction made by philosophers between *types* and *tokens*. Consider the sentence: "The cat is on the mat." How many words are in that sentence? The answer depends on whether we count "the" once or twice. If we count "the" as one word, we are counting it by *type*; if we count it twice (since it appears twice in the sentence) we are counting its *tokens*. There are *five* different words in the sentence if we count word types, and *six* if we count word tokens. What is true of words is also true of mental states and brain states (and pretty much everything else, for that matter). We can, for instance, distinguish between a general type of mental state (for example, the belief that it is raining) and particular tokens of that type (for example, the belief that it is raining that I had earlier this summer, the belief that it is raining that I had last April 16, the belief that it is raining that you had on May 1, and so on). The identity theory was originally intended as what might be called a "type-identity" theory: it claimed that for each *type* of mental state (the belief that it is raining, the belief that it is sunny, the desire for a cheeseburger, the desire for a cookie, and so on and on) there could ultimately be matched, one-to-one, a specific *type* of brain state (neuronal firing pattern of type A, neuronal firing pattern of type B, and so forth).

The trouble is that it seems clear that there *can't* be such a neat matching, because there can't be such a thing as a law-like correlation between mental states and brain states. Recall a point made above in response to behaviorism: a person will typically desire not to get wet only if he or she has other mental states, such as a fear of catching cold and a belief that getting wet tends to cause colds; moreover, he or she will have *those* mental states only if he or she also believes that catching a cold will be unpleasant, and desires to avoid this unpleasantness more than desiring to frolic in the rain, etc. Any given mental state, then, is never had individually, but involves the having of other mental states as well; and it typically also involves there being rational connections between the mental states one has. It is *because* one believes that catching cold is unpleasant and that getting wet tends to cause colds that one *infers* that one had better not get wet, and then draws the further inference that since going out in the rain, however pleasant, will cause getting wet, one had better not go out in the rain.

So there are *logical relations* between mental states that partially determine precisely which mental states one will have, if one has any at all. But there seem just obviously to be no such relations between neurons firing in the brain. It would be absurd to say – indeed, it isn't clear what it could even *mean* to say – that "neuronal firing pattern of type A logically entails neuronal firing pattern of type B," or that "the secretion of luteinizing hormone is logically inconsistent with the firing of neurons 6,092 through 8,887." Neurons and hormone secretions have *causal* relations between them; but *logical* relations – the sort of relations between propositions like "It is raining outside" and "It is wet outside" – are not causal. There seems to be no way to match up sets of logically interrelated mental states with sets of merely causally interrelated brain states, and thus no way to reduce the mental to the physical. The best we can hope for is a kind of "token-identity" theory:

particular mental state tokens are identical to particular brain state tokens – your belief that it's raining is identical to the firing of some neurons or other – but there is no way to correlate mental state and brain state types in a law-like way, no way to describe the relationship between them in terms of a rigorous scientific theory. This sort of view is sometimes called *anomalous monism*, a label coined by Donald Davidson (1917–2003), the philosopher most closely associated with it: mental events are identical to physical events, the physical being all that ultimately exists (hence "monism"); but there is no way to formulate any scientific laws connecting the mental and the physical (hence the adjective "anomalous").

A related problem with the identity theory is that it seems possible that there could be creatures that have minds even though they lack brains; the mind, that is to say, seems "multiply realizable" – something that could be "realized," or exist in, systems other than those composed of neurons. Divine beings and angels would be obvious examples, and even most atheists would admit that such beings are at least metaphysically possible, whether or not they exist in the actual world. Extraterrestrials with physiological characteristics utterly different from our own – with nothing remotely similar to human brains or nervous systems – and androids with artificial brains composed of silicon, plastic, and copper wiring, would also seem potential candidates for creatures that can be said to think and feel despite lacking our neurological makeup. But then, if minds could possibly exist in physical systems other than brains, how can they be *identical* to brains?

Functionalism

The multiple realizability objection leads us naturally – as it historically led most materialists – to the form of materialism that has been dominant in the philosophy of mind since the 1970s.

Functionalism takes as its starting point the observation that many things are properly characterized not in terms of the stuff out of which they are made, but rather by reference to the functions they perform. A knife is defined by its ability to cut, not its material composition; whether the knife is made of steel or plastic is irrelevant to its status as a knife. The game pieces of checkers are defined in terms of the functions each piece plays in the course of the game: usually the pieces are made out of plastic and moved about on a cardboard surface, but in principle one could draw a checkers board on the beach, and play the game using crushed beer cans and dead crabs. Of course, not just *any* sort of material composition will do: it would be difficult to play checkers with game pieces made of shaving cream, and a knife made out of shaving cream wouldn't truly be a knife at all. But the point is that there is still no *specific* kind of physical stuff that knives or checkers pieces have to be made out of; lots of things could do the job, as long as they have the right sort of structure to perform the requisite functions.

The functionalist claims that something similar is true of mental states and processes. It is not the stuff of which it is made that makes a particular mental state the kind it is – whether the firing of neurons or otherwise – but rather what it does, and, in particular, what sorts of causes and effects it has. What makes a sensation of pain the kind of thing it is, is that it is caused by damage to the body and tends to cause in turn certain other mental states, like anxiety, as well as behaviors like screaming and crying. What makes the belief that it is raining the sort of thing it is, is that it tends to be caused by light reflected from raindrops striking the retinas, tends in turn, and when a desire to stay dry is also present, to cause certain other mental states such as the intention to get an umbrella, and tends, in tandem with these other mental states, to cause bodily behavior like going to the closet to get an umbrella. Mental states are to be defined, then, in terms of their causal relations to other mental states, and ultimately this system of mental states is itself to be defined in terms of its causal relations to the inputs provided by environmental influences on the sensory organs and the outputs manifested in bodily behavior. That the whole system manifests the *specific kinds* of causal relations it does is what makes each element within it a distinctly *mental* state or process, and what makes the system as a whole a *mind*; whether this system is instantiated in a human brain, the slimy innards of an extra-terrestrial, or the silicon central processing unit of a sophisticated robot is irrelevant. Just as anything performing the right sort of function is a knife, whether made of plastic, steel, or something else, so too can anything manifesting the right sort of causal relations be said to have a mind, whether it is a creature with a nervous system like ours or some very different sort of being altogether: an ET, an android, or an angel.

One of the advantages claimed for this view is that it allows for an analysis of the mind that is, in principle, neutral between materialism and dualism. Functionalism *per se* holds only that mental states are to be defined in terms of their causal relations; it does not rule out the possibility that these causal relations might be instantiated in a Cartesian immaterial substance rather than in something physical. But of course the theory also allows that something that *is* entirely material could have a mind, as long as it is complex enough to manifest the relevant causal relations, and the human brain, being the most complex object known to us, surely fulfills this requirement. Functionalism thereby makes possible an explanation of the mind in purely physical terms, and this, together with Occam's razor, seems to favor materialism over dualism. Moreover, since the theory holds that minds could be instantiated in systems other than brains, it is sometimes suggested that functionalism allows the materialist to rebut the dualist's conceivability argument: if it seems conceivable that the mind could exist apart from the brain, this might simply be because mental states are multiply realizable – possibly instantiated in physical systems other than brains – and not because they can exist totally independent of *any* material substrate. Thus functionalism, even if in principle consistent with dualism, has in practice become the favored theory of materialists.

Some might question whether the idea of multiple realizability, on which functionalism rests, is really all that plausible in the first place. Should we accept so readily the suggestion that a sophisticated robot, of the sort described in the science-fiction novels of Isaac Asimov, in the *Terminator* movies, or the character Data on *Star Trek*, can be said *literally* to think and feel as we do? If we accept that such creations of fiction are at least conceivable – that we can coherently imagine a creature constructed of nothing but steel and plastic, yet which has a mind – then this would seem to give some support to the functionalist. After all, if you could really meet Data or the Terminator and engage in a conversation with them, would you really have any doubt that they were as intelligent as you? If Data asked you what time it was, wouldn't this be reason to think he *desired* to know the time? If the Terminator told you he had come from the far future, wouldn't this be evidence that he *believed* that that's where he came from? Beliefs and desires are kinds of mental states; so anything that possessed them could surely be said to have a mind. One might, nevertheless, object that such creatures wouldn't have the *feelings* and *emotions* we have. But why couldn't they? Doesn't this objection reflect merely the bias of science-fiction writers for the stereotype of the cold, unfeeling machine rather than any objective limits on the kind of robots that might in theory be constructed? The functionalist, it must be remembered, holds that feelings and emotions too are nothing but states having certain kinds of causal relations. Why couldn't such states be built into a robot? If a robot had an internal state that was caused by damage to its body, that caused it to scream and cry out and look frantically for ways to repair the damage, why wouldn't this count as pain? If you saw Data flailing on the ground, shrieking and sobbing and holding his side after having been shot with a ray gun, wouldn't you try to help him? Would you say to him "Cut it out, you're just a robot – you don't *really* feel anything!" (And what if he told you that it hurt his feelings to hear you say that? Mightn't you wonder at least a *little* whether he really did have feelings after all?)

The functionalist would argue further that the suggestion that there could be thinking and feeling robots cannot in any event be dismissed by anyone who takes seriously the general materialist claim that mental states and processes are entirely explicable by reference to states and processes of the brain. A clump of neurons is, after all, no less purely physical than a cluster of silicon computer chips in the head of a robot. Why should it be so outrageous to suggest that something whose "brain" is made of such computer chips can think and feel as we do? Why should electrical current passing between computer chips be any less capable of producing mental states than electrochemical signals sent between neurons?

A single neuron performs a relatively simple task: it gets signals from some neurons and then sends signals to others. Why couldn't a computer chip do that? Suppose a very small clump of your neurons were replaced by tiny computer chips, and that they received and sent signals in just the way the original neurons did. Is there any doubt that you'd be just as conscious and capable of thought as you were before? An artificial heart doesn't make the person receiving it any less capable of pumping blood: an artificial heart is still a heart, because it performs the functions of a heart. So why should artificial neurons be any less capable of supporting thought and feeling, if they do exactly what real neurons do? Suppose further that the nerve endings in your hand were replaced by artificial nerve endings – made of microscopic wires, or the sorts of tiny mechanisms familiar from nanotechnology – that functioned exactly as the originals did, registering damage to the body, the presence of heat and cold, and so forth. Is there any reason to doubt that you'd be just as capable of feeling pain, warmth, or coolness as you were before? If so, why exactly? The artificial nerve endings function physically in exactly the same way as the originals; so why shouldn't their ultimate effects be the same? Now imagine that other neurons and nerve endings are gradually replaced in a similar fashion, and also that various organs – a liver, a kidney, a lung – are replaced by extremely complex and sophisticated duplicates, constructed of plastic, steel, and silicon but which exactly mimic the functioning of the originals. Is there any reason to doubt that you would be able to think and feel just as well as you ever did? The new organs and neurons function physically *exactly* as the originals did; so why wouldn't their end results be identical as well? (And if you *do* somehow lose the ability to think and feel as before, exactly *when* does this happen? Replacing *one* clump of neurons or nerve endings had no such effect – so why should replacing two, three, two thousand, or two million?) Finally, imagine that eventually your *entire* body and nervous system is replaced by these artificial duplicates. Is there any doubt that you'd be just as conscious as you were before? Again, if so, why exactly? Your new parts are entirely physical, but so were your original neurons and organs, and the new parts function exactly as the originals did. So what reason could there be for doubting that you still have a mind? Notice, however, that you would in effect have become a robot. But if you, having been transformed gradually into a robot, could nevertheless think and feel, why deny that *other* robots – the kind made in a factory or laboratory – might also?

As this argument indicates, functionalism is closely tied to the idea that the brain is a kind of *computer*, with the mind a kind of *program*: the software that runs on the hardware of the brain. We will explore this in greater detail in chapter 6. Suffice it for now to note that this suggestion provides the materialist with a way of elucidating the functionalist thesis, and of arguing that it eliminates the mystery of how something purely material could have a mind. A computer program is something abstract – a mathematical structure that can be understood and specified, on paper or in the programmer's mind, long before anyone implements it in a machine. Yet for the program to become "real" – for it to have any impact on the physical world and be usable by us – it must be so implemented. Unless you can download it on to an actual piece of computer hardware, it remains purely abstract and inefficacious. It needn't be any *particular* computer that does the job – some programs could be run on almost *any* computer – but there must be *some* computer or other that does it. This may serve as a fitting analogy for the mind: we can understand the mind in functionalist terms, by abstracting away from it any of the physical details of its implementation in human brains and focusing only on its causal structure. This may give the illusion that it is capable of existing apart from some implementation; but in fact, just like a computer program, it must be implemented in some physical system or other – and if not necessarily in a human brain, then perhaps in a robotic or extraterrestrial brain. Furthermore, despite a program's abstract character, there is no mystery about how it can be run on a piece of computer hardware. But then, by analogy, there need be no mystery about how the mind can be instantiated in the brain: like computer software, it is merely an instance of a complex abstract structure being realized in a complex piece of matter.

The burden of proof

Despite the ambiguities that plague attempts to give the materialist thesis a precise formulation, then, it remains powerful. If the commonsense, down to earth character of materialism is sometimes overstated by its advocates, it nevertheless seems to get strong support from general trends in modern science. Moreover, in functionalism, materialists have a promising general philosophical theory of how the mind might be realized in something purely material, and there is compelling evidence from neuroscience that mental states and processes are indeed inextricably tied to states and processes of the brain.

What implications does all of this have for the dispute between materialism and dualism? Many materialists are of the opinion that the considerations adduced so far are sufficient by themselves to establish the rational superiority of their creed. Materialism is, in their estimation, fully capable in principle of explaining the mind. The work remaining is little more than a mopping up operation, the mere filling in of details. Dualists have effectively been refuted; at the very least, the burden of proof lies with them, not with the materialists. Given the overall evidence, materialism has a presumption in its favor. It is innocent until proven guilty.

So it might seem. Dualists could reply, however, that the philosophical advantage claimed by materialism may be illusory, with the current consensus in its favor a reflection more of intellectual fashion than of objective, dispassionate evaluation of the relevant arguments. In particular, dualists might argue that there is no good reason to take seriously the suggestion that, in the debate between materialism and dualism, it is materialism which must get the benefit of the doubt. The purported historical justification for such an attitude is familiar enough: for centuries, it is said, materialists and their opponents did philosophical battle, with neither side gaining the advantage; but then along came modern science, and phenomena which previously seemed inexplicable except in terms of supernatural forces increasingly succumbed to materialistic explanation. The mind is merely the last holdout, and that circumstance is only temporary; for with the rise of neuroscience, we now stand on the threshold of finally explaining the mental in entirely physical terms, and the materialist worldview will thereafter be completely vindicated. But however influential it has been, this historical-philosophical case has, arguably, been overstated.

First, the advance of science, far from settling the mind-body problem in favor of materialism, seems to have made it more acute. Modern science has, as noted in chapter 2, revealed that physical objects are composed of intrinsically colorless, tasteless, and odorless particles. Colors, tastes, and odors thus, in some sense, exist only in the mind of the observer. But then it is mysterious how they are related to the brain, which, like other material objects, is composed of nothing more than colorless, tasteless, and odorless particles. Science also tells us that the appearance of purpose in nature is an illusion: strictly speaking, fins, for example, don't have the purpose of propelling fish through the water, for they have in fact *no purpose at all*, being the products of the same meaningless and impersonal causal processes that are supposed to have brought about all complex phenomena, including organic phenomena. Rather, fins merely operate *as if* they had such a purpose, because the creatures that first developed them, as a result of a random genetic mutation, *just happened* thereby to have a competitive advantage over those that did not. The result mimicked the products of purposeful design; in reality, it is said, there was no design at all. But if purposes are thus "mind dependent" – not truly present in the physical world but only projected on to it by us – then this makes that act of projection, and the intentionality of which it is an instance (as are human purposes, for that matter) at least difficult to explain in terms of processes occurring in the brain, which seem intrinsically as brutely meaningless and purposeless as are all other purely physical processes. In short, science has "explained" the sensible qualities and meaning that seem to common sense to exist in reality only by sweeping them under the rug of the mind; that is, it hasn't really explained them at all, but merely put off any explanation by relocating them out of the physical and into the mental realm. There they remain, however, forming a considerable bump under the rug – one that seemingly cannot be removed by further scientific sweeping.

Second, the debate over materialism has arguably never been more than tangentially concerned with how best to explain physical phenomena – the motions of the planets, the nature of chemical reactions, or even the origins of life. That is to say, straightforwardly scientific issues seem never to have been the crucial ones. Rather, the debate has, for two and a half millennia, focused primarily on three fundamental metaphysical issues: the nature of the mind and its relation to the body, the ontological and epistemological status of mathematical and other apparently abstract objects, and the question of the existence of God. For materialism now genuinely to have the upper hand would require that materialist arguments have been victorious, or have at least been shown to be considerably more plausible, in each of these subject domains. Has this happened? No one familiar with the recent history of philosophy can honestly think so.

This is obviously so in the case of the first domain, which is the very subject presently at issue. Materialism may be the majority position in contemporary philosophy of mind, but not because anyone has proved it true. Indeed, as we will see in succeeding chapters, virtually all the work done today by materialist philosophers of mind consists, at bottom, of trying to defend their favored brands of materialism against various objections, which are implicitly or explicitly anti-materialist in character, that is, to the effect that the brand of materialism in question fails genuinely to explain some given mental phenomenon (intentionality, qualia, etc.) in entirely physical terms. Moreover, these objections are typically variations on the same criticisms of materialism that have been given for 2,500 years, with modern materialists no closer to answering them decisively than were their intellectual forebears. Dualists might argue that the fact that the project of naturalizing the mind – of attempting to show it to be explicable without resorting to non-physical properties – is as popular as it is a sign of the weakness of materialist philosophy of mind, rather than of strength; for if there were no serious doubt that the mind is explicable in purely material terms, the naturalization project should have been largely accomplished long ago. Again, the dominance of materialism in the philosophy of mind would seem to rest largely on the belief that materialism has been established everywhere *else*, so that it is reasonable to expect it to succeed where the mind is concerned.

But it seems clear that materialism has not been established everywhere else, at least if we keep in mind that it is metaphysical disputes, not scientific ones, which have historically been at issue.

Consider the second domain of debate between materialists and their opponents, namely, the debate over abstract objects. Among philosophers, mathematics has long been the paradigm of knowledge that is absolutely certain, and that is because the truths of mathematics are *necessary* truths, true in all possible worlds. For this reason, it seems clear that these truths cannot be truths about anything either mental or material: facts about the mental are facts about a subjective realm, but mathematics is objectively true, utterly independent of human interests; facts about the material world are facts about a realm that is constantly in flux, a domain of contingency, but mathematical facts are unchanging and eternal. Mathematics thus seems to describe a third realm, a domain of abstract entities – numbers, geometrical forms – that cannot be reduced to either the mental or the physical; that is, it seems to lead to what is called *Platonism* (after Plato, the philosopher most widely associated with this sort of view). Many philosophers have of course attempted to disprove this conception of mathematics, and to show that mathematical truth can, despite appearances, be naturalized. The point is that such attempts have, at best, consistently proven to be highly controversial, and, more commonly, rejected by most philosophers as ultimately implausible. The dialectic is familiar to philosophers of mathematics: the nature of mathematical truth seems inevitably to lead to Platonism; naturalistically inclined philosophers try to show otherwise; their attempts then prove to be riddled with insuperable difficulties, or even subtly to entail Platonism of a different kind. This pattern seems to be the same today as it has been for the whole history of philosophy. And if anything, it is not naturalism but Platonism – appearing as it does to follow inevitably from the nature of mathematics, and having withstood every attempt to disprove it – which ought to get the benefit of the doubt, especially given that many mathematicians themselves, in their philosophical moments, tend to be Platonists.

What holds for mathematical objects holds no less for other apparently abstract entities. When we understand a truth of mathematics, we grasp a *proposition* – the proposition that $2 + 2 = 4$, say. But we also grasp propositions when we understand any other kind of truth, and, as in mathematics, the objects of our understanding seem clearly to be neither mental nor physical. In understanding the Pythagorean theorem, or that Caesar was assassinated on the Ides of March, you and I understand the *same thing* in each case. It is not that I understand my own subjective Pythagorean theorem and you understand yours; what we understand is something objective, something that holds true independently of either of our minds. So it cannot be something mental. But neither can it be something material, for the fact the theorem describes would hold true whatever occurs in the physical world, and even if there were no physical world. This, again, is no less true of propositions about physical things: the proposition that Caesar was assassinated on the Ides of March would remain true even if the entire physical universe disappeared tomorrow; in grasping it, you can't be grasping something material. This way of putting the argument for propositions as abstract, immaterial entities is associated with Gottlob Frege (1848–1925), but the basic idea goes back a long way in the history of philosophy, and ultimately, to Plato. Plato is also associated, of course, with the idea that our words for the properties of things – redness, roundness, or goodness – refer to *universals* or *forms* which exist in some sense abstractly, independently of particular concrete objects (that is, particular red, round, or good things). Nominalists famously deny this, but equally famously, their attempts to make sense of properties without appealing to abstract universals tend either to be implausible or to entail a subtle commitment to universals after all.

All of this is controversial; indeed, that is precisely the point. The debate over these matters is simply no closer today to being *settled*, much less settled in favor of materialism or naturalism, than it ever was. There have always been critics of Platonism about mathematics, propositions, and properties, and they have always failed decisively to make their case. For all that, they may turn out to be correct. But if so, no one has yet shown that they will. If naturalism about these purportedly abstract entities is favored by many today, that may be only because, as in the philosophy of mind, philosophers assume that naturalism or materialism has been somehow established in other contexts, and so must be the correct view to take in this one. But then the state of things in the debate over abstract objects cannot be appealed to as independent evidence of there being a reasonable presumption in favor of materialism generally.

The same thing appears to be true where the debate over the existence of God is concerned. There are, of course, a number of standard objections to the traditional arguments for God's existence. But there has also been in recent decades a great revival of interest among philosophers in the philosophy of religion in general and in the traditional theistic arguments in particular. Many contemporary philosophers of religion hold that the traditional arguments can be reformulated in a way that makes them immune to the usual objections, and that many of those objections rest in the first place on misunderstandings or even caricatures. So philosophically sophisticated is the work of these recent defenders of traditional religious belief, and so significant is the challenge it poses to atheistic naturalism, that the prominent atheist philosopher Quentin Smith has gone as far as to concede that "the great majority of naturalist philosophers have an unjustified belief that naturalism is true and an unjustified belief that theism (or supernaturalism) is false." Smith's view is not that these naturalistic philosophers are mistaken – as an atheist, he shares their naturalism – but rather that most of his fellow naturalists and atheists have not made a serious attempt to grapple with the powerful arguments that can and have been made for the other side, so that the level of confidence they have in the truth of their own position is unwarranted. The question of whether God exists is, in short, as live a philosophical issue as it ever was, and cannot reasonably be assumed to have been settled in a way that would provide support for a presumption in favor of naturalism and materialism.

A materialist could accept these points about the debate over mathematics, propositions, properties, and God (as Smith appears to do) – nothing said in this section shows, or is intended to show, that materialism is false. But to accept them would be to acknowledge that there is no basis for a *presumption* in favor of a materialist account of the mind. Such an account may have to stand or fall entirely on its own merits. Of course, if one can independently argue for a broadly naturalistic account of mathematics, propositions, properties, and the origins of the universe, then one could reasonably hold materialism to be the natural default position to take in the philosophy of mind. But by the same token, if one has instead independent reasons to endorse Platonism and/or theism, one would thereby have strong grounds for giving dualism the benefit of the doubt. The a priori plausibility of either side in the debate between materialism and dualism depends largely on the background metaphysical assumptions brought to bear in evaluating that debate. If those metaphysical issues have not been settled in favor of materialism, then there are no grounds for putting the burden of proof on the dualist.

Materialism, then, whatever its merits, may not be in quite as overwhelmingly strong a position as is often assumed. This is especially so when one considers that nothing said so far has really undermined the arguments for dualism discussed in the previous chapter. Even the claim made by some materialists that the mind's multiple realizability suffices to explain away the dualist conceivability argument is dubious: for the point of that argument is not that it is conceivable that the mind could exist in physical systems other than the brain, but rather that it is conceivable that it could exist apart from *anything physical at all*. So far we have seen no reason for doubting this.

Yet to *give* a reason for doubting it would seem necessary if materialism is to be established; and accomplishing this – showing that it is *not even conceivable* that the mind could exist apart from the physical world – is surely a tall order. If the interaction problem poses a difficulty for dualism, the dualistic arguments we've examined pose an equally daunting challenge to materialism. Accordingly, the materialist has so far achieved stalemate at most, and appeals to the advance of science, the greater parsimony of a materialist ontology, general correlations between the mind and brain, etc., ultimately cannot break it. Materialists must go beyond this, and show that all the various specific aspects of the mind – qualia and consciousness, thought and intentionality – are, despite appearances to the contrary, purely material properties, features that *cannot conceivably* exist apart from some physical substrate. The devil is in the details, and materialism and dualism stand or fall with their ability to account for those details. It is to those details that we now at last turn.

Further reading

Materialism or naturalism as a general metaphysical position is defended by David Papineau in his *Philosophical Naturalism* (Oxford: Blackwell, 1993); as a theory of the mind in particular, it is defended by D. M. Armstrong in his *A Materialist Theory of the Mind*, revised edition (London: Routledge, 1993). Paul K. Moser and J. D. Trout, eds. *Contemporary Materialism: A Reader* (London: Routledge, 1995) is a useful anthology, as is Howard Robinson, ed. *Objections to Physicalism* (Oxford: Clarendon Press, 1993), which contains essays critical of materialism.

Reductionism is the subject of the articles in David Charles and Kathleen Lennon, eds., *Reduction, Explanation, and Realism* (Oxford: Clarendon Press, 1992). An influential work on supervenience is Jaegwon Kim's *Supervenience and Mind* (Cambridge: Cambridge University Press, 1993). Chalmers' "naturalistic dualism" is defended in *The Conscious Mind* (New York: Oxford University Press, 1996). The "materialist conceivability argument" outlined in the text is developed in chapter 10 of Peter van Inwagen, *Metaphysics* (San Francisco: Westview, 1993).

Behaviorism is most widely associated with Gilbert Ryle's *The Concept of Mind* (London: Hutchinson, 1949). The identity theory is famously presented in J. J. C. Smart's "Sensations and Brain Processes," anomalous monism in Donald Davidson's "Mental Events," and functionalism in D. M. Armstrong's "The Causal Theory of the Mind" and Hilary Putnam's "The Nature of Mental States." These classic essays are widely anthologized, and all four can be found (alongside other important related articles) in either David M. Rosenthal, ed. *The Nature of Mind* (New York: Oxford University Press, 1991) or David J. Chalmers, *Philosophy of Mind: Classical and Contemporary Readings* (New York: Oxford University Press, 2002).

The debate over the metaphysical status of numbers, propositions, and properties is surveyed in Michael Jubien, *Contemporary Metaphysics: An Introduction* (Oxford: Blackwell, 1997). Frege's argument for propositions as abstract entities can be found in his famous essay "Thought," reprinted in Michael Beaney, ed. *The Frege Reader* (Oxford: Blackwell, 1997). A more recent defense of the same idea (along with a response to a common epistemic objection to belief in abstract objects) is in chapter 6 of Alvin Plantinga, *Warrant and Proper Function* (New York: Oxford University Press, 1993). J. J. C. Smart and J. J. Haldane, *Atheism and Theism*, second edition (Oxford: Blackwell, 2003) contains a good overview of the recent debate over the existence of God and an excellent bibliography of recent work in the philosophy of religion. Quentin Smith discusses the current state of atheistic naturalism in "The Metaphilosophy of Naturalism," *Philo: A Journal of Philosophy*, vol. 4, no. 2 (Fall 2001).

4

Qualia

If Descartes is right, pinching yourself will not suffice to prove that you are awake. It may suffice, however, to prove something more philosophically momentous: that materialism is false. That, at any rate, is the claim of a number of recent anti-materialist arguments in the philosophy of mind. The feel of the pinch – the subjective, "inner" element that makes it true that there is "something it is like" to be pinched – appears to be distinct from and additional to objective "outer" phenomena such as the reddening of the pinched skin, the stimulation of nerve endings, or indeed anything material or physical. It seems, in short, to be *im*material or *non*-physical, and, if it is, its very existence refutes the materialist claim that everything real is really material.

Qualia – the feel of a pinch or an itch or a pain, the taste of apple or whiskey, the redness of a fire engine or an after-image, and so on for all the sensory modalities – constitute, in the minds of many philosophers, the most serious challenge to materialism. The little said about them so far in this book has perhaps given an intuitive sense of why this is. And then again, perhaps not; for it is easy to understand why someone might not be clear on exactly what the problem is. After all, isn't the pain of your toothache, in an obvious sense, in your tooth? And if it is, doesn't that show that it is phys-ical? Your tooth is physical, after all, so wouldn't anything in it – blood vessels or pain – have to be physical too? But the pain isn't "in" your tooth in quite the same sense in which blood vessels are – you can't observe or pin-point the pain the way you can the blood vessels – and that should be a hint that there might indeed be something philosophically mysterious going on here. In any case, a number of recent arguments have attempted to make plain precisely what qualia are and how they are supposed to be impossible to account for in purely material terms.

The inverted spectrum

The idea of the "inverted spectrum" has a long history in philosophy, going back at least to Locke, but it has served recent philosophers well as a means of motivating the problem of qualia. It goes like this: it seems possible that another person, even one who is physically, behaviorally, and functionally identical to you could have color experiences which are inverted relative to your own; that is, what you see when you look at what you both call red, for instance, is what the other person sees when he or she looks at what you both call green, and vice versa, and this difference would, nevertheless, not register in what either of you said about red and green objects or in how you interacted with them. If you were somehow able to look inside the other person's mind when he or she was looking at what you both call red, you would say "Wait a second, that's what *I* would call *green*!" and if he or she could look inside your mind when you're looking at what you both call green, the other person would say "Wait a second, that's what *I* would call *red*!" Since neither of you can do this, however, the difference in the subjective character of your experiences goes unnoticed. The scenario is similar to the difference in experiences between those who are color-blind and those with normal vision: color-blind people can make many of the same discriminations between objects that everyone else can, so their color-blindness can, in principle, go undetected for quite some time. From the "outside" it might appear that the experiences of color-blind people and those of normally sighted people are identical, but they are not. The inverted spectrum scenario is just an extension of this, a case where the difference between your experiences and those of the other person is *absolutely* undetectable from the outside. It would seem to follow from the possibility of such inverted color experiences that facts about color qualia – about what it is like to experience red and green – are facts *over and above* the facts about one's physical make-up and functional organization; for those latter, purely physical facts would, in this case, not be enough by themselves to determine the nature of the color experiences one is having. But then materialism, which holds that the physical facts involved in color experiences are all the facts there are, would seem to be false.

Similar scenarios can be described in which what is inverted are not color, but some other kind of qualia. We can imagine, for example, that what you taste when eating what you and other people both call sweet is what they taste when eating what you would both call savory; that what you feel when experiencing what you would both call pain is what they feel when experiencing what you would both call pleasure, and so on. The color inversion is probably the easiest to imagine because of its similarity to the real-world phenomenon of color-blindness. But it also suggests how the materialist might be able to get around the problem. The inverted spectrum scenario will only be a difficulty for materialism if indeed there is absolutely no way *in principle* for the inversion to be detected from the outside – no way for it to manifest itself in differences in behavior, or in differences in the functional organization of you and the other person. But there seems to be good reason to doubt that this would be impossible in principle. As philosophers of mind like C. L. Hardin and Austen Clark have emphasized, the scientific study of color and color vision has revealed there to be highly complex relations between the various colors, such that any particular color can be given a detailed description in terms of its relations to the others. These form, when made thoroughly explicit, an abstract structure sometimes referred to as "color space," a system of relations within which each color can be given a precise location. This structure appears to be asymmetrical, however. Features characteristic of one part of color space – the "warmth" of red, say – are absent in other parts, such as the area where blue lies, which is characteristically "cool." The number of shades that can be discriminated in the case of one color might not match the number discriminable in the case of another: we believe, for instance, we can discriminate more shades of red than of yellow. And so forth. But these asymmetries would surely manifest themselves in the functional organization and behavior of color perceivers whose color qualia had been inverted: if you saw what I would call blue whenever you looked at what we both call red objects, you presumably would not, as I would, react to those objects in a way that corresponded to the "warmth" that their color seems to me to exhibit; if you saw what I would call yellow when you looked at what we both call red objects, you surely would not be able to distinguish the same number of shades of their color as I would be able to; and so forth. It seems likely, then, that a qualia inversion *would* in principle be detectable "from the outside" – from differences in the physical facts. Materialism, which holds that the physical facts are all the facts there are, would thus not be refuted by the inverted spectrum idea after all.

It is sometimes replied to this that even if *our* color experiences could not be inverted undetectably, it is nevertheless possible that there could be other creatures who perceived two different colors whose relations were symmetrical, so that an inversion of *their* experiences *would* be undetectable from the outside. If so, then the facts about their color experiences would be facts over and above the facts about their physical constitutions and functional organization, and the anti-materialist implications of the inverted spectrum idea would still stand. But it is not at all clear that this is possible. What exactly would these hypothetical colors be like? Certainly not like our colors (e.g. red and blue), whose structure is asymmetrical (e.g. warmth versus coolness). What we need to conceive of, then, in order to be sure that the suggestion really is possible, are colors totally unlike ours, whose structure is symmetrical and yet could be inverted without detection. But it is hard to see how anyone could, with any confidence, claim that this really is conceivable. In particular, it is hard to see how we can be confident that two colors whose relations were *entirely* symmetrical would count as *different* colors in the first place. The inverted spectrum scenario thus seems difficult to salvage as a decisive argument against materialism.

The "Chinese nation" argument

Even the inverted spectrum scenario doesn't claim to show that the physical features of the nervous system, behavior, etc. are completely divorced from qualia. What is at issue is whether the purely physical properties of your nervous system are sufficient to determine the precise character of your qualia; that you have qualia of some sort or other is not in question. But there is another famous thought experiment that attempts to show that at least the functionalist version of materialism – the version which, as we've seen, is currently the most popular – fails to explain not only the specific character of qualia but even why we have any qualia at all. This is the "Chinese nation" argument, named after a thought experiment devised by Ned Block.

Functionalism, as we've seen, takes mental states to be properly definable in terms of their causal relations, not in terms of the particular kind of stuff in which those causal relations happen to be instantiated. A belief is a belief, whether it is realized in the firing of neurons or in the passing of electrical current through computer circuitry. Anything that plays the requisite functional role will do the job. If computer chips can perform the same function as neurons – which is, basically, nothing more than the receiving and transmitting of simple signals – then they can, when organized into a system as complex as the system constituted by our neurons, generate a mental life just as rich as ours. But what is true of computer chips should, if functionalism is correct, be true of any number of other possible elements. We can imagine, for instance, that an enormous number of people – the population of China, let's suppose – could be mobilized to interact with one another in a way that exactly parallels the interaction of neurons in the brain. At the most basic level, those neurons merely send signals to fire or refrain from firing to other neurons. So we can imagine that each member of the population is given instructions to do something similar, perhaps by sending signals to each other via walkie-talkie or cell phone to the effect that the people receiving them should either go on to send a further signal down the line or to refrain from sending one. Suppose also that this vast network of people is connected, via a radio transmitter, to a complex robotic body sophisticated enough in its construction to receive, through its artificial sensory organs, just the sorts of information our senses receive and to exhibit just the sorts of behavior we exhibit. The network of walkie-talkie or cell phone-wielding signalers serves, collectively, as the "brain" of this robotic body. When the robot is kicked in the shins, the artificial nerve endings in the legs send signals up to the radio transmitter in the robot's head which in turn sends signals to a few hundred thousand members of the walkie-talkie network, who in turn send signals to a few hundred thousand others, who in turn send signals to others, and so on until at the end of the line the last members of the network send signals back to the robot, as a result of which the robot yelps "Ouch!" and rubs its shins. The signals sent between the members of the network parallel exactly the signals sent between neurons when a human being is kicked in the shins, and produce the same behavioral response. And we can imagine that the network of Chinese signalers is so organized that their interactions parallel those of neurons in every other respect as well, so that in general, the robot body behaves exactly as we do in exactly the same sorts of circumstances: conversing with others, laughing at jokes, and crying at injuries.

As in the case of the original robot example we used to motivate functionalism, we have, in this robot controlled by the population of China – "China-head," as some philosophers have affectionately dubbed it – a system which is functionally identical to us: it produces the same sorts of behavior in response to the same sorts of stimulation, and via exactly parallel intermediate processing, but instantiated in walkie-talkie-using people rather than in neurons. If the functionalist is right, this system, however eccentric, should have mental states just like ours, and in particular qualia just like ours. But would it? It is, for instance, hard to believe that when you kick China-head in the shins, the entire population of China *collectively*, as a vast super-mind, feels pain! But if it doesn't, then functionalism is false: for if a system could be functionally identical to us and yet lack qualia, then there is more to having a mind, and in particular more to having qualia, than having a certain sort of functional organization.

That is the conclusion Block and others take to be the intuitive one. But the "Chinese nation" argument, like the inverted spectrum argument, seems less than conclusive as a qualia-based argument against materialism. For it seems that the gradual transformation scenario which, as we saw in the previous chapter, the functionalist can use to defend the claim that a Data-type robot would be conscious, can be adapted for use against the "China-head" example. Consider a case we can call the "Spaghetti-head" scenario.

Even if you doubt that China-head would be conscious, you surely have no doubt that *you* are. Now imagine that you are kidnapped by mad, philosophically inclined neuroscientists who strap you to a table in their laboratory and remove the top of your skull, exposing your brain. Suppose they've figured out how to disentangle the billions of tiny nerve fibers constituting it in a way that their functioning is not affected. Slowly and carefully, they hang them from hooks above the table, labeling each one with a number. Then they treat them with a special chemical that allows the fibers to be stretched almost indefinitely without breaking or losing their conductivity. Eventually the room becomes filled with billions of tiny strands hanging from the ceiling. All this time, though, you continue to be as capable of having thoughts and experiences as you were before, and notice no difference in your mental life. Of course, all of this is science-fiction of the sort not likely ever to be realizable. But it seems perfectly conceivable, and thus metaphysically possible.

Now suppose that, as in the gradual transformation described in chapter 3, each of your stretched-out neurons is gradually replaced – only this time, they are not replaced with computer chips, but with people. Specifically, when a neuron is removed, the neuroscientists attach a radio unit to each neuron with which it had been connected, and give another radio unit to the person replacing it. Instead of sending an electro-chemical signal, the neurons which previously triggered the replaced neuron now send a radio signal which is picked up on the human replacement's radio, and that person in turn sends further radio signals, in lieu of electro-chemical ones, to other neurons, just as the original neuron used to. Suppose that at first only a hundred or so neurons are replaced in this way. As in our original replacement scenario last chapter, it seems highly implausible that this would affect mental functioning in any way: the people with the radio units are doing exactly what the original neurons did, so your mental life – including your qualia – should be just as they were before.

The reader has no doubt guessed where all this is going. We can imagine that all your neurons are eventually replaced in this way – perhaps by the population of China. Spaghetti-head is transformed into China-head. Yet at no point in this gradual transformation is it plausible that your qualia disappear, for as in the computer-chip replacement scenario described in chapter 3, the functioning of your nervous system remains exactly the same, whether composed of neurons or people with radios: why, then, should it cease generating the mental states it did before? At the very least, it seems possible, given the gradualness of the change, that your qualia would remain the same. But then Block's original "Chinese nation" example seems much less compelling. If you, having been gradually transformed into China-head, would remain conscious, why couldn't the original China-head – who is, after all, functionally identical to you – also be conscious? It seems at least arguable that it would be: in which case Block's argument also fails decisively to refute functionalism.

The zombie argument

For all that has been said so far, it might still seem that there is something fishy about the suggestion that China-head would truly be conscious. In any event, many critics of materialism hold that the basic thrust of the Chinese nation argument – that it is metaphysically possible for a creature functionally identical to us nevertheless to lack qualia – can be defended without having to appeal to systems as eccentric as the one Block envisages. This brings us to the "zombie argument."

It seems perfectly conceivable, and thus metaphysically possible, for there to be a creature which is (unlike China-head) physically identical to you, down to the last molecule – one which looks and acts exactly the same, which is absolutely indistinguishable in its material and functional characteristics even after the most detailed examination – and yet is totally devoid of conscious experience. When you step on a tack, there is damage to the skin of your foot, stimulation of the nerve endings, signals sent up the leg to the spinal cord, a consequent reflexive pulling away of your foot, further signals sent up to the brain, and complex neural processing that climaxes in you clenching your teeth and yelling "Ouch!" Also, associated with all this physical activity, there is a subjective throbbing feeling of the sort we normally associate with pain. When the creature steps on a tack, there is also damage to the skin of its foot, stimulation of its nerve endings, signals sent up its leg to the spinal cord, a consequent reflexive pulling away of its foot, further signals sent up to its brain, and complex neural processing that climaxes in it clenching its teeth and yelling "Ouch!" But there is in this case no subjective feeling of pain, or any other conscious experience associated with these physical processes at all. Anyone observing the creature from the outside would be unable to tell it apart from you, for your physical characteristics and behavior are identical. Indeed, just like you, the creature would, if asked whether it was conscious and whether it was really in pain, respond, with apparent indignation, "Of course I am!" Still, there is a dramatic difference on the *inside*: in your case, there is a rich and vivid stream of sensations and experiences; in its case, all is dark. Such a creature is what philosophers of mind have come to call a *zombie*: a creature exactly like us in all its behavioral, physical, and functional properties but totally lacking qualia.

If zombies are metaphysically possible, then materialism would seem to be false, for it holds that behavioral, physical, and functional properties are all the properties there are, and that they are entirely sufficient for the having of any mental state. But the possibility of zombies entails that facts about qualia are *additional* to, *over and above*, the having of behavioral, physical, and functional properties: if a creature could have all those properties and yet lack qualia, then to have mental states involving qualia is something more than just having those properties. The zombie argument is the flip side of the conceivability argument for dualism discussed in chapter 2. There the claim was that it is conceivable, and thus metaphysically possible, for the mind to exist apart from the body, brain, or any physical substrate at all. Here the claim is that it is conceivable, and thus metaphysically possible, for a fully functioning body and brain to exist without any mind present at all (or at least without certain aspects of the mind – qualia – being present). The upshot is the same in both cases: the mind is not merely the body or brain (or anything physical for that matter), but is something additional to them.

The zombie argument also sometimes goes by the name of the *conceivability argument*, though unlike the argument of chapter 2, it attempts to undermine materialism without necessarily committing itself to full-blooded Cartesian substance dualism. One could accept the zombie argument without holding that the mind can exist entirely apart from the brain and body; the claim would just be that even if conscious experiences are causally dependent on the brain for their existence, they are nevertheless not reducible to (or metaphysically supervenient upon) purely physical or functional properties of the brain. So some of the objections the materialist might make against Descartes's brand of dualism (to the effect that the mind seems too dependent on specific features of the brain to exist completely independently of it) are without force against this argument. The argument is also sometimes called the *modal argument* against materialism because, like the argument of chapter 2, it appeals to such modal notions as metaphysical possibility; indeed, an early version of this argument was presented by Kripke, whose work on possibility and necessity has been enormously influential in contemporary philosophy of mind, as our earlier discussion of the conceivability argument indicated. And the defense of that argument made in chapter 2 by appealing to some of Kripke's ideas would also apply more or less without alteration to defending the zombie argument against any parallel objections one might think to raise (such parallel objections being, indeed, the standard objections to the zombie argument).

The zombie argument thus seems to exacerbate the problem for materialism posed by the original conceivability argument: it is at least as strong as the latter, and maybe stronger, since it shows that the critique of materialism by no means stands or falls with the acceptability of substance dualism.

The knowledge argument

The zombie argument tries to show that physical reality does not, on its own, add up to mental reality. A related argument, which reinforces this basic idea, tries to show that knowledge of physical reality does not on its own add up to knowledge of mental reality. It is accordingly generally known as the *knowledge argument*, and derives from the contemporary philosopher Frank Jackson.

Jackson asks us to consider Mary, a neuroscientist living in the far future when we have a complete knowledge of the details of the structure and functioning of the nervous system. Mary is in the unique situation of having lived her entire life in a black-and-white room, interacting with the outside world via a black-and-white television monitor. So she has never had any experience of color. (We can even imagine that she has always worn a suit that covers her entire body, and which has kept her from seeing the color of her skin and hair, etc.) While in this room she has come to master the science of the brain, and in particular she has acquired a thorough knowledge of the physics and physiology of color perception. She has never seen the color red herself, but she knows exactly what happens in the eyes, nervous system, and on the surface of the object whenever anyone does see red. She knows down to the last detail, that is to say, all the physical facts there are to know about the perception of color. Now let's imagine that one day Mary is allowed to leave the room, and upon her release she is shown a red apple in full living color for the very first time. Will she learn anything from this experience? Surely she will: she will learn what it is like to see red. And what this shows, according to the argument, is that materialism is false.

The reasoning is this. Materialism claims that the physical facts about perception and the like are all the facts there are. But Mary, hypothetically, knew all the physical facts there were to know about perception – the sorts of facts that could be written down in neuroscience textbooks or conveyed in lectures heard over the television monitor. Yet she did not know all the facts there were to know about perception, because she learned something new about it upon leaving the room – and you can't learn something you knew already. So what she learned must be a *non*-physical fact. In particular, knowledge about qualia – about what it's like to see red, for instance – must be knowledge about something non-physical.

The suggestion that knowledge of all the relevant physical facts cannot yield knowledge of all the facts about conscious experience has also been illustrated vividly in an example given by Thomas Nagel. Bats, Nagel notes, navigate via senses very different from our own: where we rely chiefly on vision and hearing, they use a kind of sonar or echolocation, putting together a sensory map of the external world by emitting shrieks and then registering the sound waves that bounce back to them from the objects in their immediate environment. The experiences bats have in perceiving the world in this way must be radically dissimilar to ours. Scientific investigation into the structure and functioning of a bat's nervous system may well give us insight into the mechanics underlying its perceptions. But the nature of the perceptual experiences themselves – what it is like to *be* a bat – cannot be revealed by such inquiry, Nagel argues. For science gives us only the objective, third-person facts about any phenomenon, leaving aside any aspect tied to a particular point of view. But it is only from the particular, subjective point of view of a bat that a bat's experiences can be understood. Materialistic scientific accounts must necessarily be inadequate to capture all the facts about a bat's consciousness – or any consciousness, for that matter.

One response sometimes made to arguments like this is that they simply assume that future neuroscience won't be able to explain all there is to explain about conscious experiences: how can we know for sure that Mary wouldn't know what it is like to see red, simply from having mastered the material in her textbooks while in the black-and-white room? There are two problems with this suggestion. The first is that it seems intuitively implausible. Any facts the neuroscientists of the future are likely to discover are bound to be facts of the same general sort they already know: facts about how neurons are wired, or about which biochemical substances are involved in which processes. It is hard to see how any further knowledge of that sort – of yet more objective, third-person phenomena – could reveal the subjective, first-person facts about what it is like to experience red or to get about by echo-location; there is just a basic and straightforward conceptual difference between the former sort of fact and the latter. The second problem is that the suggestion at hand seems inevitably beset by the same indeterminacy that plagues some versions of physicalism, as we saw in the previous chapter: what if the way neuroscientists of the future explain conscious experience is by positing non-physical properties? This would vindicate the knowledge argument rather than undermine it. Yet there is nothing about the current course of neuroscience that can reasonably lead us to expect any other way in which it might explain consciousness.

More formidable responses to the knowledge argument usually proceed by conceding that there is a sense in which Mary would learn something upon leaving the room, even though she's mastered the neuroscience of the future. The strategy is then to argue that what she learns can, when rightly understood, be seen not genuinely to threaten materialism. Paul Churchland argues that on leaving the room, Mary would not actually learn any new *facts*; rather, she would just learn, in a new *way*, facts she *already* knew. So since she already knew all the physical facts, and there are no new facts (non-physical or otherwise) she learns after leaving the room, the conclusion that the physical facts cannot be all the facts there are is blocked. Churchland elaborates upon this suggestion by appealing to Russell's famous distinction between "knowledge by acquaintance" and "knowledge by description": you might now know about giraffes only by descriptions you've heard or read in a book, but you might someday know about them by becoming directly acquainted with them in perceptual experience; similarly, Mary, while still in the room, knew all the facts about the experience of red only by description, and then becomes directly acquainted with those very same facts after leaving the room.

One possible objection to this argument is that it seems implausible to suggest that Mary doesn't learn a new fact on leaving the room: surely the fact that red looks like *this* (where "this" refers to the immediate sensation she has of the color) is a fact she did not know before leaving the room, but learns afterward. Another problem is that the Russellian distinction Churchland appeals to is not as philosophically neutral as it might appear. Russell himself held that all we really know by acquaintance are, not external physical objects like giraffes, but rather (what philosophers these days would call) the subjective qualia we normally suppose to have been produced by such external objects; the external physical world in its totality is something we know only indirectly, by description. This goes hand in hand with the sort of indirect realist theory of perception discussed in chapter 1, of which Russell was a proponent (as is Jackson, for that matter). It also raises the question of precisely what these qualia are with which we are directly acquainted; Jackson and (as we'll see in the next chapter) Russell take them to be irreducible to the sorts of properties revealed by physical science, properties which, unlike qualia, we cannot know by acquaintance. So to appeal to Russell's conception of knowledge by acquaintance can hardly help Churchland in rebutting an argument against materialism. But to reject Russell's conception and insist instead that knowledge by acquaintance does not involve knowledge of non-physical qualia would be to beg the question. Either way, it seems that Churchland's response to Jackson's argument fails.

Another response is put forward by David Lewis, who, like Churchland, denies that what Mary learns is a fact she didn't know before. Rather, the knowledge she gets is knowledge of new *abilities*: knowledge of *how* to do something rather than knowledge *that* something is the case, and in particular knowledge of how to recognize red objects, the ability to imagine red, and so forth. But this reply seems to have problems parallel to those undermining Churchland's: for one thing, it seems implausible to assert that Mary learns no new facts, since knowledge that red looks like *this* (referring to a subjective sensation) is knowledge of a new fact; for another, the distinction Lewis appeals to is itself not necessarily a neutral one. Mary may well gain new abilities or knowledge upon leaving the room, but it is arguable that some of those abilities are gained only because she learns new facts: Mary now has the ability to imagine what red looks like, but only because she has also learned the fact that red looks like *this*.

Robert van Gulick presents a somewhat technical reply to Jackson's argument. He claims that what Mary gains is knowledge of a new concept, and that if she also learns new propositions this is so only on a fine-grained scheme of individuating or distinguishing between propositions. What this means can best be explained by example. Whether the proposition that water freezes at 32 degrees Fahrenheit and the proposition that H_2O freezes at 32 degrees Fahrenheit are the *same* proposition depends on whether we individuate propositions in a fine- or coarse-grained mode. A fine-grained mode would be one which took account of the fact that "water" and "H_2O" are associated with different concepts (even though they refer to the same substance) and thus would count these propositions as distinct; a coarse-grained mode would ignore the difference in concepts and (since "water" and "H_2O" refer to the same substance) count them as identical. Similarly, the proposition that $5 + 7 = 12$ and the proposition that 38 is the square root of 1,444 are the same proposition on a coarse-grained mode of individuating propositions (one that takes account only of the fact that these mathematical propositions, being necessarily true, both have exactly the same truth value in every possible world); but they are different propositions on a fine-grained scheme, one that takes account of the different concepts associated with "5," "+," "7," "=," "12," "38," "square root," and "1,444." In the first example, it is clear that even if we count the propositions as different, the fact they refer to is the same: water is identical to H_2O, so the fact that water freezes at 32 degrees Fahrenheit is the same fact as the fact that H_2O freezes at 32 degrees Fahrenheit. Similarly, van Gulick suggests, even if Mary, having learned a new concept after leaving the room, is thereby also able to learn a new proposition, it would not follow that the fact that proposition describes is a fact she didn't already know. Perhaps it is a physical fact of the same sort she already knew while still in the room.

As with the other responses to the knowledge argument, one could object to this one that it seems intuitively implausible: the fact that red looks like *this* (where "this" refers to an immediate sensation) seems obviously to be a different fact than the fact that Mary is in a brain state of type B (or whatever). Of course, van Gulick might suggest that the way things seem might nevertheless in this case be wrong: it might also seem to someone ignorant of chemistry that the fact that water freezes at 32 degrees Fahrenheit is a different fact from the fact that H_2O freezes at 32 degrees Fahrenheit, even though they are in reality the same. But it isn't clear that this suggestion will work. After all, few people would find it a satisfactory defense of the highly dubious claim that the fact that $5 + 7 = 12$ is the same fact as the fact that 38 is the square root of 1,444. In the case of this mathematical example, we surely have two different facts, not just two different fine-grained propositions. Indeed, it is partly our sense that this is so that leads us to see the need for a fine-grained mode of individuating propositions in the first place: we don't suppose this is necessary merely in order to take account of differences in concepts, but also because the propositions of which concepts are constituents often seem (as in the mathematical example) to be about different facts. But the suggestion that the facts that Mary learns on leaving the room are the very same facts as those she knew before seems just as intuitively implausible as the suggestion that the mathematical facts in our example are the same. And if such an implausibility is, in the one case, itself precisely what leads us to accept a more fine-grained account of mathematical propositions – so that it would be absurd to suppose that one could defend the claim that the mathematical facts in question are the same by appealing to a fine-grained account – then it would be (equally) absurd and implausible to suppose that one could refute the knowledge argument by a parallel appeal to a fine-grained scheme of individuating propositions. In other words, it is in part precisely because it seems so intuitively plausible that facts about qualia and physical facts are just different sorts of fact that we find a fine-grained mode of individuating propositions about them to be necessary in the first place. So it won't do to appeal to such a mode in order to defend the claim that they aren't different.

Subjectivity

Most of the criticisms of the knowledge argument are more or less along the same lines, and would therefore be open to similar objections. But there is another possible reply, suggested by what was said earlier about the inverted spectrum scenario, which may be more formidable. Suppose that each color can indeed be given a precise location in color space, and thus analyzed in terms of its relations to every other color. It then seems possible, at least in principle, that one might be able to deduce the nature of one color from its relations to the others. Consider a simple example involving three very close shades of blue, A, B, and C, where A is the lightest, C the darkest, and B intermediate. It is certainly plausible that someone who had only ever experienced A and C would be able to figure out what it would be like to experience B simply by considering its relations to A and C (the relations being "darker than" and "lighter than"). By extension, it may also be plausible to

suggest that someone who had never seen orange could, in principle, determine what it would be like to experience it if he or she
had experienced red and yellow: one could deduce the appearance
of orange from its being similar to, and intermediate between,
these other colors. Why not conclude, then, that someone who had
had at least *some* visual experience – of black and white, of gray as
intermediate between them, of light and dark – might in principle
be capable of deducing what the various colors looked like based
on a sufficiently detailed description of their relations? Why not
conclude in particular that Mary – who studied the theory of color
and the structure of color space – would have been able in principle to deduce what it would be like to experience red while still in
the room, so that she would in fact not have learned anything new
when leaving it?

This sort of strategy could in theory be extended to all qualia –
auditory, tactile, olfactory and gustatory as well as visual – which
could all be described in terms of their relations to other qualia of
the same sort, and even their relations to qualia of different
sorts: "warmth," "coolness," "hardness," softness," "sharpness,"
smoothness," seem to be qualities applicable to many different
kinds of qualia, so that (to some extent at least) visual qualia can be
described in terms of their similarity relations to auditory qualia,
auditory qualia in terms of their similarity relations to tactile
qualia, and so forth. Rudolf Carnap (1891–1970) attempted just
such a detailed and systematic analysis of all qualia in terms of their
relations to each other, which relations he took to be grounded
ultimately in the basic relation of "recollection of similarity." If
such an analysis could be carried out completely, then it is arguable
that anyone thoroughly familiar with it could, on the basis of even
the most limited sensory experience, determine what it would be
like to have any experience that he or she has never in fact had.

This approach seems promising, though it would take a great
deal of argument convincingly to defend it. But even if successful,
the critic of materialism could hold that this strategy would not

undermine the deeper truth captured by the knowledge argument, in Nagel's version more than in Jackson's. That truth is, arguably, just this: while Mary might at least in principle be able to deduce, from what she knows while still in the room, what it is like to experience red, she would not be able to deduce from it *why it is like anything at all*. The real mystery is not that red "feels" specifically like this rather than that; it is that it has any "feel" in the first place. Nagel captures the problem by noting that it is the fact that there is "something it is like" to be conscious that makes consciousness so difficult to account for in purely material terms. The zombie argument captures it by suggesting that it is metaphysically possible for there to be creatures physically identical to us but without consciousness, creatures who exhibit exactly the same behavior – and thus, for example, make exactly the same discriminations between red and other colors – but who do not experience red, for whom there is nothing it is like to discriminate red from other colors. That there is something it is like for us to experience it would seem to be a further fact about us, over and above the physical ones.

This goes hand in hand with Nagel's point that a conscious being is one with a first-person point of view on the world, who is a locus of subjectivity. Consciousness of what an experience is like is always consciousness of what it is like "for me," for a subject of experience; and for Mary to deduce what experiencing red would be like from its similarity relations to other experiences presupposes that she is a conscious subject *for whom* it would be similar. One might think to deflate this notion of subjectivity by suggesting that lots of purely physical things have points of view on the world as well – a camera, for instance, which can photograph only what is in front of it; its images produced by reflecting its particular point of view – so that it shouldn't be so mysterious why we, with our specific sensory organs and physical limitations, should have points of view too. But such a suggestion would seem fallacious. A camera is just a mechanism sensitive to light such that it can be used to generate patterns on film that correspond to the light patterns reflected by physical objects. It has no literal "point of view," for it doesn't view anything in the first place in the sense in which we do. It is we who understand the pictures the camera produces to have significance – indeed, it is we who regard them as pictures rather than splotches of chemicals on paper. It is also true that the particular point of view any of us occupies is, like the camera, limited by our specific position in space and the physical constraints imposed by the structure of the human body. But (to make a point that parallels the point made above about the experience of seeing red) it is not our having this or that particular point of view that is claimed to be difficult or impossible to explain in materialistic terms; it is rather our having any point of view at all that is mysterious.

In the dualist's view, that science, at least as understood by materialists, cannot *in principle* solve this mystery seems to follow necessarily from the very nature of scientific explanation: it is not a matter of our not yet having gathered all the relevant neurological evidence or hit upon the right theory. For, as noted in the last chapter, the method of modern scientific explanation has historically been precisely to carve off and ignore the subjective, observer-relative aspect of any phenomenon it investigates and identify such phenomena exclusively with the objective, third-person residue which remains. We can take the explanation of temperature as a paradigm. A hoary philosophical example illustrates the subjectivity of temperature considered as a felt experience: someone who first puts his or her right hand in a bucket of ice cold water and his or her left in a bucket of hot, then puts both in a bucket of lukewarm water, will find that the lukewarm water feels warm to the right hand and cold to the left. We can also imagine extraterrestrials who would feel what we would call coolness when putting their hands (or tentacles) in hot water and heat when putting them in ice cold water. If by "heat" and "cold" we mean the subjective sensations or feelings produced by hot and cold objects, there is no objective fact about whether a particular object is hot or cold. Science thus ignores subjective feelings and instead defines (or re-defines) heat and cold exclusively in terms of the objective, mind-independent physical facts which (in us, anyway) cause the relevant sensations: facts about mean molecular kinetic energy. But if the method of science is in every case to strip away the subjective appearance a phenomenon exhibits and, as it were, push it into the mind, it seems obvious that the same procedure cannot in principle be applied to an explanation of the mind itself: for the mind *just is* (in part) the collection of the subjective appearances of the things it experiences; the subjective element cannot in *this* case be stripped away without thereby stripping away and ignoring the very phenomenon to be explained – in which case it hasn't really been explained at all.

Subjectivity – comprising the phenomena of being present to an experiencing subject, of being directly accessible only from the point of view of that subject, and of being capable of existing in experience even when (as in dreams or hallucinations) an apparent objective correlate of the experience does not exist – thus appears to be the essential core to the concept of qualia, and the feature that is most plausibly inexplicable in physical terms. Philosophers often attribute other supposedly problematic features to qualia, such as ineffability and intrinsicality, but to a very great extent these appear to be reducible to or parasitic upon subjectivity. For example, qualia seem ineffable only because our language is typically used to communicate thoughts about *objective*, *public* phenomena, and words are typically learned by reference to such phenomena; communicating thoughts about private and subjective phenomena thus seems difficult or impossible. To the extent that qualia are ineffable, this is just a consequence of their being subjective.

Qualia are often claimed to be intrinsic in the sense of not being analyzable in terms of their relations to other things, for example, in terms of the causal relations functionalism claims all mental phenomena can be analyzed in terms of; for, as was suggested by the zombie argument, it seems logically possible for any such set of causal relations to exist without qualia. But here too subjectivity seems to be what's really at issue. It is because qualia are not analyzable into relations instantiated in *objective*, *third-person* phenomena – causal relations between firing patterns in clumps of neurons, say – that they seem to be intrinsic. Yet this leaves open that they may be analyzable into *subjective*, *first-person* similarity relations of the sort Carnap, Clark, and Hardin have tried to elucidate: that they may well in this sense be *both* irreducibly subjective and yet non-intrinsic. Indeed, it is arguable that it is precisely because they are so analyzable that we can communicate about them despite their subjectivity (so that they are *not* ineffable in the strict sense): if we were not able to describe and convey to one another the systematic similarities and differences between qualia, we would not be able to know (as we surely do know) that we are all talking about the *same* phenomena when we discuss qualia and argue about whether materialism can account for them. Our knowledge of the relational structure of qualia makes our claims about them cognitively meaningful and rationally assessable, despite the fact that the relations comprising that structure are directly knowable only from the subjective, first-person point of view.

It seems arguable then that the key difference between qualia on the one hand and such physical phenomena as functional organization, neurophysiology, and behavior on the other, is that the former are irreducibly subjective, "private," and first-person in character while the latter are inherently objective, publicly accessible, and third-person. The dualist concludes that since the two sorts of phenomena have such irreconcilable essential properties, the former cannot be accounted for in terms of the latter – in which case materialism, which claims that everything real is explicable in terms of objective, third-person physical phenomena, must be false.

Property dualism

Interestingly, most of the philosophers typically associated with the sorts of arguments surveyed in this chapter are, though critics of mainstream materialism, nevertheless not Cartesian dualists. Some of them endorse an agnostic materialism as a fallback position: Joseph Levine, for example, suggests that what such arguments really prove is at most that there is an "explanatory gap" between the physical and the mental – that we do not understand *how* materialism can be true, but that this doesn't show that it *isn't* true; Colin McGinn adds that it might simply be that evolution has not given us the conceptual resources fully to grasp the manner in which material processes generate mental ones. But such moves arguably miss the point: if the arguments of Chalmers, Jackson, Kripke, et al. work at all, they seem to prove that qualia are just not reducible to physical properties, not that we can't understand how they are reducible. (No one would think it reasonable to reply to Gödel's arguments for his famous incompleteness theorems by suggesting that perhaps we just don't understand how the consistency of a formal system containing computable arithmetic is internally provable.)

Most philosophers sympathetic to the arguments in question opt instead for what has come to be known as *property dualism*, the view (alluded to earlier when discussing the zombie argument) that there is, contrary to Cartesian substance dualism, only one kind of substance – material substance – but that there are also, contrary to materialism, two kinds of properties, physical and non-physical. In this view, the mind, considered as a substance, is indeed identical to the brain, but mental properties – or at least qualia – are not physical properties of the brain, but non-physical properties inhering in its physical substance. The advantage claimed for this view is that it can accommodate both the Cartesian dualist's conviction that mind is irreducible to matter and the materialist's insistence that mind is inseparable from matter.

Property dualists also often take other mental phenomena – those which don't essentially involve qualia – to be susceptible of explanation in terms of materialistic functionalism in a way qualia are not. This is held to be true in particular of the *propositional attitudes* – belief, desire, hope, fear – so called because they involve a subject taking a certain attitude toward a proposition, such as the attitude of belief you take toward the proposition that it is raining when you believe that it is raining, or the attitude of hope you take toward the proposition that you will pass your exams when you hope that you will pass your exams. The idea is that since these sorts of mental states are not necessarily associated with qualia (for you could believe that it is raining even if you aren't consciously entertaining the belief at the moment), there is no objection to be made to reducing them to physical states of the brain on the basis of arguments of the "inverted spectrum," "Chinese nation," "zombie," or "knowledge" sort.

Whether this suggestion is as plausible as property dualists generally take it to be is something we will explore in chapters 6 and 7. But it might seem to give the property dualist a significant advantage over the Cartesian dualist where defending a broadly dualist view of the world is concerned. As we saw in chapter 2, the Cartesian dualist appears to have a difficult time explaining exactly how a non-physical substance could possibly interact with the body. How, for example, your belief that it is raining can be what causes you to go get your umbrella becomes metaphysically mysterious. Epiphenomenalism looms. But the property dualist might appear to have avoided this problem: your belief is, most property dualists would allow, a physical state of your brain, so there need be no mystery about how it can have a causal influence on behavior. Even your perception that it is raining can, in so far as it involves having a propositional attitude as much as a belief does, be identified with a physical process in your brain, so that there is no problem in explaining how it too can cause behavior. True, the perception, unlike many beliefs, may well be associated with certain qualia (such as the sensation of water droplets hitting one's arm), and these cannot be identified with physical properties of the brain. Indeed, it seems that qualia, unlike propositional attitudes, must at the end of the day be regarded as epiphenomenal, playing no role whatever in the production of behavior, since the behavior of a zombie would be exactly the same as that of someone who has qualia. But as long as the perception itself is physical, this shouldn't matter: your perception of the raindrops really does cause you to get your umbrella, even if the qualia associated with it do not.

In fact, however, it matters a great deal, and property dualism seems if anything to have a worse problem with epiphenomenalism than does Cartesian dualism. Recall that the Cartesian dualist who opts for epiphenomenalism seems to be committed to the absurd consequence that we cannot even so much as talk about our mental states, because if epiphenomenalism is true, those mental states have no effect at all on our bodies, including our larynxes, tongues, and lips. But as Daniel Dennett has pointed out, the property dualist seems committed to something even more absurd: the conclusion that we cannot even *think* about our mental states, or at least about our qualia! For if your beliefs – including your belief that you have qualia – are physical states of your brain, and qualia can have no effect whatsoever on anything physical, then whether you really have qualia has nothing to do with whether you believe you have them. The experience of pain you have in your back has absolutely no connection to your *belief* that you have an experience of pain in your back; for, being incapable of having any causal influence on the physical world, it cannot be what caused you to have beliefs about it. Indeed, it would also seem to follow that you can have no confidence that the pain even *exists* in the first place; for you would have exactly the same beliefs about it whether it existed or not. Property dualism thus appears to lead to a skepticism even more radical than that entailed by Descartes's evil spirit scenario: if property dualism is true, then you cannot even be certain that your own conscious experiences exist; you might, for all you know, be a zombie!

This is not only bizarre, it is incoherent. The whole point of property dualism is to insist that there are non-physical qualia; if the theory also entails that we can never know that there are such qualia, then how (and why) are we even considering it? How can property dualists themselves so much as formulate their hypothesis? Chalmers attempts to deal with this problem by suggesting that the assumption that there must be a causal connection between the knower and what is known, though appropriate where knowledge of physical objects is concerned, is inappropriate for knowledge of qualia. The existence of a causal chain implies the possibility of error, since (as we saw in chapter 1) it seems to entail a gap between the experience of the thing known and the thing itself, a gap between appearance and reality: it is at least possible that the normal causal chain connecting us to the thing experienced has been disrupted, so that the experience is misleading (as in hallucination or deception by a Cartesian evil spirit). But knowledge of qualia, Chalmers says, is absolutely certain. Here there is no gap between appearance and reality, because the appearance – the way things seem, which is constituted by qualia themselves – *is* the reality. Knowledge of qualia must therefore somehow be direct and unmediated by causal chains between them and our beliefs about them. The fact that they can have no causal influence on our beliefs thus does not, after all, entail that we can't think or talk about them.

But an objection to this is that it seems question-begging, since whether our knowledge of qualia really is certain is part of what is at issue in Dennett's argument. Moreover, Chalmers' claim that there is no gap between appearance and reality where knowledge of qualia is concerned seems problematic, given the assumption he shares with other property dualists that propositional attitudes can, unlike qualia, be reduced to physical processes in the brain. For while there is a sense of "appearance" and "seeming" which involves the having of qualia (a sense we can call the "qualitative" sense), there is also a sense of these words (call it the "cognitive" sense) which does not, but instead involves only the having of certain beliefs: one might say, for example, that at first it seemed or appeared to him that Chalmers' arguments were sound, but on further reflection he concluded that they were not. Here there need be no qualia present, but only a mistake in judgment or the having of a false belief. But the having of beliefs and the making of judgments are, by Chalmers' own lights, identical with being in certain brain states, so that there is a sense in which even a zombie has beliefs (including false beliefs) and makes judgments (including mistakes in judgment). But in that case, it could "seem" or "appear" even to a zombie that it had qualia, even though by definition it does not. So there can be a gap between appearance and reality even where qualia are concerned. Dennett's challenge remains: how can property dualists so much as think about the qualia they say exist? How can they know that they aren't zombies?

Chalmers' view seems to be that this sort of objection can be avoided by arguing that it is just in the very nature of having an experience that one is justified in believing one has it, that there is a *conceptual connection* between having it and knowing one is having it. The evidence for my belief that I'm having the experience and the experience itself are the same thing; so I don't infer the existence of the experience from the evidence, but just know directly from the mere having of the evidence. But this seems merely to push the problem back a stage, for now the question is how one can know one really has that evidence – the experience – in the first place, given that an experienceless zombie would also believe that it has it (and, if it's read Chalmers, that there is a conceptual connection between having it and being justified in believing it does). Chalmers' claim seems to amount to the conditional: *if* you have qualia, *then* you can know you have them. But that raises the question of how one can know the antecedent of this conditional, i.e. of how one can know one *does* in fact have qualia. Chalmers' reply is "Because it *seems* to me that I do, and its seeming that way is all the justification I need." But a zombie would believe the same thing! "But *I* have evidence the zombie doesn't have – my experience!" Chalmers would retort. Yet the zombie believes *that too*, because it also seems to it (in the cognitive sense) that it has such evidence. Any response Chalmers could give to such questions would seem to invite further questions about whether he *really* has the evidence he thinks he does. His only possible reply can be to say that he has it because he *seems* to have it, but if he says that he seems to in the *cognitive* sense of "seems," then he's saying something even a zombie would believe, while if he says, even to himself, that he seems to in the *qualitative* sense of "seems," then he's begging the question, for whether he has the qualia that this sense of "seems" presupposes is precisely what's at issue. Chalmers' reply to the sort of criticism raised by Dennett thus seems to fail.

Property dualism would thus appear to lead to absurdity as long as it concedes to materialism the reducibility of the propositional attitudes. If it instead takes the attitudes to be, like qualia, irreducible to physical states of the brain, this absurdity can be avoided: for in that case, your beliefs and judgments are as non-physical as your qualia are, and there is thus no barrier (at least of the usual mental-to-physical epiphenomenalist sort) to your qualia being the causes of your beliefs about them. But should it take this route, there seems much less motivation for adopting property dualism rather than full-blown Cartesian substance dualism: it was precisely the concession of the materiality of propositional attitudes that seemed to allow the property dualist to make headway on the interaction problem, an advantage that is lost if that concession is revoked; and while taking at least beliefs, desires, and the like to be purely material undermines the plausibility of the existence of a distinct non-physical mental substance, such plausibility would seem to be restored if all mental properties, beliefs and desires, as much as qualia, are non-physical. Moreover, property dualism raises a puzzle of its own, namely that of explaining exactly how non-physical properties could inhere in a physical substance.

Property dualism, then, is arguably not a genuine advance over substance dualism, though some of the arguments of property dualists appear to pose a significant challenge to materialism and thereby to advance the cause of dualism generally. Yet the materialist still has the interaction problem to wield against the dualist, along with the less paradoxical but still unsatisfactory form of epiphenomenalism that threatens even Cartesian dualism. Moreover, the materialist's last word about qualia has not yet been spoken. We've seen that the problem qualia pose for the materialist is, at bottom, the problem of accounting for the existence of a conscious subject having a first-person point of view on the world. An adequate understanding of the qualia problem cannot be had, then, unless it is considered as part of the broader problem of the nature of consciousness itself. If consciousness in general can be explained in entirely materialistic terms, maybe a materialist account of qualia in particular would be possible after all, as a by-product of this more general theory. That, at any rate, is the hope of a number of contemporary materialist philosophers. A look at the problem of consciousness must therefore be the next item on our agenda.

Further reading

Block's Chinese nation scenario is from his "Troubles with Functionalism," reprinted in both the Rosenthal and Chalmers anthologies cited at the end of the last chapter. Jackson's version of the knowledge argument is presented in "What Mary Didn't Know" and Nagel's in "What is it Like to Be a Bat?"; Churchland's reply is in "Knowing Qualia: A Reply to Jackson," Lewis's in "What Experience Teaches," and van Gulick's in "Understanding the Phenomenal Mind: Are We All Just Armadillos?" These essays have been reprinted in numerous places (some of them in the Chalmers and Rosenthal anthologies), but they can all be found together in Ned Block, Owen Flanagan, and Guven Guzeldere, eds. *The Nature of Consciousness: Philosophical Debates* (Cambridge, MA: MIT Press, 1997). Sydney Shoemaker's "The Inverted Spectrum," which discusses that famous thought experiment, can also be found in this anthology. The structure of color space is the subject of C. L. Hardin's *Color for Philosophers* (Indianapolis: Hackett, 1988) and Austen Clark's *Sensory Qualities* (Oxford: Clarendon Press, 1993). Carnap's analysis is in his classic *Der logische Aufbau der Welt*, translated by R. George as *The Logical Structure of the World* (Berkeley and Los Angeles: University of California Press, 1967). The section of Kripke's *Naming and Necessity* defending the modal or zombie argument (though not by that name) is reprinted in the Chalmers, Rosenthal, and Block et al. anthologies. Levine's "Materialism and Qualia: The Explanatory Gap" and McGinn's "Can We Solve the Mind-Body Problem?" are also available in the Chalmers anthology. Chalmers defends property dualism and the zombie argument at great length in *The Conscious Mind* (New York: Oxford University Press, 1996). Dennett's critique of property dualism is in his *Consciousness Explained* (Boston, MA: Little, Brown, and Company, 1991). That subjectivity rather than intrinsicality is the core of the concept of qualia is a thesis I defended earlier in "Qualia: Irreducibly Subjective but not Intrinsic," *Journal of Consciousness Studies*, Vol. 8, No. 8 (August 2001).

5

Consciousness

Consciousness has in recent years become *the* hot topic among philosophers of mind, and among not a few neuroscientists and cognitive scientists too. The reason has largely to do with the qualia problem surveyed in the last chapter. The received wisdom is that if we distinguish between, on the one hand, the conscious mind's capacity to represent the world beyond itself (that is, its intentionality) and to reason on the basis of such representations, and on the other, the qualia associated with these mental states and processes, then (a) it is the latter – the qualia – rather than rationality or intentionality, that are essential to conscious states *qua* conscious, and (b) it is these qualia that make consciousness difficult to account for in materialist terms, with rationality and intentionality being readily amenable to a reductionist explanation.

My own suspicion is that this received wisdom has things backwards, on both counts: it is not qualia but the other mental phenomena – rationality and, especially, intentionality – which are essential to consciousness, and which pose the most important challenge to materialism. Ironically, consideration of the views of some contemporary theorists representative of the received wisdom will help us to see this. Their strategy is to give a materialistic explanation of consciousness by first reducing qualitative states (those characterized by qualia) to intentional states (those characterized by intentionality), and then completing their explanation by carrying out (what they suppose to be) the easier task of reducing intentional states to material states of the brain. In this chapter we will examine, among other theories of consciousness, some attempts to develop the first part of this strategy – often called the *intentionalist* approach – and see that, while none proposed so far is free of difficulties, each of them plausibly contains elements of truth, and can be combined into a general intentionalist account of consciousness. Chapters 6 and 7 will then consider whether intentional mental states and processes really can be accounted for in purely materialistic terms.

Eliminativism

The intentionalist approach to consciousness holds that conscious states are nothing more than intentional states: states exhibiting intentionality, or the capacity to represent something beyond themselves. The difficulty with this approach is that qualia seem devoid of intentionality: the throb of a toothache, for example, doesn't seem to represent anything; it just hurts. So qualia seem to be an extra element, an aspect of conscious experiences over and above their intentional content. The overall experience of a toothache may include the thought that one is in pain – a thought which, representing as it does one's current situation, exhibits intentionality – but the pain itself is a further, non-intentional, component. Conscious experiences, therefore, cannot be completely reduced to intentional states. In particular, qualia are irreducible to intentional properties, and must somehow be accounted for separately, independently of any materialist analysis of intentionality.

Daniel Dennett's response to this difficulty is, whatever else one might say about it, bold: he simply denies that there really are any qualia to account for in the first place. His is what philosophers call an *eliminativist* position, one that deals with a philosophically problematic phenomenon by suggesting that its problematic nature gives us reason to doubt its existence – to "eliminate" it entirely from our picture of the world, rather than attempting to explain it. He does not deny that we really do have conscious experiences – feeling pain, tasting coffee, smelling flowers, hearing music, and all the rest – but denies only that any of these experiences feature properties of the sort qualia are taken to be. There are, that is to say, no properties that are essentially intrinsic – that is, unanalyzable in terms of their relations; or subjective – that is, directly accessible only from the first-person point of view. The throb of a toothache, appearances notwithstanding, is neither of these things. It was suggested in the previous chapter that qualia might not be essentially intrinsic in the sense they are often claimed to be; to this extent Dennett may be right. But it was also suggested that they do seem to be essentially subjective. So what of Dennett's claim that there are no essentially subjective properties? Isn't it just obviously false, given what we know from introspection?

Recall from chapter 3 that materialists often take our common-sense concept of the mind to constitute a kind of theory, that can be described as "folk psychology." If one grants this assumption, then the entities supposedly "postulated" by folk psychology – such as qualia – count as *theoretical* entities: they might turn out to exist, as the best explanation of the phenomena they are postulated to explain; but then again, they might turn out not to exist, for there might be a better explanation that does not postulate them. But even if we do grant this, is there really any reason to doubt that qualia, even if theoretical, are real? Dennett thinks there is, and in defending his eliminativism he revisits the sort of qualia inversion scenarios considered in the last chapter. Suppose you wake up after neurosurgery and are baffled to find that grass looks red, and the sky looks yellow. It might seem obvious that your color qualia had been inverted, presumably due to some playful rewiring of your neurons. But, as Dennett argues, that is not the only possibility. The neurosurgeons might have produced your bafflement by tampering with whatever neural connections underlie your perceptions of color, thereby inverting your qualia, but they might instead have done it by tampering with the connections underlying *memory*: maybe your qualia are the same now as they always have been, and you are only misremembering how they seemed before. The only way you could possibly determine which of these possibilities is actual is by asking the neurosurgeons or, perhaps, doing some sort of neurological self-inspection. But then you must necessarily rely on *objective, third-person* evidence to know whether your qualia have been inverted; and in that case, Dennett says, qualia can't be subjective. But if qualia are held to be essentially subjective – subjectivity being part of their very essence – then this just entails that there really are no qualia. Whatever the inverted spectrum scenario, and color vision in general, involve, they do not involve the having of qualia, and we ought therefore to prefer a theory of mind that does not make reference to qualia.

One could object that this argument appears to be a *non sequitur*. That whether your memory of your qualia has been tampered with is something you need to appeal to third-person neurological evidence to determine does not seem to show that your qualia themselves – past or present – can be known only by appealing to that evidence. You might, for all Dennett has said, still be directly aware of your qualia from the first-person, subjective point of view even if you don't know whether they are the same as or different from the sort of qualia you had yesterday – just as you might really be aware of the book in front of you even if you don't know whether it was the same as or different from the book you saw yesterday. Questions about memory do not necessarily have a bearing on the nature of your awareness of objects present here and now (even if they have an obvious bearing on what you can justifiably claim to know about such objects), whatever those objects happen to be.

Of course, the analogy isn't exact. There is no doubt that you really are aware of your qualia now even if you don't know whether or not they're like the ones you had yesterday; in the case of the book, you might not really be aware of it right now, for you might be merely hallucinating it. And if the indirect realist theory discussed in chapter 1 is correct, then even if you are aware of it, you are not aware of it directly, in the way you are aware of your qualia. But all this seems only to strengthen the suggested reply to Dennett. For, if indirect realism is correct, it is only through the *first-person, subjective* realm of qualia that we know that there is an objective, third-person realm – including neurosurgeons and the brains they might tamper with – in the first place. Indeed, puzzles concerning memory, of the sort Dennett makes use of, when one pushes through their implications consistently, serve to underline (rather than undermine) the reality of the first-person, subjective realm of qualia: that the entire past is a figment of my imagination, and the universe really only five minutes old, is yet another skeptical scenario of the sort considered in chapter 1, one raised this time by consideration of the possibility of faulty memory. Nor will appeal to third-person neurological evidence by itself serve to refute such skeptical worries, for such an appeal would itself assume the reliability of one's memory (that is, it would assume that one was correctly remembering what the neurologists had told one or what one had read in textbooks about the links between certain neural structures and memory). So even to trust the evidence from the neurosurgery requires first being able to show you can trust the subjective evidence of your senses, via arguments (of the sort also considered in chapter 1) that can themselves be defended entirely from the first-person point of view.

It seems we ought, for these reasons, also to reject the assumption that qualia are theoretical entities in the first place. Far from being the postulates of a theory, they are, rather, among the data to which all empirical theorizing and postulating must appeal. Dennett would object that appeal to such first-person, subjective data is incompatible with the objectivity demanded by scientific method. He holds, accordingly, that only evidence available from the third-person objective point of view ought to form the basis of a scientifically respectable theory of the mind. Given such a constraint, materialism, and indeed eliminativism, seem to follow automatically, even trivially. But to insist on this constraint seems, by the same token, simply to beg all the important questions. It is also to take a position that is prima facie implausible, especially if one accepts the indirect realist view considered in chapter 1. In any case, Dennett's assertion that scientific objectivity requires appealing exclusively to third-person evidence appears mistaken. It certainly would have come as a surprise to a thinker like Carnap, whose regard for science as the touchstone of objective knowledge was legendary (indeed, legendarily excessive), yet who regarded respect for the first-person (or, as he called it, *autopsychological*) point of view as fully consistent with such objectivity. What scientific objectivity requires is, not denial of the first-person subjective point of view, but rather a means of communicating inter-subjectively about what one can grasp only from that point of view. Given the relational structure first-person phenomena like qualia appear to exhibit – a structure that, as we saw in the last chapter, Carnap devoted great effort to elucidating – such a means seems available: we can communicate what we know about qualia in terms of their structural relations to one another. Dennett's position rests on a failure to see that qualia being essentially subjective is fully compatible with their being relational or non-intrinsic, and thus communicable. This communicability ensures that claims about qualia are epistemologically objective, that is, they can in principle be grasped and evaluated by all competent observers, even though they are claims about phenomena that are arguably not metaphysically objective, that is, they are about entities that exist only as grasped by a subject of experience. It is only the former sort of objectivity that science requires. It does not require the latter – and cannot plausibly require it if the first-person realm of qualia is what we know better than anything else.

Representationalism and higher-order theories

If qualia cannot be dismissed as unreal, then, how can an intentionalist theory of consciousness deal with them? The most straightforward answer is *representationalism*, the view that qualia are nothing more than representational properties of conscious experiences. The redness of your experience of seeing an apple, for instance, is just a representation of the objective redness of the apple itself, of the physical property of the surface of the skin of the apple by virtue of which it absorbs some wavelengths of light and reflects others. There is, on this view, nothing more to the redness than that: its intentionality or representational content is all the content it has, and there is no distinctly qualitative element over and above that. So, the problem of qualia reduces to the problem of intentionality; it does not pose a separate challenge to materialism.

What about bodily sensations that do not seem to have such representational content? To return to the example of a toothache, its nagging quality does not seem to represent anything; it appears to be nothing more than what philosophers sometimes call a "raw feel," a pure sensation without any intentionality or meaning (even though, again, one's thoughts about the pain would of course have intentionality or meaning). But the representationalist would hold that such cases are not genuine counter-examples. The qualia associated with toothache can plausibly be taken to represent something, namely the damage to the tooth that causes the toothache. By the same token, pains in general can be taken to represent damage to the parts of the body in which they are felt, and other bodily sensations can be taken to represent other states of the body.

Even if we accept all this, there is still the problem of accounting for why representational states like seeing an apple or feeling pain are associated with consciousness, while other representational states (for example your belief that $2 + 2 = 4$ which you have even when you are not conscious of it) are unconscious. If to be a conscious experience is just to be a state having a certain representational content, wouldn't all states with representational content be conscious? But they aren't all conscious; so some extra element, in addition to their representational content, must be what makes certain states with representational content conscious, and representationalism thus cannot be the full story about consciousness.

Here is where some philosophers would appeal to a *higher-order theory* of consciousness. The idea here is that what makes any particular mental state a conscious state is that it is the object of a higher-order mental state that represents it. Some versions of this theory would take such higher-order states to be thoughts, while others would take them to be more akin to perceptions: in the first version, just as one might have a thought about some object in the external world, one might also have a thought *about a thought*, or about some other kind of mental state; in the second, just as one might have a perception of an object in the external world, one might also have an "inner" perception *of the perception itself.*

The overall picture of consciousness that emerges from these theories is this: what gives a particular conscious experience the particular qualitative character it has – that is, what makes it the case that it is associated with particular qualia – is the unique representational content embodied in those qualia. Some theorists would also add that the structural relations, alluded to above and discussed in the previous chapter, by which each quale can be uniquely identified in terms of its similarities and dissimilarities to other qualia, also play a role in determining the precise character of a conscious experience. But representational content and/or structural relations between qualia, even if they can account for why an experience has this qualitative character rather than that, still do not explain why it has any such character at all. To explain that requires appeal to a higher-order account: a state is conscious when there is another, higher-order state which represents it. The presence of such a higher-order state thus ensures that the particular mental state represented by it counts as a conscious experience; and the elements of that conscious experience having the particular representational content and/or structural relations they do ensures that it is a conscious experience of this sort rather than that.

There is much to be said for this approach (or combination of approaches), but it seems insufficient as it stands. Representationalists and higher-order theorists (and structural relation theorists like Clark and Hardin too, for that matter) generally see their accounts as variations on functionalism: representational states and higher-order states are interpreted by them as fully analyzable in terms of the causal relations they bear to stimulation of the sensory organs, other internal states, and behavior. But then their accounts would appear to be as vulnerable to the anti-materialist arguments of the previous chapter as is any other version of functionalism. For example, a zombie duplicate of you would not only have an internal state caused by light reflected from an apple striking its retinas, signals from the retinas being sent to the visual centers of the brain, and so on, but would also have a further ("higher-order") internal state caused by the first internal state, and all these states together would produce behaviors like salivating, or saying "Look, an apple!"; yet such a zombie would, nevertheless, lack any subjective conscious experience of the apple. So, the notion of higher-order mental states, *understood in functionalist terms*, appears to add little to a materialist account of consciousness.

If representationalist and higher-order theories are to shed new light on the problems of consciousness and qualia, then, it seems they must somehow go beyond the standard functionalism in which they are usually embedded. To see one way in which this might be accomplished requires a digression.

Russellian identity theory and neutral monism

Thus far in this book we have focused on dualism and materialism as the main alternative general metaphysical approaches in the philosophy of mind. That is, we have considered the views that everything is ultimately material (materialism), and that the material and the mental are equally ultimate (dualism). These alternatives are paid the most attention by contemporary philosophers of mind, but they are not the only alternatives to be proposed in the history of the subject. A third view, known as *idealism*, holds that everything is ultimately mental – for example, the version associated with George Berkeley (1685–1753) holds that purportedly physical objects like tables and chairs really exist only in so far as a mind perceives them to exist. But though idealism has had some illustrious defenders in the history of philosophy, it is not generally regarded as a serious option by most contemporary philosophers (with some important exceptions). There are two other, more promising, alternatives that we will be exploring, one in this chapter and the other in chapter 8. The first holds that neither mind nor matter is metaphysically ultimate: what is ultimate is rather a single kind of stuff that is neutral between, and more fundamental than, either of them. This is, in a nutshell, the metaphysical theory known as *neutral monism*.

The most important proponent of this view in the twentieth century was Bertrand Russell. His formulation of it evolved significantly through the course of his long career; what we want to focus on is the final, settled version. Russell begins by drawing out the implications of the indirect realism he endorsed, and which we discussed in chapter 1. If in perception we are directly aware, not of external physical objects themselves, but rather only representations of those objects, then we have in Russell's view no grounds for supposing that those objects really have the properties they are presented to us by perception as having. We have no reason to assume, for example, that the redness and sweetness of the apples we perceive is really in the apples themselves, as opposed to being merely an artefact of our perceptual machinery – just as the redness you see on the wall in front of you when you are wearing glasses with red lenses is, for all you know, not really in the wall itself but only an artefact of the glasses. As we've noted before, physics seems to give us positive reason to believe that the redness and sweetness are *not* in the apples: for like every other physical object, an apple is in reality nothing but a collection of colorless, odorless, tasteless particles. What the physical world is really like "in itself," apart from our perceptual representations of it, is not something perception can tell us.

What does tell us what the physical world is really like is science. But science, Russell argues, does not tell us nearly as much as we often assume it does. For instance, what exactly *are* these colorless, odorless, tasteless particles of which physics speaks – molecules, atoms, quarks, gluons and so forth? Physics defines these entities entirely in terms of their causal relations to one another: a molecule is whatever plays such-and-such a causal role at the microscopic level, an atom is, among other things, what plays the role of serving as a component of a molecule, and so on. But what exactly it is that happens to play these roles is something physics does not tell us. We know from science only that the material world is a collection of fundamental entities having a certain causal structure, a structure described in mathematically precise detail by the physical sciences; but what it is that fleshes out this causal structure, the intrinsic nature of the specific entities that bear these causal relations to one another by filling out each place in the vast causal network described by science, is something we do not know. (This is a view about the nature of scientific knowledge known as *structural realism*: realist because it holds that there really is a physical world existing external to our minds, structuralist because it holds that all we know of that world is its structure rather than intrinsic nature.)

Our knowledge of the external physical world turns out to be highly abstract; including our knowledge of the brain, considered as the object of neuroscientific research, as one external physical thing among others. The brain is not in reality the greyish, squishy thing we encounter in perception: that is only a subjective, perceptual representation of the brain. The brain is, rather, a complex causal structure of neural events, where these neural events are defined in terms of their characteristic causes and effects rather than in terms of the qualities presented to us in visual or tactile inspection of the brain. The inner nature of what specifically has these cause and effect relations is something we do not know – or at least, we do not know from either perception or neuro-scientific study.

But are perception and scientific inquiry (whether neuro-science, physics, chemistry or whatever) the only possible sources of knowledge about the nature of the brain? Russell suggests that there is one further possibility: introspection. In introspecting or looking within itself, the mind is directly aware of its own contents – of thoughts, experiences, and their associated qualia. As materi-alists have argued, there are, at least in general, correlations between various mental events on the one hand and brain events on the other. Perhaps in introspecting these mental events, and in particular our qualia, we are directly aware of precisely the inner natures of the entities that play the causal roles specified by neuro-science. Perhaps neural events *just are* the thoughts, qualia, and so forth encountered in introspection. In being immediately aware of the taste of an apple or a sensation of pain, maybe what we're directly aware of are events occurring in the brain, as it really is "in itself."

This is obviously a mind-brain identity theory. But it is not the *materialist* kind of identity theory discussed in chapter 3. Materialism in general seems to take it for granted that we know exactly what the intrinsic nature of the physical world is, and seems to assume also – especially in the case of functionalism – that we do not know (or at least that pre-philosophical and pre-scientific common sense does not know) what is the intrinsic nature of the mental realm: the functionalist claims that mental states and processes are to be defined entirely in terms of their causes and effects. Russell's view is that this has things precisely backwards. It is in fact the mental world that we know most directly and inti-mately, and the external physical world that we grasp only in terms of its causal structure. In identifying the mind and the brain, Russell is not, as the materialist identity theorist is, reducing the mind to the brain; if anything it is the other way around. The brain turns out to be the mind; more exactly, the neural events and processes defined only abstractly, in causal terms, by neuroscience turn out to be nothing other than mental events and processes – thoughts, experiences, and the like. The grey squishy thing you've seen pictures of in textbooks or that a neurologist looks at when doing surgery is not what the brain is really like intrinsically. If you want to know what it is really like, you need only focus on the qualia you're experiencing right now. The whiteness and blackness of the paper and ink of the book you're reading, the colors on the cover, the smell and warmth of the coffee in the cup beside you, the feel of your back against the chair: those are the brain's true qualities. In introspecting those qualia, you are directly aware of nothing other than the inner nature of your own brain. Or, as Russell paradoxically put it: "I should say that what the physiologist sees when he looks at a brain is part of his own brain, not part of the brain he is examining"!

If this sounds strange, it is supposed to. But it makes perfect sense when one combines indirect realism with the mind-brain identity thesis. For what Russell means is that the physiologist is not *directly* aware of the (patient's) brain he is examining, though of course he is aware of it *indirectly*; what he is directly aware of is a constellation of qualia – greyishness, squishiness, etc. – which are, given the identity theory, identical to features of his own brain, and which are ultimately a distant effect of the light reflected from the patient's brain traveling to the physiologist's retinas, which sets up a sequence of neural firing patterns eventually culminating in the visual experience. Still, the theory definitely counts as a revision of common sense. More importantly, for our purposes, it counts as a rejection of materialism, for, both epistemologically and metaphysically, it gives priority to the subjective, first-person realm of qualia rather than the objective third-person external physical world. Yet it also seems to count as a rejection of dualism, in so far as it identifies the brain with the mind, rather than seeing them as distinct substances.

Indeed, it might seem at first glance to lead instead to a kind of idealism: for if qualia are the intrinsic qualities of the brain, and the brain is – as far as we know from science – made of exactly the same kind of stuff as everything else in the physical universe, wouldn't this entail that everything else in that universe also has qualia as intrinsic qualities? Wouldn't qualia be what ultimately make up tables, chairs, rocks, trees, and every other object of every-day experience? If so, this would seem to entail that, in some sense, *everything physical is really mental*, which is precisely what idealism claims. But Russell and some other philosophers who have endorsed and developed his position, such as Michael Lockwood, have resisted this conclusion. They have suggested that what con-temporary philosophers have come to call qualia (this was not Russell's own expression) – reddishness, the nagging character of pain, the pungency of an odor – may well indeed be the intrinsic properties of every physical thing; but they have also suggested that these properties are, contrary to the standard view, not in fact essentially mental properties at all. Reddishness and all the rest need not necessarily exist in the mind of an experiencing subject: they can exist unsensed by any mind, and do so exist when they enter into the constitution of physical objects other than the brain. The Russellian view is thus interpreted – at least by Russell him-self and Russellians like Lockwood – as a version of neutral monism: qualia comprise the single ultimate kind of stuff out of which everything in the world is composed (hence "monism"), but they are intrinsically neither mental nor non-mental (hence "neutral"); they count as mental only when organized into the sort of causal structure described by neuroscience (that is, a brain), and count as non-mental when organized into other sorts of causal structures (rocks, trees, tables, chairs, galaxies). Since it identifies qualia with properties of the brain, this account is also a kind of identity theory – sometimes labeled the *Russellian identity theory*, to distinguish it from materialist identity theories of the sort described in chapter 3.

One of the advantages of this theory, whatever one wishes to call it, is that it seems to be immune to the sorts of objections that, as we've seen, plague materialist theories. In response to the zombie argument, for instance, the Russellian can hold that zombies can be shown not truly to be conceivable when one's exercise in conception is informed by indirect realism (and the structural realism Russell conjoins to indirect realism). Zombies seem conceivable only if, when imagining them to be "physically identical to us," we imagine their brains being the greyish, squishy things we encounter in perception. But of course, to imagine that sort of thing is really only to imagine a perceptual representation of a brain; it no more involves imagining the brain as it really is intrinsically than does imagining a linguistic representation like the word "brain." To note that a greyish, squishy thing can be imagined to exist apart from qualia no more undermines a mind-brain identity theory than the fact that you can imagine the symbol "H_2O" existing in the absence of water undermines the claim that water = H_2O. Really to imagine the brain as it is "in itself" would, on the Russellian view, require imagining it as constituted by qualia. But to imagine that is, by definition, not to imagine a zombie, since a zombie is supposed to be a creature devoid of qualia. In that case, however, zombies turn out to be *in*conceivable after all.

Troubles with Russellianism

Or do they? A number of philosophers take the Russellian position – long neglected in the philosophy of mind, but in recent years making something of a comeback – to be a great advance over the standard alternatives. But arguably, it will not do as it stands. First, the suggestion that qualia can exist independently of any experiencing conscious subject is highly counter-intuitive, indeed highly implausible. The very notion of qualia is, after all, introduced as the notion of properties of immediate conscious experience. So it is questionable whether we can coherently abstract away from the notion of qualia the presence of a conscious subject, a mind, to whom they are presented.

Some philosophers sympathetic with the Russellian approach, such as David Chalmers, acknowledge that qualia require a conscious subject for their existence – and thereby accept the idealism (or *panpsychism*, as they often prefer to call it, to distinguish their view from the sort of idealism associated with Berkeley) to which this commits them. They don't hold that qualia quite like ours – pains, itches, color sensations, odors, and the like – make up the physical universe outside our minds, for our qualia are no doubt more complex, given the complexity of our brains. At the level of molecules, atoms, and subatomic particles, there are instead what might be called *proto*-qualia playing the relevant causal roles, properties simpler than, and only vaguely analogous to, our qualia. Associated with these proto-qualia, and thus with molecules, atoms, and subatomic particles, would have to be proto-subjects – simple, tiny minds (or proto-minds) having extremely simple experiences (or proto-experiences). It is only when these proto-qualia get organized into highly complex structures like our nervous systems that they somehow, in combination, give rise to complex minds like our own.

The initial, uncharitable objection to all of this is that it is just plain crazy, and Chalmers' critics have not been shy about raising it. For most philosophers, if a theory has implications as bizarre as that basic physical particles are associated with minds (proto- or otherwise) experiencing qualia (proto- or otherwise), that is reason enough to reject it. A more technical objection is that it is hard to see how proto-qualia could combine in such a manner as to "add up to" the sort of conscious experience we're familiar with in everyday life – an experience which seems to be a *single* conscious experience rather than a composite of billions of tiny proto-experiences, and which is present to a single conscious subject rather than to a collection of billions of tiny proto-subjects. A conscious experience, that is to say, has a unified character it would not have if it were an aggregate of simpler elements.

We will return later to the question of the unity of consciousness – a question which by no means poses a challenge to panpsychism alone. Its potentially panpsychist implications are, in any case, not the only problem for the Russellian theory. For it seems that the theory does not in fact avoid the zombie argument the way some of its defenders seem to think it does. Recall that what is essential to a molecule, atom, or subatomic particle *qua* molecule, atom, or subatomic particle is, in the Russellian view, that it plays a certain causal role, the role assigned to it in theoretical physics. The Russellian believes that qualia or proto-qualia are what play these roles. But could something else have played them instead? There seems no reason not to think so. An analogy might help: what is essential to the particular philosophy professor Feser *qua* being a philosophy professor is that he is capable of teaching certain classes, directing students in their research, etc. Could someone other than Feser have performed those functions just as well? Much as he'd like to think otherwise, it is true that someone could. There is nothing about Feser *qua* Feser that is necessary to playing the role of being a philosophy professor: plenty of non-Fesers can and do play the role just as well. Similarly, there seems to be nothing about a quale or proto-quale *qua* proto-quale that is necessary to performing the functions of a basic physical particle. Something other than a proto-quale, something absolutely devoid of anything even vaguely analogous to qualitative character, could play the role just as well.

This would seem to entail that it really is perfectly possible for there to be a creature physical-particle-for-physical-particle identical to you which is utterly devoid of proto-qualia, and thus of qualia – a creature which has something other than proto-qualia playing the relevant causal roles. But then such a creature would be a zombie, in which case zombies really are conceivable even on the Russellian view. And if that is so, then even the Russellian view entails a kind of dualism: for it entails that qualia are one kind of thing, and the basic physical components of the universe *qua* physical (that is, *qua* having the causal properties described by physical science), which can exist either with or without qualia, are another. Indeed, though Russell and Lockwood take themselves to be identity theorists of a sort, Chalmers does not, and explicitly presents his own panpsychist brand of Russellianism as a version of property dualism.

Would a Russellian property dualism, like other forms of property dualism, be threatened with epiphenomenalism? At first glance, it might seem not: if qualia or proto-qualia are what play the causal roles physics associates with molecules, atoms, subatomic particles, etc., then they might indeed appear just obviously to have a causal influence on the physical world. But appearances are deceiving. Given that something other than proto-qualia could equally well play those same roles, there is nothing about their distinctly mental, qualitative character that is relevant to their playing it. Feser is a husband and father, but his being a husband and father is completely irrelevant to his playing the role of a professor: someone who was neither a husband nor a father could play that role in exactly the same way. So Feser's being a husband and father is, we might say, epiphenomenal relative to his effects on the world *qua* philosophy professor. Similarly, a proto-quale's qualitative character – being proto-reddish, or proto-pungent – is completely irrelevant to its playing the role of a subatomic particle: something lacking proto-reddishness or proto-pungency could have played the role in exactly the same way, so that these proto-qualitative features are epiphenomenal. So not only does the Russellian view lead to property dualism, but it seems to lead to epiphenomenalism too – with all the problems we've seen that entails.

A more consistent Russellianism

Despite these problems Russell's theory might yet prove to be an advance over the usual alternatives. The reason lies not in the theory's metaphysical component – taking qualia to be the intrinsic properties of the material world, with all the weirdness this seems to lead to – but rather in its epistemology, its account of the nature of perceptual knowledge. Russell's central insight was, arguably, to see that indirect realism has dramatic implications for the mind-body problem; but it may have been an insight neither he nor his followers have taken seriously enough, or far enough.

Russell's own defense of indirect realism emphasized the causal element in perception, the way in which all our experiences of the external world are mediated by causal chains. The gap represented by these chains – by, for instance, the myriad neural firing patterns, retinal cell activity, and stream of photons that come between the surface of an apple and your experience of it – entails, in his view, that you never directly get at external objects themselves, but at best only at mental representations of them. Russell assumed, however, that you do indeed, in introspection, directly get at these representations themselves. But do you?

In Russell's view, those perceptual representations are, like all other mental states, identical with certain brain processes, which come at the end of a long causal chain beginning with the surface of an external object. But then the introspection of these representations must be as dependent on the causal workings of the brain as perception is. If your perception of external objects is mediated by causal chains, surely so is your introspection of those perceptions, as brain events subserving perception, triggered by impulses from the sensory organs, in turn trigger further brain events subserving introspection. As with perception, introspection would thus seem to provide you with only a representation – an introspective representation – of what you are made aware of through it. It gives you a representation, that is to say, *of your perceptual representations themselves*; it does not acquaint you with the intrinsic nature of those representations. And if we imagine yet higher-order mental events directed on to introspection itself – instances of meta-introspection, if you will – then these too must, on the Russellian model, be regarded as involving yet further causal chains and thus yet higher-level representations (that is, representations of representations of representations).

If this is right, then there is reason to believe that we have, contrary to Russell, no more knowledge of the inner world of the brain as it is "in itself" than we have knowledge of the external physical world as it is in *it*self. All such knowledge would be mediated by representations. One consequence of this seems to be that the Russellian response to the zombie argument can be salvaged after all. Zombies really are inconceivable, for in conceiving of perceptual experiences and qualia *as I encounter them in introspection* existing apart from the abstract causal structure of the brain (or whatever), I am not conceiving of those experiences and qualia as they are in themselves, but only of *introspective representations* of them. As with Russell's original proposal, we can conclude that conceiving of that sort of thing existing apart from the brain is of no more consequence than is the fact that the symbol "H_2O" can be imagined to exist in the absence of water. This would also appear to restore to the Russellian view its status as a version of neutral monism rather than property dualism. There is, at least where the question of the relationship between consciousness and the brain is concerned, only one kind of stuff, but it is intrinsically neither mental nor material. We count it as material when it is presented to us via perception, and as mental when presented to us via introspection: hence the brain seems "material" when one examines it during brain surgery, but "mental" when one "looks within" at thoughts, experiences, and feelings; but one is aware of exactly the same object in both cases. The difference between material processes and qualia is a difference only in how we represent things, not a difference in the things themselves as they exist independently of us. It is, that is to say, an epistemological difference, not a metaphysical one.

Consciousness, intentionality, and subjectivity

When the Russellian view is modified in the way suggested, we have a position that is in many respects reminiscent of the representationalist and higher-order theories considered earlier: the features we are introspectively aware of as qualia are just features of perceptual representational states, and features of those states, not intrinsically, but only as represented by yet higher-order representational states. Unlike other versions of those theories, this one is not a materialistic functionalist account, since it does not try to reduce qualia to features of objective, third-person material phenomena, and it is therefore not subject to the usual objections to functionalism and materialism.

Of course, this still leaves us needing to explain representation or intentionality itself. But if the problem of qualia can indeed be reduced to the problem of intentionality, that is no mean achievement. And the other common objections to the intentionalist account do seem answerable. The question of how intentionalism can deal with intentional states that are not conscious – such as one's belief that $2 + 2 = 4$, of which one is usually not conscious – is best dealt with by denying the assumption that there are such states in the first place. As John Searle has argued, strictly speaking there really are no processes that are both totally unconscious and literally intentional; rather, what exist are non-intentional, unconscious processes – neural wiring patterns, say – which have come into existence as a result of past learning (for example, one's study of basic arithmetic) and which have a tendency under the right circumstances (for example, when one is balancing one's check-book) to cause certain states which are both intentional and conscious, such as the conscious belief that $2 + 2 = 4$. Searle's reasons for endorsing this *connection principle* (the connection in question being an inherent connection between intentionality and consciousness) can only be fully understood after we have more closely examined the issues surrounding intentionality; but the principle shows that the objection from so-called unconscious intentional states is hardly fatal.

Intentionalism is also plausible for reasons other than those already considered. As Tim Crane has argued, the essential features of an intentional state include *directedness* on an object, and what he calls (following Searle) *aspectual shape*, or the object's being presented in a certain aspect or in a certain way: thinking about the 43rd President of the United States involves your mind's being directed upon a particular man and considering him *as* the President (rather than as the former Governor of Texas or the son of a previous President). But conscious states characterized by qualia seem to involve exactly these features. To have a toothache, for instance, is for your mind to be directed upon a particular part of the body – your tooth – and in a certain aspect – as hurting. Furthermore, in both intentional states and conscious states, sub-jectivity is essential. The directedness of an intentional mental state is always the directedness of the mind of a subject upon an object of thought, and aspectual shape is always the way that object is presented to that subject; similarly, qualitative conscious states always involve things appearing or seeming a certain way to a subject, where the qualia determining the character of that appearing or seeming (such as the particular shape of the reddish patch of color you see when you look at a tomato) always reflect the perspective or point of view of a particular subject (who is, say, to the left of the tomato).

The centrality of intentionality to consciousness and of subject-ivity to both is made more evident by a consideration of the *unity of consciousness.* Consider the experience you're having right now: you see and feel a book and your hands holding it, perhaps against the background of a table, and hear the rustling of the pages as you turn them. We know from modern neuroscience that discrete processes in the brain register each aspect of the physical world you are experiencing – the colors, shapes, and sounds, the motion of the book's pages, the feel of their texture, and so forth, are each correlated with a different neural event. Yet the experience you are having is neither an incoherent jumble of distinct and disconnected features (pages, ink, motion, colors, etc.) nor is it a collection of distinct and disconnected experiences of distinct and disconnected features; it is a *single, unified* experience of a book, the hands holding it, and a table. The experience has a coherent significance or meaning, and significance or meaning *for a single subject* of experience. You are not only aware of the shape, texture, colors, etc. as separate elements, but are aware of them as a book; and it is you who are aware of them, rather than myriad neural events somehow each being "aware" of one particular aspect of the book. In this unity of conscious experience, we see again how deeply tied consciousness is to intentionality, and how both consciousness and intentionality are tied to the presence of a subject.

The overall view suggested by the considerations adduced in this and the previous chapter is this. In perceptual experiences, the conscious subject represents the world external to the mind, and in introspection of those perceptual experiences, the subject represents those experiences themselves. In the first case, the subject is only indirectly aware of the external world; in the second, he or she is only indirectly aware of the perceptual experiences. In both cases, the subject is directly aware of a representation: in the former a first-order representation (of the external world), in the latter a second-order representation (of the first-order representation). In the latter, the first-order representation is represented as being, in various ways, more or less similar to other representations

– that is, it is represented as exhibiting certain qualia, where qualia are analyzed in terms of their similarity relations to each other. In so far as conscious experiences, whether first-order perceptual ones or higher-order introspective ones, are ultimately representational, consciousness is at bottom a manifestation of intentionality; in so far as intentionality in general and qualitative similarity judgments in particular require the presence of a subject, and in so far as the indirectness of perception and introspection entail the primacy of the first-person point of view, consciousness-cum-intentionality appears to be inherently and irreducibly subjective.

Despite the advances in our understanding of consciousness made possible by the theories examined in this chapter we seem left, metaphysically, in much the same position we found ourselves at the end of the previous chapter: with subjectivity laying at the core of the mental, and persisting as the main obstacle in the way of a materialist account of conscious experience. There is, as we've seen, a sense in which qualitative conscious states might be identified with states of the brain: perception of a brain state and introspection of a mental state can be seen as two different ways of representing the same thing. Still, since the characteristically "material" and "mental" aspects of this thing, whatever it is, turn out to exist not in the thing itself but only in the subject's representations of it, the sense in which the mental and physical can be identified would be a neutral monist sense, not a materialist sense. Moreover, the metaphysical status of the subject who does the representing of these conscious states/brain states has yet to be determined; in particular, nothing said in this chapter adds plausibility to the suggestion that this representing subject is material in nature.

The binding problem

These matters have not been settled conclusively in favor of the dualist. For, if it is true that the problem of consciousness cannot be divorced from the problem of intentionality, the question of whether materialism can account for subjectivity cannot ultimately be answered until we consider whether it can account for intentionality.

Providing such an account will be difficult, as evidenced by what was said earlier about the unity of consciousness. We noted that though the various aspects of the scene you experience are separately encoded by distinct processes in the brain, your experience is, nevertheless, unified: it is an experience of the book, hands, and table all together, and of the book, hands, and table as book, hands, and table rather than as a meaningless sequence of colors, shapes, textures, and sounds. But how exactly is this possible? How do discrete brain processes manage to add up to a meaningful, unified experience?

This is known among neuroscientists, cognitive scientists, and philosophers of mind as the *binding problem*; and while it is often discussed as if it reflected merely a temporary gap in our scientific knowledge, William Hasker has argued (following leads found in the writings of Descartes, Leibniz, and Kant) that it is most likely impossible in principle for there to be a materialistic, neuroscientific, solution to it. Even if each of the processes in the brain encoding different aspects of the experienced objects were somehow individually conscious (in a manner reminiscent of Chalmers' panpsychism) – this brain process conscious of this shape, that process conscious of that color, a further process conscious of a certain sound – this would not account for the existence of a unified experience, on the part of the conscious subject, of the book, hands, and table as a whole. As Hasker notes, if each student in a class knows the answer to at least one question in an examination, it doesn't follow that there is anyone who knows all the answers all at once. Their individual consciousnesses of the answers don't add up to a single, unified, collective consciousness of everything on the exam. Similarly, distinct neural processes correlated with different aspects of an object or scene by themselves do not, even if they are individually conscious, add up to consciousness of the object or scene as a whole. (And things are only more mysterious when we keep in mind that these processes are not individually conscious.) Nor will positing the existence of some neural scanning mechanism along the lines of the higher-order states we've discussed in this chapter, which integrates the information in each distinct neural process, solve the problem. For now all the relevant information would have to be gathered together in this mechanism, which itself would be composed of yet further distinct neural processes encoding distinct aspects of the visual field, and the binding problem would arise again at a higher level.

The implication seems to be that whatever it is that ultimately binds together the information presented either in perceptual experience or in higher-order introspective awareness cannot be composed of parts which individually correlate with different aspects of the information. This would seem to lend some credence to Descartes's indivisibility argument, according to which the mind is a simple, and thus immaterial, substance. And it indicates that giving a materialist account of intentionality – which must ultimately be an account of the subject whose mind is directed upon an object when in an intentional state – is going to be a tall order indeed. Nevertheless, as we will see in the next two chapters, many materialists have tried to demonstrate that their view can meet this challenge.

Further reading

The Block, Flanagan, and Guzeldere anthology *The Nature of Consciousness*, cited in the previous chapter, gives a large and representative sample of the enormous literature on consciousness that has developed over the last twenty years or so. Other important anthologies are Martin Davies and Glyn W. Humphreys, eds., *Consciousness* (Oxford: Blackwell, 1993), Thomas Metzinger, ed.,

Conscious Experience (Thorverton: Imprint Academic, 1995), and Quentin Smith and Aleksandar Jokic, eds., *Consciousness: New Philosophical Perspectives* (Oxford: Clarendon Press, 2003).

Dennett's eliminativism is defended in his influential book *Consciousness Explained*, cited in the previous chapter, and in "Quining Qualia," available in the Chalmers *Philosophy of Mind* anthology, also cited there. Cited there too was Chalmers' *The Conscious Mind*, in which he gives sympathetic treatments of both Russellianism and panpsychism. Other important book-length studies of the problem of consciousness include Owen Flanagan, *Consciousness Reconsidered* (Cambridge, MA: The MIT Press, 1992), William G. Lycan, *Consciousness* (Cambridge, MA: The MIT Press, 1987), and David Papineau, *Thinking About Consciousness* (Oxford: Oxford University Press, 2002). Joseph Levine's *Purple Haze: The Puzzle of Consciousness* (Oxford: Oxford University Press, 2001) is a rigorous critical analysis of all the most influential theories of consciousness, though the beginner will find it very hard going in places.

Representationalism is defended by Fred Dretske in *Naturalizing the Mind* (Cambridge, MA: The MIT Press, 1995), William G. Lycan in *Consciousness and Experience* (Cambridge, MA: The MIT Press, 1996), and Michael Tye in *Ten Problems of Consciousness* (Cambridge, MA: The MIT Press, 1995). Higher-Order theories are defended in Lycan's *Consciousness and Experience*, D. M. Armstrong's "What Is Consciousness?" and David Rosenthal's "A Theory of Consciousness," the latter two essays being available in the Block, Flanagan, and Guzeldere anthology. Tim Crane's *Elements of Mind* (Oxford: Oxford University Press, 2001) contains his fullest exposition and defense of intentionalism.

Berkeley's *Principles of Human Knowledge* is available in many editions. An important contemporary defense of idealism is to be found in John Foster, *The Case for Idealism* (London: Routledge and Kegan Paul, 1982).

Russell's position is most fully developed in his *The Analysis of Matter* (London: Kegan Paul, 1927). (His remark about what the physiologist sees is on p. 383 of that book.) He briefly and lucidly summarizes it in chapter 2 of *My Philosophical Development* (London: Unwin Paperbacks, 1985). Recent defenders of the Russellian view include, in addition to Chalmers, Michael Lockwood, *Mind, Brain, and the Quantum* (Oxford: Basil Blackwell, 1989), Grover Maxwell, "Rigid Designators and Mind-Brain Identity," available in Chalmers' *Philosophy of Mind* anthology, and Galen Strawson, "Real Materialism," in Louise M. Antony and Norbert Hornstein, eds., *Chomsky and His Critics* (Oxford: Blackwell, 2003). Lockwood's book includes his defense of the notion of unsensed qualia (or phenomenal qualities, as he refers to them), a defense I criticize at greater length in "Can Phenomenal Qualities Exist Unperceived?", *Journal of Consciousness Studies* Vol. 5, No. 4 (September 1998).

Searle develops the notion of aspectual shape, defends the connection principle, and criticizes materialist theories of consciousness in *The Rediscovery of the Mind* (Cambridge, MA: The MIT Press, 1992). Also of interest is Searle's *The Mystery of Consciousness* (New York: The New York Review of Books, 1997), which includes trenchant criticisms of, and testy exchanges with, Chalmers and Dennett. Hasker presents his argument from the unity of consciousness in *The Emergent Self* (Ithaca: Cornell University Press, 1999).

6

Thought

In hitting upon the formulation "I think, therefore I am," Descartes took himself to have established not only his existence, but his nature: he is essentially a thing that thinks. Thought, that is to say, is the essence of mind. There are two aspects of thought that are of particular philosophical interest: its representation of things beyond itself, that is, its intentionality; and its movement from one representation to another in accordance with the laws of logic, that is, its rationality. But, as indicated in the previous chapter, contemporary philosophers of mind typically take the problems of qualia and consciousness to pose the most serious challenge to a materialist concept of the mind, with intentionality and rationality being more readily explicable in naturalistic terms. There is a certain irony in this view, in so far as it effectively takes sensation and feeling – capacities we seem to share with other (obviously material) animals – to be more mysterious than thought, which we (arguably) do not share with them. One would have thought it more natural to see things the other way around; indeed, most philosophers of the past have seen things the other way around. The suggestion that what we share with the beasts is scientifically puzzling, while what appears to be unique to us is merely one, relatively unproblematic material capacity among others, would have struck Plato and Aristotle, Augustine and Aquinas, Descartes, Leibniz, and Kant as odd, even perverse.

We also saw, in the previous chapter, that there is a strain in contemporary thinking that holds qualia and consciousness ultimately to be explicable in terms of intentionality, and it was suggested that a strong case could be made for this view. But, in so far as the same strain typically takes the task of explaining intentionality itself in materialistic terms to be little more than a comparatively trivial mop-up operation, it is, arguably, misguided. As we shall see, a number of contemporary philosophers hold that the older philosophical tradition was correct, and that there are considerable difficulties involved in carrying out a naturalistic explanation of thought. In this chapter and the next we will examine recent attempts at such an explanation. This chapter will focus on attempts to account for rationality in particular; and we will see that, as with our investigation of qualia and consciousness, the investigation of rationality leads us inexorably to intentionality. Chapter 7 will then deal, at last, with that most ubiquitous of mental phenomena.

Reasons and causes

Suppose you witness Ethel crying out in pain after stubbing her toe, and then watch as she removes her shoe and examines her foot. If asked to explain the first event, you would probably say something to the effect that the damage to her body resulted in her crying out; if asked to explain the second, you would say that she wanted to determine the extent of the damage and thought that removing her shoe would be the best way to do so. In the first case, you would be pin-pointing the *causes* of *her* behavior; in the second you would be giving the *reasons* for it. In both cases you are giving an explanation of human behavior, but the sort of explanation is very different in each. In the first you are appealing to brute physical forces – an impact on skin and muscle tissues, together with the stimulation of nerve endings – while in the second you are appealing to what a person takes to be a rational course of action given her beliefs and desires.

This distinction between reasons for and causes of behavior is a crucial one, and raises in a vivid way the question of how human beings fit into the natural world. The role of causes seems unproblematic. The human body is, after all, a material system alongside other ones, and it is, as much as they are, governed by the causal regularities enshrined in the laws of physics. So it is not surprising that much of human behavior should be explicable in causal terms. But what about behavior that seems to involve more than this? What about behavior that results from choice, after reflection about which course of action would be best? To understand such behavior, it seems insufficient to speak in terms of ordinary causal factors – the stimulation of nerve endings, the secretion of chemicals, the firing of neurons and the like. Reasons for the action taken are relevant also, and appear to be just different sorts of things from causal factors. To say that neural processes cause the muscles in my fingers to move as I type these sentences is true enough; but my desire to write these sentences, my belief that using a word processor would be the most efficient way of doing so, and my consequent decision to start typing are clearly just as important, and seem irreducible to the sorts of causal processes alluded to. For A to be *the cause of* B is one sort of relation; for A to *be a reason for* B is another. The first concerns the impersonal realm of meaningless material forces; the latter concerns the personal sphere of rational deliberation. It's a straightforward case of comparing apples and oranges.

The trouble is that giving a materialistic or naturalistic explanation of any phenomenon seems somehow to require fitting it into the causal network described by physical science. If the materialist picture of the world is correct, there can be no true explanation of human behavior that does not ultimately amount to a causal explanation. But are the reasons one has for an action really analyzable in terms of causes of that action, appearances notwithstanding? Many philosophers have thought so. They would argue that since the action of my typing these sentences was the result of the reason for action constituted by my beliefs and desires, there is a clear sense in which it was caused by that reason for action. Reasons are, on this view, just a species of causes. But other philosophers have, following Ludwig Wittgenstein (1889–1951), argued that, in many cases, it is simply a conceptual confusion to treat reasons as causes of action. The smile with which I greet you is, in this view, not caused by the happiness I feel at your return from a long trip, even if the happiness was the reason for my smile; rather, the smile partially constitutes the happiness. The behavior and the happiness are not two neatly distinguishable elements related, like events as described in physical science, by some causal law. The tie between them is an intrinsic, conceptual one.

What we want to focus on, however, is not the question of whether this or that isolated reason for an action might plausibly be said to be a cause of the action, but instead on the larger question of whether the vast network of beliefs, desires, thoughts, and other propositional attitudes as a whole, which largely constitutes the mind, can plausibly be explained in terms of the network of causal processes that constitutes the brain. We noted in chapter 3 that the elements of the first network are related by logical connections, whereas the elements of the latter are causally related. When one set of neural processes brings about another, this is at most an instance of a contingent causal regularity. But when the thought that *all men are mortal* and *Socrates is a man* brings about the thought that *Socrates is mortal*, this is a case of logical inference, where the second thought follows of necessity. So how can the latter sort of phenomenon possibly be explained by reference to the former? How can the wholly contingent tendency of certain neural processes to trigger certain other ones account for our ability to think in accordance with the utterly inflexible laws of logic?

The computational/representational theory of thought

The answer, in the view of many contemporary philosophers of mind, lies in the digital computer. We saw in chapter 3 that one way of expanding on the generic functionalist idea that mental states are definable in terms of their characteristic causes and effects is to think of those causes and effects as the inputs, outputs, and transitional states of a computer program. The mind, in this view, is literally a complex piece of computer software implemented on the hardware of the brain. The modern theory of computation owes much to the mathematician Alan Turing (1912–1954), whose concept of a *Universal Turing Machine* – an abstract specification of a mechanical device capable of implementing any algorithm – was the model for the modern computer. The view in question is thus sometimes called *Turing machine functionalism*.

The beauty of an algorithm is that it provides a way of carrying out a highly complex task – including such tasks as performing a difficult mathematical computation, or reasoning through a long chain of argument to a conclusion – in a series of simple steps. The steps can in fact be so simple that we often speak of carrying them out "mechanically." And what a computer does is essentially to mimic, in this mechanical way, what we do when we follow an algorithm. Your pocket calculator or computer perform a number of elementary operations, realized in nothing more than the sending of electrical signals, which collectively add up to something significant: the display of "4" following upon the inputs "2," "+," "2," and "=," or the generation of text following upon the pressing of keys on a keyboard. Since the elementary operations are so extremely simple, it is possible to construct a machine which is capable of performing them with a very high degree of reliability. And this means that it is possible to construct a purely material system whose operations parallel exactly the laws of logic. A suitably programmed computer can be depended upon always to display "4" following the inputs "2," "+," "2," and "=," and always to generate "Socrates is mortal" following the inputs "All men are mortal" and "Socrates is a man."

If an artificial device can do this, why not a brain? Why can't we suppose that neural processes are as capable of implementing algorithms as are computers? Indeed, perhaps this is exactly what human thought, including the most abstract and rigorous mathematical and logical reasoning, really is: the implementation of a set of algorithms constituting a program. And if so, the way would be opened to fitting the sphere of reasons for action, and reasoning in general, into the sphere of physical causation. Just as the implementation of a computer program is ultimately reducible to the network of causes and effects instantiated in a piece of computer hardware, so too would the implementation of the program that is the human mind be reducible to the network of neuronal firing patterns constituting the brain. The capacity of the brain, considered as a purely material system governed by the same laws of physics that govern everything else in the universe, to generate patterns of thought that correspond to the laws of logic would be no more mysterious in principle than the capacity of a calculator reliably to function in accordance with the laws of arithmetic.

In a computer there are identifiable symbols – numerals like "2" and "4," and the signs "+" and "=" and so forth – that correlate with the numbers and functions of a mathematical computation. Is there anything analogous in the case of the computer that is the brain? Many philosophers have argued that there is, in the form of *sentences*. In their view, a particular mental state, such as the belief that Socrates is a man, is to be understood as a relation between the person having the belief and a sentence that has the meaning that Socrates is a man. Where is this sentence, though? Surely it can't be in the brain itself – there is nothing in the brain that looks like the sentence "Socrates is a man." And what language is this sentence written in? Surely not English, since lots of people who do not speak English have the belief that Socrates is a man.

It is a mistake, however, to suppose that a sentence having the meaning that Socrates is a man has to look like the sentence "Socrates is a man." After all, the sentence "Socrates is a man" could be handwritten instead of typed on paper, and remain the same sentence despite the difference in appearance. Moreover the sentence could be spoken, existing only as sound-waves rather than splotches of ink on paper; if spoken into a tape recorder, it would exist as a pattern on recording tape. So why couldn't it exist as a neuronal firing pattern in the brain? Why couldn't there literally be "sentences in the head," as some theorists have put it?

If there are such sentences they would indeed not plausibly be sentences of English – or Spanish, Chinese, German, or any other natural language. But they could well be sentences of some other, universal language – a "language of thought" common to all human beings, one we all think in unconsciously, and the sentences of which get manifested in our conscious thinking, speaking, and writing as translations (as it were) into sentences of English, Spanish, Chinese, German, and all the rest. Philosophers who take the view that there is such a language of thought often refer to it as *Mentalese*; and since the overall theory of which the Mentalese hypothesis is a part is one that takes thought to be computation of a sort analogous to the computation performed by modern digital computers, where this computation involves transitions between states directed on to sentential representations in a language of thought, the theory is often referred to as the *computational/representational theory of thought* or *CRTT* (in the words of Jerry Fodor, the theory's best-known advocate). Its defenders claim that, whatever else one thinks of this theory, it shows that there is, in principle, no problem in explaining our capacity for rational thought in purely materialistic terms.

The argument from reason

There are, however, a number of serious objections to this proposal. Consider first the implications of taking mental states to be states of a computer program whose causal efficacy derives entirely from their implementation in electrochemical processes in the brain. When you type "2," "+," "2," and "=" on the keyboard of an electronic calculator, various electrical signals are sent through the device which ultimately cause the symbol "4" to appear on the display screen. But that that symbol signifies to us the number 4, and that the other symbols signify the number 2, the function of addition, and the relation of being equal, plays no role whatsoever in the causal process. If we decided to change the meanings of these symbols – for instance, by using the sequence "2 + 2 =" to mean "Please display the message that it is raining" and the symbol "4" to mean "it is raining" – this would have no effect on how the device operates. Nor would it have any effect if we all forgot the meaning of the symbols, and came to regard calculators merely as toys that displayed different shapes whenever one pressed their keys. The meanings of the symbols are, in short, completely irrelevant to their causal efficacy, for they would have the same causal properties whatever meanings they had, or even if they had no meanings.

If this is true of the symbols processed by a calculator it would be true also of the symbols "processed" by the brain – it would be true, that is to say, of the contents of our thoughts as they are characterized by the CRTT. If your thought that "Socrates is a man" is identical with a neural process instantiating a sentence in Mentalese which has the meaning or content that Socrates is a man, then that meaning *per se* plays absolutely no role in causing whatever events the neural process, and thus the thought, causes. The causal properties of the neural process/thought would be just as they are even if it had instead the meaning that "it is raining," or even if it had no meaning at all. And that entails that the fact that your thought has the content that "Socrates is a man" plays absolutely no role whatsoever in causing you, for example, to say or write the sentence "Socrates is a man." You would have written or uttered the same sentence even if your thought had been about the rain or even if it had had no meaning at all. The electrochemical properties of the neural process implementing the thought are all that matter to its causal efficacy, just as the electronic properties of the symbols in a calculator are all that matter to their causal efficacy.

What this seems to mean is that distinctively mental properties turn out in the materialistic CRTT to be no less epiphenomenal than they do with property dualism. Nor is the CRTT the only materialist theory to have this consequence; indeed, any theory that takes mental states to have whatever causal efficacy they have only because of their identity with or supervenience upon physical states seems destined to have the same result: the physical properties of such states end up doing all the causal work, with the mental properties being an irrelevant, epiphenomenal extra. Epiphenomenalism would thus appear to threaten materialist theories no less than it does dualist ones – in which case the claim of materialist theories to be better able than dualist ones to account for the causal relations between mind and body seems to dissolve.

The problem, however, seems especially poignant for the CRTT, given its claim to provide a materialistic explanation of our capacity for rational thought. If the content or meaning of thoughts has, in the CRTT, no causal influence on behavior, neither does it have any causal influence on other thoughts. That your thoughts have the content that *Socrates is a man* and that *all men are mortal* can have no influence whatever on producing the thought that *Socrates is mortal*, for that last thought would have been caused by the others even if those others had instead had the content that *Fido is a dog* and *all fish have fins*, or even if they had no content or meaning at all. The electrochemical properties of the neural processes with which the thoughts are associated are entirely sufficient to bring about whatever effects they do bring about. The meaning or content of the thoughts is irrelevant.

That this result is as counter-intuitive as it is is bad enough, but the problem goes deeper. It is only in virtue of the meaning or content of thoughts that they can serve as a rational justification for other thoughts: your thoughts that *Socrates is a man* and that *all men are mortal* are a rational justification for believing that *Socrates is mortal* only because they have the meaning they do, and they would not serve as a rational justification for the latter thought if they meant instead that *Fido is a dog*, etc. Yet if the meaning or content of a particular thought plays absolutely no role in bringing about any other thought, it would seem to follow that it can provide no rational justification for any other thought. You'd have exactly the same beliefs you have now whatever the content had been of the further beliefs you appeal to in justifying them. In that case, however, your beliefs would seem to have no rational justification at all. But surely this cannot be right – surely you do have a rational justification for at least many of your beliefs. Yet the CRTT, it seems, cannot account for this – ironically enough, given that its very rationale was to account for our capacity for rational thought. Even worse, advocates of the CRTT obviously think they have a rational justification for their own belief in the CRTT; but if the theory is correct, it would seem that they can't! The theory appears to undermine itself.

The CRTT defender might appeal to evolution as a guarantee of the reliability of our thought processes: wouldn't natural selection ensure that our brains are wired in such a way that the thoughts we generate are, for the most part, true? Wouldn't we have died out long ago if things were otherwise? One quick reply to this would be to suggest that it is question-begging: for it assumes that we can be rationally justified, in the CRTT, in believing the Darwinian evolutionary story (or believing anything else) in the first place, which is precisely what is at issue. Another reply would be to note that what natural selection tends to maximize is the capacity of an organism to survive and reproduce, and there is no reason to assume that having a true system of beliefs really is what is most conducive to survival: maybe our environment is such that we have been able to survive and reproduce as well as we have only because we have developed a mostly *false* system of beliefs, a kind of elaborate fantasy world that shields us from certain truths, the knowledge of which would tend toward our destruction (perhaps because they would be too horrifying for us to bear). But there appears to be an even deeper problem. The general truth or falsity of a system of beliefs can only be affected by natural selection if that system of beliefs has, *by virtue of its truth or falsity*, some causal influence on behavior – that is, if the truth or falsity *per se* causes behavior which is either adaptive or maladaptive, and which will tend therefore to get either selected for or selected out. But a belief's being either true or false is bound up with its having the particular content it has, and as has been suggested, there seems to be no way, in the CRTT (or perhaps in any materialistic account of thought), for the content or meaning of a thought to have any causal influence on behavior. The purely neurophysiological properties which, according the CRTT, instantiate the thought are the only ones that can have any causal relevance. So there is no way for the truth or falsity of a belief to have any effect on behavior, and thus natural selection cannot affect in any way the general truth or falsity of a system of belief. But in that case, if the CRTT (or any purely materialistic account of thought) is true, evolution cannot account for the reliability of our thought processes.

The sort of argument described in this section is sometimes called *the argument from reason*, and versions of it have been presented by C. S. Lewis (1898–1963), Karl Popper (1902–1994), and, most recently, Alvin Plantinga and William Hasker. In so far as it depends on the claim that materialist theories cannot avoid epiphenomenalism any more than property dualism can – the claim, that is, that materialists cannot solve what philosophers of mind have come to refer to as the "problem of mental causation" – it rests on a premise that is bound to be controversial. But it shows, at the very least, that the suggestion that our capacity for rational thought is in principle easily explicable in naturalistic terms is far from having been demonstrated.

The Chinese room argument

Many think that this conclusion is bolstered by an important set of arguments associated with John Searle – perhaps the foremost critic of the notion that the human mind ought to be thought of as a kind of software and the brain as a kind of computer hardware. The first and most famous of these arguments involves a thought experiment that has come to be known as the "Chinese room," and is directed at the claim that the implementation of the right sort of program – whether in a computer, a sophisticated robot, or a human being – is sufficient for genuine intelligence. Searle asks us to imagine a scenario in which he is locked in a room with a collection of Chinese symbols and a rulebook, written in English, which tells him which combination of symbols to put together in response to questions written in Chinese and slipped to him through a slot in the door. Searle doesn't speak a word of Chinese, and the rulebook doesn't tell him the meanings of the symbols he's combining – all it tells him, in effect, is that when he's given a set of symbols that look like *this* (where *this* refers to some specific set of shapes on the page), he should reply with a set of symbols that look like *that* (where *that* refers to some other set of shapes). It is possible that Searle could get so good at combining the shapes that a native Chinese speaker who is putting questions to him through the slot and is unaware of what is going on would assume that Searle really speaks Chinese.

Turing famously suggested that a way of determining whether a suitably programmed machine could be said truly to think would be to put it in a situation where a human being would have to carry on a conversation with both the machine and another human being, and try to determine which participant in the conversation was the machine and which the other human being. If, after a sufficient period of time, the interlocutor couldn't determine which was which – if, that is to say, the machine's performance was indistinguishable from that of the human being – then, Turing suggested, the machine could be regarded as having exhibited real intelligence. The appropriate way to test for intelligence, on this view, is to see whether something *behaves* intelligently, and the machine will have passed what has come to be known as the "Turing test."

Searle, in his Chinese room, exhibiting behavior that is indistinguishable from that of a native Chinese speaker, has thereby passed the Turing test for understanding of Chinese. Moreover, he has done so by doing what a computer program does, namely, manipulating symbols in accordance with an algorithmic procedure to which only the symbols' physical properties (in this case their shape), and not their meanings, are relevant: he is, in effect, "running the program" for competence in the Chinese language. Yet for all that, he still does not understand a word of Chinese, and has no inkling of what the answers he's giving out mean. (Perhaps he occasionally hears some yelling on the other side of the door and wonders whether he's just "said" something insulting, or hears laughing and wonders whether he's told a joke or committed a *faux pas*!) But then it follows, Searle concludes, that running a program, of whatever level of complexity, cannot suffice for understanding or intelligence; for if it did suffice, then he would, simply by virtue of "running" the Chinese language program, have understood the language. So human intelligence just isn't what the CRTT says it is: it is not the implementation of a kind of computer software.

Searle considers the possible reply to this argument that even if *he* doesn't understand Chinese, it doesn't follow that no understanding of Chinese is present. After all, it isn't just a part of a computer, even the central processor, that runs a program, but the computer as a whole; and Searle is, in the thought experiment, part of a larger system that comprises also the rulebook, symbols, and door slot. It is this entire system which, strictly speaking, runs the Chinese language program. So maybe the system *taken as a whole* understands Chinese, even if one part of it (Searle) does not. This "systems reply" (as it is known) may sound bizarre: how can a room, even one as eccentric as the Chinese room, be said to "understand" Chinese, or anything else for that matter? But if one is willing to take seriously the suggestion that intelligence consists of the running of a program in the first place, one is bound to have to swallow some unusual consequences, given the great variety of systems which could, in principle, implement a program. In any event, Searle argues that the room is not really essential to the thought experiment. We could instead imagine that he memorizes the symbols and rulebook, and responds to questions put to him by quickly recollecting what symbols to give out in response to whatever symbols are put to him. Perhaps he even memorizes the sound of each symbol as well as its shape, and, following the rulebook, can now respond verbally to whatever is said to him by uttering the appropriate sequence of (what to him sound like) noises. In this scenario, Searle himself *just is* the entire system – yet he still doesn't understand a word of Chinese.

Some have suggested that in this scenario – in which, we can suppose, Searle interacts directly with other speakers and with the external world – he inevitably would pick up on the meanings of the Chinese words he's uttering. If a certain sequence of sounds tends to be uttered only when it is raining, he's bound to be able to infer that it means "it's raining"; if another sequence tends to be uttered when cheeseburgers are in the vicinity, he might conclude that it means "cheeseburger," and so forth. Whether such causal interaction with the world would suffice to generate a grasp of meaning is something we'll explore in the next chapter. But, as Searle notes, even if such an account is correct, the reply to his argument just sketched essentially concedes its main point, namely, that running a program is by itself insufficient for understanding.

There is a way to argue that in Searle's revised scenario, genuine understanding of Chinese would, for all Searle has shown, exist even in the absence of causal interaction with the world. Consider the fact that computers often run a number of programs simultaneously; for example, you might surf the Internet, and thus be running your web browser, while also playing a video game and typing a paper with your word processing software. Yet though the same machine is running all three programs, none of the programs necessarily has any influence on any of the others. Your word processing has no effect on your score in the game, and your score has no impact on which websites you visit. You might say that none of the programs "knows" what the others are doing. But maybe something similar is happening with Searle: his conscious understanding of English might be identical to his running a certain program (the program for English competence), while at the same time, by virtue of his following the rules in the rulebook and implementing the program for Chinese understanding, there is a second stream of consciousness that *is* consciously aware of speaking and understanding Chinese, even if the English-speaking program isn't. Since they are different programs, neither has any access to what is going on with the other one, any more than your word processor "knows" what your web browser is up to; but that doesn't mean that each one isn't aware of what is going on within itself. The result would be something like Multiple Personality Disorder: by virtue of his running both the English- and Chinese-speaking programs, more than one mind has taken up residence in Searle's body, though Searle is aware only of the thoughts of the first. If this is possible, then the fact that Searle's English-speaking stream of consciousness wouldn't be aware of understanding Chinese would nevertheless be consistent with there being some stream of consciousness within him that does understand it, and if that possibility hasn't been ruled out, the computational picture of the mind hasn't been refuted.

Other defenders of the CRTT have suggested that the replies to Searle's argument just surveyed fail to get at its main problem, which is that it is really directed at a straw man. Fodor, in particular, has argued that it is a mistake to view the computational/representational approach to the mind as a theory of *understanding* in the first place. Advocates of that approach do not hold – or at least need not hold, and should not hold – that it gives an account of *meaning* or *intentionality*: it has nothing to say about how symbols, Chinese or otherwise, come to have any content, or about how we come to understand that content. Rather, it is merely a theory about *rationality*, about our ability to go from one thought to another in accordance with the laws of logic; and what it holds, as we've seen, is that we are able to do this because our thought processes are computational processes implemented in the hardware of the brain. Nothing in Searle's argument undermines this claim: he is, by virtue of "running" the Chinese language program, genuinely engaging in rational thought, even if he is unable to understand the contents of the thoughts he's having. Of course, this doesn't show how the CRTT can get around the other objection we've looked at – the argument from reason – but it does seem to show that the Chinese room argument cannot provide compelling, further, independent grounds for rejecting the CRTT.

The mind-dependence of computation

The Chinese room argument seems, at best, inconclusive. But Searle has other arrows in his quiver. The claim of computational-ism is that the human mind is identical to a computer program, a piece of software implemented in the brain. The brain, that is to say, is on this view literally a kind of computer. But by virtue of what, exactly, does something count as a computer in the first place? Consider the computer sitting on your desk. You use it to surf the Internet and do word processing, and part of what this involves is the generation of text and images on the computer screen in response to inputs typed on the keypad. As we've noted earlier, the words and images appearing on the screen are intrinsically just meaningless patterns, shapes, and colors: it is *we* who give them whatever meaning they have; the same images could, in principle, have come into existence accidentally, and been associated with no meaning whatever. But Searle argues that the same thing is true of the electrical impulses produced by the striking of the keys, and of every other electrical impulse or mechanical operation that occurs within the machine in the course of its carrying out the functions enshrined in its programming. All of these are, intrinsically, just meaningless physical events, and they get their significance as stages in the implementation of a program only because we take them to have such a significance.

But your computer's being a computer at all just consists of its implementing various programs; and its implementing such programs just consists of our taking it to be doing so, of our using it to run the programs. In itself, the machine is nothing more than a hunk of plastic, steel, silicon, and wires, with electrical current running through it. It counts as a computer, Searle suggests, only *relative to us and our interests*. Indeed, it is not strictly speaking a computer even then; it is we who literally compute when we use "computers." By the same token, it is *we* who really calculate when we use "calculators": the calculator itself is just a mechanical device, and the electrical current running through it, the images displayed on its screen, and the markings on its keypad are intrinsically without meaning. We give these things meaning and we do the calculating, with the device being merely an external aid, vastly different in degree of complexity from an abacus or a pencil and paper, but not (relevantly) different from them in kind.

For this reason, anything could in principle be used as a computer; all that matters is that the system thus used has a structure complex enough for us to be able to interpret its states as being stages in the program. To use an example of Searle's, the atomic structure of the wall of his study is complex enough for there to be some configuration of events taking place within it, at the micro-level, that could be interpreted as the implementation of a word processing program; in a sense, his wall is therefore "running"

Word Perfect. Of course, we have no access to that system of micro-level events, so we could never actually find a workable way of isolating one part of the set of events and labeling it the "input," of isolating another part and labeling it the "output," and so on. But all that means is that we have no practical use for the wall as a potential word processor. Relative to our interests, it doesn't count as one, but in principle it could (and perhaps there might be creatures who would be able to make use of it). And the things that do count as word processors and the like do so only because we find it useful so to count them.

Computation, Searle concludes, is an *observer-relative* phenomenon. There is nothing intrinsic to the nature of anything in the material world that makes it a computer, or that makes it true that it is implementing a program. It is all a matter of interpretation: our interpretation. If we decide to count something as a computer, it is one; if not, then it isn't. There is nothing more to it than that. The most complex machine that rolls off the assembly line at IBM will not count as a computer if we have no use at all for it; by contrast, even the pen sitting on the desk in front of you counts as a computer in the trivial sense that we can interpret it as "implementing" the following "program": "Lie there and don't move."

The problem Searle wants to pose for the computational conception of the mind should now be evident. If computation is observer-relative, then that means that its existence presupposes the existence of observers, and thus the existence of minds; so obviously, it cannot be appealed to in order to explain observers or minds themselves. That would be to put the cart before the horse. It would be like trying to "explain" someone's appearance by appealing to a painting of her: "See, the painting looks like this; so that must be why she does too." Obviously, in this case, things are in reality the other way around: the painting's looking the way it does is to be explained in terms of the appearance of the person it is a painting of. By the same token, it is computation that must get explained in terms of the human mind, not the human mind in terms of computation. The brain is not intrinsically a digital computer, because nothing is. So the mind's ability to think in accordance with the laws of logic cannot be explained in terms of the brain's running a certain kind of program. The computational/representational theory of thought thus seems incoherent.

Another way to see the point is to recall that the computationalist account regards mental processes as the implementation of a set of algorithms. To implement an algorithm is to follow a set of explicit rules. As Hubert Dreyfus, another influential critic of computationalism, has pointed out, an apparent problem with the view that the mind can be explained entirely in terms of the following of some basic set of algorithmic rules is that any set of rules is capable of a variety of interpretations. It is possible to fix the interpretation of a given set of rules by appealing to a set of higher-order rules, but that just pushes the problem back a stage, since these higher-order rules are themselves going to be susceptible to various interpretations. So, another way to understand Searle's argument is as follows: the fact that a computer is following some basic set of algorithmic rules cannot fully account for its behavior, because that the set of rules (and thereby its behavior) is to be understood in *this* way rather than *that* requires some interpretation to be put on those basic rules; and since there is, by definition, no more basic set to appeal to in order to fix the interpretation, we need to appeal to something outside the computer – a mind that interprets the rules. In that case, we cannot explain the mind itself in terms of the following of algorithmic rules, for that such rules are to be given this interpretation rather than that presupposes the existence of a mind. Indeed, strictly speaking, that they truly count as rules at all presupposes that there is a mind interpreting them as rules; otherwise all that is present are regularities of behavior that can be described *as if* they amounted to the following of rules.

Some have tried to reply to Searle's argument by noting that, strictly speaking, more is required of something if it is to count as a computer than merely that we could interpret some isolated set of its states as a computation. It is not enough, for example, for a system plausibly to count as implementing the computation "$1 + 2 = 3$" that it has states that correspond to "1" and "2" which are followed by a state that corresponds to "3." For what it does genuinely to count as addition, it must also be true that had we instead counted the first two states as "3" and "4," the third state would have counted as "7" – and so on for other counter-factual inputs and outputs. But this does not seem to undermine Searle's basic point. All it shows is that a system is only going to be useful to us as a computer or calculator if it is complex enough to mirror all the possible computations we might want to perform with it, and not just some limited range. But this does not at all show that computation is not observer-relative. We couldn't make a knife out of just anything – steel and plastic will do, but shaving cream and butter won't – but that doesn't undermine the point that something counts as a knife only relative to our interests. Not everything can effectively be used to express a word or sentence – ink marks and sounds will do, but cigarette smoke trails and water droplets are too formless and unstable – but that doesn't affect the point that a given physical object only counts as a word or sentence if we use it as a word or sentence. Similarly, a machine has to have a certain level of complexity if it is going to be useful to us as a word processor or calculator, but that doesn't change the fact that its being a word processor or calculator is ultimately a mind-dependent phenomenon.

These last examples indicate that if Searle is right, his argument would apply not only to the "computational" part of the CRTT, but also to the "representational" part of it. The CRTT, as we've seen, holds that we think in a "language of thought," where this language is realized in "sentences" somehow instantiated in the neural wiring of the brain. But as we've seen, physical shapes, patterns of sound, electrical impulses, and the like by themselves have no meaning. And the point is not merely that the word "cat" does not refer to cats apart from our taking it so to refer; it doesn't even count as a word in the first place, whatever we take it to refer to, unless we so count it. But the same is true of sentences. Nothing is intrinsically a sentence; something's status as a sentence is entirely relative to our using it as one. In itself, a sentence is just a string of marks on paper, a series of noises, or whatever. And this seems no less true of neural wiring patterns: as one set of physical phenomena among others, they appear to have no intrinsic meaning or status as sentences, any more than do ink marks or sound-waves. But in that case, there cannot literally be sentences in our heads unless we interpret some neural processes occurring there as being instances of certain sentences – something which, quite obviously, happens only extremely rarely, if ever. More to the point, if sentences too are observer-relative, then they cannot be appealed to in an explanation of the mind and its thoughts. If one accepts the basic thrust of Searle's position, then, the "representational" aspect of the CRTT seems as incoherent as the "computational" aspect.

Thought and consciousness

Finally, there is arguably a problem with the claim of the "language of thought" hypothesis that the thoughts which have that language as their medium are never brought to consciousness – a claim that the theory must make, seeing as we are never aware of thinking in any such language, but only in the natural languages (English, German, French, Chinese, etc.) we use to speak. Searle argues that there can in principle be no such thing as an entity which is both literally a thought and totally unconscious. This is the "connection principle," alluded to in the previous chapter, in which there is an inherent connection between something's being a thought and its being conscious. If this principle is true, it would seem to follow that there is yet another reason to regard the language of thought hypothesis, and the CRTT of which it forms a part, as incoherent.

Searle's argument for this principle brings into sharper focus the deep connections that, as we suggested in the previous chapter, seem to hold between consciousness, subjectivity, and intentionality. Boiled down to its essence, it goes like this: unconscious mental states, such as one's unconscious belief that water quenches thirst, have intentionality: in this case, the belief *represents, is directed at*, or is *about* the fact of water's being thirst-quenching. But as with all intentional states, such unconscious states have "aspectual shape," in that they represent whatever it is they represent in some particular aspects rather than others. In the case at hand, the belief represents the fact in question as the fact that *water* is a thirst-quencher, and not necessarily as the fact that H_2O is a thirst-quencher (for the person who has the belief may know nothing about H_2O, and thus not know that water = H_2O). But aspectual shape is not something that can in principle be analyzed in exclusively objective, third-person neurophysiological or behavioral terms. If we observe someone going to a spigot and turning it, there is nothing about this behavior by itself that determines conclusively that the person is seeking water rather than H_2O, for the behavior might be the same either way. Even asking him which one he is seeking won't be enough, because saying "I'm seeking water and not H_2O" won't by itself tell you whether what the person means by the sounds "water" and "H_2O" is the same as what you mean by those sounds. (And asking what the person does mean will just raise the same problem at another level: what does the person mean by these other sounds, which are made in order to explain what is meant by the first ones?)

The upshot, Searle concludes, is that it is only from the first-person point of view of the subjective experience of the person having the belief that the meaning of the person's words can be conclusively determined. It is important to note that Searle's claim isn't merely that we can't know for certain from the external, objective point of view what the meaning of the words is, but rather that *there would be no fact of the matter at all* what those words mean if the only evidence that existed was the external, third-person evidence alone. Here Searle appeals to a famous set of arguments given by the philosopher W. V. O. Quine (1908–2000) for what Quine called the *indeterminacy of translation*. Quine argued that an anthropologist who notes that a member of a previously unknown tribe constantly uses the expression "gavagai" in the presence of rabbits might naturally interpret that expression as meaning "rabbit," and go on to translate the rest of the speaker's language accordingly. But it is also possible, going by the speaker's behavior alone, that the expression could be translated instead as "undetached rabbit part" or "temporal stage of a rabbit" – assuming that the speaker's language reflects, unlike our own, a special interest in body parts that remain attached to the body, or in objects of ordinary experience considered as mere temporal stages of larger four-dimensional space-time structures (that is, the entire history of the rabbit from conception to death) – and that the rest of the speaker's language could be translated in light of these unusual assumptions. There is nothing *in the speaker's behavior alone* that could possibly favor one system of translation over the other, Quine argues, provided that each system of translation was thorough enough to account for all of the speaker's behavior. Quine, who was a kind of behaviorist – he held that there just is nothing to the mind over and above patterns of behavior – took this to have the startling consequence that there is no fact of the matter, period, about what any of us means whenever we utter any expression: whether we decide to regard others, or even ourselves, as meaning "rabbit" or "temporal stage in the life of a rabbit" when we talk about rabbits, is entirely a pragmatic affair, a matter of which translation we find more useful. Neither interpretation is objectively closer to the truth than the other, for there is no object-ive truth of the matter in this case. Searle rejects this view utterly: there is, he insists, clearly more to the mind than behavior – there is also the subjective, first-person point of view of the conscious subject – and from this point of view a person does know that as a matter of fact it is, say, "rabbit" that he means, and not "temporal stage of a rabbit." But Searle does agree with Quine that if third-person, behavioral (and neurophysiological) evidence were all we had to go on, there wouldn't be such a fact of the matter. The third-person, external evidence just isn't by itself enough to determine meaning – or, in particular, to determine aspectual shape.

If objective, third-person facts are not enough to determine aspectual shape, then they are also not enough to determine the content of an intentional mental state like a belief that water quenches thirst. But when a person has such a mental state *unconsciously*, such objective, third-person facts – facts about neural connections in the brain, about behavioral dispositions and the like – are all the relevant facts there are. So, strictly speaking, when he or she is not consciously aware of believing that water quenches thirst, he or she does not, in Searle's view, have that belief. But there is obviously a sense in which one has that belief even when one isn't conscious of it, isn't there? There is, Searle agrees, but what this amounts to is really just this: when someone isn't consciously entertaining that belief, what he or she has is a set of neural connections that have a tendency under certain circumstances to produce the conscious belief that water quenches thirst. Until the person is conscious of it, though, he or she doesn't literally have a mental state having the content that water quenches thirst; the person couldn't have it, given the inherent connection between the conscious, subjective, first-person point of view of the subject and the aspectual shape exhibited by all mental states involving intentionality.

If there is such an inherent connection there just couldn't be states which were literally mental and literally had intentionality, and yet were always in principle unconscious. That is, there couldn't be states of the sort the "language of thought" hypothesis postulates: beliefs, desires, and so on, formulated in Mentalese. In Searle's view, if we are never conscious of such thoughts, we never really have them at all.

The defender of the CRTT could reply by suggesting that perhaps what we mean by "rabbit," and what we mean by anything else for that matter, really isn't as determinate from the first-person point of view as Searle thinks. Maybe you don't really know, even via introspection, precisely what you mean when you use "rabbit," or any other expression. And if not, there would be no reason to accept Searle's suggestion that an appeal to the subjective, first-person perspective of consciousness is necessary to account for the determinate meaning of our thoughts and expressions, for they just wouldn't have any determinate meaning in the first place.

This would, to say the least, seem to be a rather extreme and counter-intuitive way to avoid Searle's conclusion – it appears to entail that there is no fact of the matter about whether you mean "rabbit" or "temporal stage of a rabbit" – and it brings us, at long last, to the issue of whether materialism can account for what seem to be the obvious facts about meaning or intentionality. The arguments considered in the previous chapter led us to conclude that this is, ultimately, the key question the materialist has to face. The arguments of this chapter have reinforced this conclusion: the argument from reason implies that the standard materialist attempts to explain human rationality fail to account for the effect intentional mental states *qua* intentional have on the physical world; and Searle's various arguments suggest that the categories these materialist theories appeal to – computation, representation, language and its elements (for example, sentences) – *presuppose* intentionality and the point of view of the conscious subject, and thus cannot form the basis for a theory *explaining* the rational intentional processes of the subject. The last of his arguments has also reinforced the previous chapter's suggestion that there is an inherent link between consciousness, intentionality, and subjectivity, and that one cannot account for one of these without accounting for the others. We will consider whether this argument is ultimately defensible as we focus on intentionality itself in the next chapter.

Further reading

An excellent introduction to many of the issues and arguments dealt with in this chapter is Tim Crane's *The Mechanical Mind: A Philosophical Introduction to Minds, Machines, and Mental Representation*, second edition (London: Routledge, 2003). The claim that reasons are a species of causes is defended by Donald Davidson is his *Essays on Actions and Events* (Oxford: Clarendon Press, 1980); the claim that they are not is defended by Wittgenstein's student G. E. M. Anscombe in her *Intention* (Oxford: Blackwell, 1959).

The language of thought hypothesis, and the computational/representational theory of thought of which it is a part, are associated most famously with Jerry Fodor, who has defended it in a series of publications. Particularly important are his *The Language of Thought* (Cambridge, MA: Harvard University Press, 1975) and *Psychosemantics* (Cambridge, MA: The MIT Press, 1987). Kim Sterelny's *The Representational Theory of Mind: An Introduction* (Oxford: Blackwell, 1990) is also helpful. Turing's ideas are presented in his famous essay "Computing Machinery and Intelligence," reprinted, with a number of other important articles relevant to the issues dealt with in this chapter, in Margaret A. Boden, ed. *The Philosophy of Artificial Intelligence* (New York: Oxford University Press, 1990).

Some important articles on the problem of mental causation are collected in John Heil and Alfred Mele, eds. *Mental Causation* (Oxford: Clarendon Press, 1995). The "argument from reason" has been presented in many different versions and by many different thinkers, most of whom did not call it by that name. C. S. Lewis is often cited as its inventor, though it seems that other people have independently developed similar ideas, both before Lewis and after. In any event, Lewis's version of the argument is to be found in his book *Miracles* (Macmillan, 1978), and is developed and defended by Victor Reppert in *C. S. Lewis's Dangerous Idea: In*

Defense of the Argument from Reason (Downers Grove: InterVarsity Press, 2003). William Hasker's version is presented in chapter 3 of *The Emergent Self* (Ithaca: Cornell University Press, 1999). Karl Popper's related argument is in chapter 6 of *Objective Knowledge*, revised edition (Oxford: Clarendon Press, 1979). Alvin Plantinga's is presented in chapter 12 of *Warrant and Proper Function* (New York: Oxford University Press, 1993) and debated in James Beilby, ed. *Naturalism Defeated?: Essays on Plantinga's Evolutionary Argument against Naturalism* (Ithaca: Cornell University Press, 2002).

Searle's Chinese room argument was originally presented in "Minds, Brains, and Programs," which has been very widely reprinted (including in the Boden anthology cited above). That article and a number of early responses can be found together in Rosenthal's anthology *The Nature of Mind*, referred to in earlier chapters. Searle's ideas on the observer-relativity of computation and the "connection principle" are developed most thoroughly in *The Rediscovery of the Mind* (Cambridge, MA: The MIT Press, 1992). All of these ideas are debated in John Preston and Mark Bishop, eds. *Views into the Chinese Room: New Essays on Searle and Artificial Intelligence* (Oxford: Clarendon Press, 2002). Dreyfus's views are developed most thoroughly in *What Computers Still Can't Do* (Cambridge, MA: The MIT Press, 1992). Quine's argument is most thoroughly developed in his *Word and Object* (Cambridge, MA: The MIT Press, 1960).

Another important challenge to the computationalist model of the mind is, in the view of some writers, posed by Gödel's famous incompleteness results in mathematical logic. An argument to that effect was first proposed by J. R. Lucas in his "Minds, Machines, and Gödel," available in Alan R. Anderson, ed. *Minds and Machines* (Englewood Cliffs, NJ: Prentice Hall, 1964) and developed at length by Roger Penrose in *The Emperor's New Mind* (New York: Oxford University Press, 1989).

7

Intentionality

The term "intentionality" derives from the Latin *intendere*, which means "to point (at)" or "to aim (at)" – hence the use of the term to signify the capacity of a mental state to "point at," or to be about, or to mean, stand for, or represent, something beyond itself. (It is important to note that *intentions*, for example, your intention to read this chapter, are only one manifestation of intentionality; your *belief* that you are reading a book, your *desire* to read it, your *perception* of the book, and so forth, exhibit intentionality just as much as your intention does.) The concept was of great interest to the medieval philosophers, but Franz Brentano (1838–1917) is the thinker most responsible for putting it at the forefront of contemporary philosophical discussion. Brentano is also famous for regarding intentionality as the "mark of the mental" – the one essential feature of all mental phenomena – and for holding that their possessing intentionality makes mental phenomena ultimately irreducible to, and inexplicable in terms of, physical phenomena. The previous two chapters gave us reason to think he was right to make the first claim. The present chapter will consider whether he was also right to make the second.

In chapters 1 and 2 we examined some reasons for taking intentionality to be mysterious and perhaps incapable of a materialistic explanation. The intuitive idea was as follows: when we consider examples of material entities that exhibit intentionality – words, sentences, pictures – we see that they do not have their intentional content inherently, but only relative to human interests; in itself, a word, sentence or picture is just a meaningless set of ink markings and has whatever meaning it has only because we use it to convey a meaning. As Searle has put it, the intentionality present here is "derived intentionality" rather than "intrinsic intentionality." (Searle also distinguishes a third category: "as-if intentionality," which something exhibits when it behaves *as if* it had intentionality though it really doesn't, for example, the way water in a river moves as if it wanted to get to the ocean, when in reality it doesn't "want" anything at all.) The derivativeness of their intentionality seems to be a necessary feature of the entities in question: since it is, intrinsically, just a collection of meaningless particles of ink, say, a written word or sentence couldn't have intrinsic intentionality. But what is true of these examples seems true of material entities in general. Sound-waves emitted by the larynx, electrical current passing through a computer and the like all have whatever intentionality they do only in a derived fashion. More to the point, brain processes, composed as they are of meaningless chemical components, seem as inherently devoid of intentionality as sound-waves or ink marks. Any intentionality they have would also have to be derived from something else. But if anything physical would be devoid of intrinsic intentionality, whatever does have intrinsic intentionality would thereby have to be *non*-physical. Since the mind is the source of the intentionality of physical entities like sentences and pictures, and doesn't get its intentionality from anything else (there's no one "using" our minds to convey meaning) it seems to follow that the mind has intrinsic intentionality, and thus is non-physical.

In chapter 5 we considered the suggestion that the objection to identifying qualitative conscious states with brain states could be overcome by arguing, in modified Russellian "neutral monist" fashion, that neither perception nor introspection reveals to us the inherent nature of its objects: the way the brain appears to us in perception and the way conscious states appear to us in introspection are not necessarily the ways those things really are intrinsically. Perception and introspection give us only *representations* of the brain and of qualia-bearing conscious experiences, respectively, and not the real nature of those things as they are "in themselves." If it seems that brain states and conscious states cannot be identical, this might reflect just a difference in the way we represent them, and not an objective difference in the things themselves; they might, for all that, really be identical after all.

Could such a move be made in answer to the argument just sketched against identifying intentional mental states with brain processes? No, and the reason should be obvious. The modified Russellian neutral monist strategy depends on holding that the greyishness and squishiness of the brain are not intrinsic to the brain and that the qualia associated with conscious experiences are not intrinsic to the experiences: the greyishness, squishiness, and qualia all exist only relative to our representations of the brain and of conscious experiences. But the same move cannot be made with respect to the intentionality of intentional mental states. It would make no sense to hold that the intentionality exhibited by the mind does not exist intrinsically in the mind itself but only relative to our representations of the mind; for a representation is itself a manifestation of intentionality. We couldn't possibly "represent" ourselves as having intentionality unless we really had it, in which case we never have it only relative to a representation. That we can represent at all shows that we have it intrinsically.

Naturalistic theories of meaning

That, anyway, is the prima facie case for holding intentionality to be inexplicable in materialist terms. But despite this apparent difficulty for materialism − or perhaps precisely because of it − the attempt to provide a materialistic or "naturalistic" account of intentionality has been one of the main preoccupations of contemporary philosophers of mind. Some of them have suggested that the variety of accounts developed in recent years give, by virtue of their very existence, reason to think that a materialist explanation of intentionality should at least in principle be possible after all. So we need to consider these accounts and see whether they overcome the intuitive difficulties that seem to face such an explanation. The major theories can be grouped into four categories:

1. Conceptual role theories

This sort of theory proposes that the meaning or intentional content of any particular mental state (a belief, desire, or whatever) derives from the role it plays within a system of mental states, all of which, as we've seen, seem logically interrelated in the manner briefly discussed in chapters 3 and 6, since to have any one mental state seems to require having a number of others along with it. The idea is that what gives the belief that *Socrates is mortal* the precise meaning it has is that it is entailed by other beliefs meaning that *all men are mortal* and that *Socrates is a man*, that together with a belief meaning that *all mortals will eventually die* it entails a belief meaning that *Socrates will eventually die*, and so on. If we think of beliefs, desires, and the like as a vast system of logically interconnected elements, the theory holds that each element in the system gets its meaning from having precisely the place in the system it has, by bearing exactly the logical and conceptual relations it bears to the other elements. (More precisely, it is the objects of beliefs, desires, and the like – sentences of Mentalese according to the CRTT, or, more generically and for those not necessarily committed to the CRTT, "mental representations" of some other, non-sentential sort – that bear meaning or intentional content. But for the sake of simplicity, we can ignore this qualification in what follows.)

There seems to be a serious problem with the conceptual role approach, namely that even if it is granted that mental states have the specific meaning or content they do only because of their relations to other mental states, this wouldn't explain how mental states have any meaning at all in the first place. That a particular belief either implies other beliefs or is implied by them presupposes that it has some meaning or other: nothing that was completely meaningless could imply (or be implied by) anything. The very having of logical and conceptual relations assumes the prior existence of meaning, so that no appeal to logical and conceptual connections can (fully) account for meaning. Moreover, if belief A gets its content from its relations to beliefs B and C, and these get their content from their relations to beliefs D, E, and F, we seem destined to be led either in a circle or to an infinite regress. Either way, no ultimate explanation of intentional content will have been given. To provide such an explanation thus inevitably requires an appeal to something outside the network, something which can impart meaning to the whole.

John Searle, who endorses something like the conceptual role theory of meaning, acknowledges that logical and conceptual relations between mental states cannot be the whole story if circularity or infinite regress is to be avoided. He therefore postulates that the entire "Network" of intentional mental states (he capitalizes Network to signify its status as a technical term) rests on what he calls a "Background" of non-intentional capacities to interact with the world around us. We have, for example, such intentional mental states as the desire to have a beer and the belief that there is beer in the refrigerator, and these mental states do, in part, get the specific meaning they have via their relations to each other and to other mental states in the broader Network. But ultimately these mental states, and the Network as a whole, function only against a Background of capacities, such as the capacity to move about the world of physical objects, pick them up, manipulate them, and so on. This capacity is not to be identified with the belief that there is a real external world of physical objects; for if it were such an intentional mental state, then it would have to get its meaning from other mental states, and thus couldn't serve as part of the Background that ends the regress of mental states. The capacity in question is rather something unconscious and without intentionality, a way of acting rather than a way of think-ing. One acts as if one had the belief in question, though one in fact does not. While this capacity could in principle become a con-scious, intentional mental state – one could come to have the explicit belief that *there is a real world of external physical objects that I can manipulate and move about within* – this would mean that this particular capacity has moved out of the Background and into the Network, and now rests on some other unconscious, non-intentional Background capacity or way of acting. There is, in short, always some set of capacities or other that comprises the Background (even if it is not always the same set for different people, or even for the same person at different times), and these capacities serve to ground the Network of intentional mental states.

There is much to be said for Searle's hypothesis of the Background, but it seems that it cannot save the conceptual role theory, for to speak of a "non-intentional capacity for acting" is to speak ambiguously. Consider that when you act without the con-scious belief that *there is an external world of physical objects*, but merely manifest a capacity to interact with the world of physical objects, your capacity isn't non-intentional in the same sense that an electric fan's capacity to interact with the world of physical objects is non-intentional. You behave "as if" you had a conscious, intentional belief in a world of physical objects, but of course you don't, because it typically never even occurs to you either to believe or doubt that there is such a world: you just interact with the world, period. The fan also behaves "as if" it believed there was a world of external physical objects (that it "wants" to cool down, say); but of course it doesn't really have this belief (or any wants) at all. In the case of the fan, this is not because it just hasn't occurred to the fan to think about whether there is such a world, for the fan isn't capable of such thoughts; it is rather because, strictly speaking, the fan doesn't really "act" or "behave" at all, as opposed to just making movements. And the reason we don't regard it as acting or behaving in the same sense we do is precisely because it doesn't have intentionality – it is a dumb, meaningless, unconscious hunk of steel and wires. We on the other hand don't merely make physical movements: the waving of your hand when your friend enters the room isn't just a meaningless movement, but an action, the action of greeting your friend. If it were just a meaningless movement – the result of a seizure, say – we wouldn't count it as an action at all; it wouldn't in that case be something you do, but rather something that happened to you. The fan, however, is capable of making nothing but meaningless movements.

For something genuinely to behave or act as we do requires that it does have intentionality – action and behavior of the sort we exhibit are themselves manifestations of intentionality, and thus presuppose it. But in that case, an appeal to a "capacity for action" cannot provide the ultimate explanation of intentionality. We need to know why our capacities for action are different from the mere capacities for movement that a fan exhibits. Merely noting, à la Searle's Background hypothesis, that our capacities are non-intentional ways of acting cannot help, for that they are genuinely ways of acting is precisely what needs to be explained. Indeed, since they are ways of acting, they cannot be literally non-intentional, for if they were, they would no more be true ways of acting than are the capacities of an electrical fan. A capacity for action is, as a matter of conceptual necessity, an intentional capacity.

In fairness to Searle, it isn't clear that he intends his hypothesis of the Background to serve as a complete explanation of intentionality. His aim may be just to draw out some implications of the fact that mental states are logically and conceptually related to one another in a Network. The point, though, is that his way of avoiding the circularity or regress that threaten any conceptual role theory cannot be appealed to in order to vindicate such a theory as a complete theory of meaning – and that it may even be incoherent, if Searle holds that the capacities and ways of acting that form the Background are literally devoid of intentionality.

2. Causal theories

The right way to break out of the circle or regress of mental states is, in the view of many contemporary philosophers, to appeal to the *causal relations* those states bear to elements of the external world. It is, in this view, not (or not merely) the relations these mental states bear to one another that give them their intentional content or meaning, but (also) the fact that those mental states tend to be generated by certain kinds of interaction with the thinker's environment. Your belief that the cat is on the mat has the particular content it has not (merely) because of the logical and conceptual relations that belief bears to other mental states, but (also) because that belief tends to be caused by the presence of a cat in your external surroundings.

Some theorists would hold that causal relations alone account for the intentional content of mental states, while others would allow that conceptual role plays a part as well. The latter would accordingly distinguish between "wide content" (that aspect of the intentional content or meaning of a mental state that is determined by its causal relations to the external world) and "narrow content" (that aspect of intentional content or meaning that is determined by a mental state's relations to other mental states). Theories which, like causal accounts, tend to emphasize wide content are typically referred to as "externalist" theories (since they focus on causal relations to elements external to the thinker), while theories, like the conceptual role account, which tend to emphasize the priority of narrow content, are called "internalist" (since they focus on logical and conceptual relations between mental states, which are internal to the thinker). Externalist theories have in recent years come to be favored by philosophers of mind interested in giving a naturalistic account of intentionality.

The reason for this is not difficult to see. As noted earlier, the mind's evident causal interaction with the physical world provides the most powerful argument for the materialist claim that the mind must be just one more part of that world; and that the best way to account for the mind in materialistic terms is to analyze it into its causal relations is the central claim of the functionalism that has come to be the most popular version of materialism. It is natural, then, for the materialist to suspect that a causal approach to intentionality, in particular, is likely to succeed if any naturalistic approach will. Moreover, the causal approach clearly has some intuitive plausibility: surely, one is inclined to say, the fact that your belief that the cat is on the mat was caused by the cat's being there has *something* to do with the fact that it has the content it does.

As it stands (and as all causal theorists recognize), the idea clearly needs development. For you could have the belief that the cat is on the mat even if that belief were *not* caused by the cat's being there, but instead caused by something else (like hallucinogenic drugs put into your coffee), and the cat's being there could cause a belief other than the belief that the cat is on the mat (for example, because of bad lighting, it could instead cause the belief that the dog is on the newspaper). So mere causal connection is not enough to account for meaning. At the very least, some kind of *regular correlation* between a mental state and a particular cause of that state also seems crucial. Many philosophers see models for such correlations in the natural world: smoke is correlated with fire, the rings of a tree with its age, and the symptoms of a disease with the disease itself. So regular are these correlations that in each case we typically take the presence of the effect to provide a reliable indication of the presence of the cause: that is to say, we take the presence of smoke to be a reliable indication that fire is present, the presence of thirty-three tree rings reliably to indicate that the tree is thirty-three years old, and the presence of red spots to be a reliable indicator of measles. Indeed, we even use the language of meaning here: we say that smoke *means* fire, and so forth. Such regular, reliably indicative correlations seem a plausible model for the sort of causal connections that could explain the meaning or intentional content of mental states.

A little thought shows that even this development of the basic idea of a causal theory of meaning cannot be the end of the story, for how could even such regular causal correlations explain our ability to have thoughts about things we don't seem to have any causal connection with – non-existent objects (Superman and Santa Claus), future objects and events, and so on? Moreover, how can it explain our ability to make mistakes? In many cases a mental state "means" something with which it isn't causally corre-lated in a regular way: as we've seen, you might, because of bad lighting, take something to be a dog which is in fact a cat. Philosophers call this the "misrepresentation problem" for causal theories of meaning. A related, though distinct problem is the "dis-junction problem": if (because there's always bad lighting in your house, or because you've got bad eyesight) a particular mental state of yours tends regularly to be caused not only by cats but also, in certain circumstances, by dogs, why (if the causal theory is true) should we regard that mental state as representing cats uniquely? Why should we not regard it as representing, disjunctively, *cats OR dogs-in-certain-circumstances*? Of course, there are going to be many cases where it does represent cats uniquely – the elderly person with bad eyesight might really only ever think that a cat is present, even when it's a dog – but that is precisely the problem: how can the causal theory explain this, given that the theory seems to entail that your mental state will represent anything that regularly causes it?

Jerry Fodor, an influential proponent of the causal theory, has suggested that the solution to such problems lies in the notion of what he calls *asymmetric dependence*. The idea is that, when a mental state typically caused by cats is also caused by dogs-in-certain-circumstances, the latter sort of causal connection is parasitic on the first. That is to say, dogs-in-certain-circumstances will cause the relevant mental state only because that mental state is already typically caused by cats – the "dogs-in-certain-circumstances" causal connection only gets set up once the "cats" connection is in place – while cats would cause the relevant mental state whether or not dogs-in-certain-circumstances ever did. The causal connection between the mental state and dogs-in-certain-circumstances is therefore asymmetrically dependent on the causal connection between the same mental state and cats: the former connection will exist only if the latter does, but the latter would exist whether or not the former did. The right way to formulate a causal theory, then, is to hold that it is causal connections that are *not* thus asymmetrically dependent that give rise to meaning: in the case at hand, the mental state represents cats uniquely because the causal connection between it and cats is not asymmetrically dependent on some other causal connection.

Fodor's is but one attempt to solve the problems facing the causal theory, and all such efforts have faced a battery of further objections. The result has been the incorporation of ever more subtle and complex technical qualifications into the causal story in terms of which causal theorists want to account for meaning, so as to stave off various counter-examples. But even if one or more of these various technical moves can successfully deal with the specific counter-examples they are designed to handle, it seems that several fundamental difficulties facing any possible causal theory would remain unanswered.

The first problem is that the theory seems to assume that it is not possible for a mental state genuinely to represent anything other than something that typically causes it. But we have already seen, in chapter 1, powerful reasons for thinking that this assumption is false: your thoughts and perceptions might represent cats even if they are never caused by cats at all, but by a Cartesian evil spirit, or a supercomputer stimulating your brain, as it sits in a vat of nutrients. A causal theorist might deny that this is really possible, but if so, he cannot appeal to the causal theory itself as grounds for this denial without begging the question.

A causal theorist willing to countenance the narrow content favored by the conceptual role theorist, in addition to the wide content emphasized by the causal theory, could perhaps reply that the possibility of these skeptical scenarios can be accounted for in terms of the former sort of content: the logical and conceptual connections one's thoughts about cats have to other mental states might suffice to make them genuinely about cats, despite the possibility that they are caused by something other than cats (for example, by a Cartesian evil spirit). It is not clear that this would work to save the causal theory – for if my thoughts would be thoughts about cats regardless of what caused them, how can causal relations play any role in generating meaning? But in any event, the causal theory would still remain open to an objection that we've already seen applied to the conceptual role theory. Like that theory, the causal theory would seem at most to account for why a particular mental state means *this* specifically, rather than *that*; it does not thereby account for why it has any meaning at all. It seems that it is only when a mind, with all its intentionality, has already come into being that there can be mental states which bear specific meanings related to their specific causes; and if so, then an appeal to such causes cannot by itself account for intentionality.

The causal theorist's appeal to alleged cases of meaning in nature does nothing to undermine the point: it supports it. When we say that "Smoke means fire," we're not speaking literally. Smoke doesn't really *mean* anything, at least not in the way that the *word* "smoke" means (given our linguistic practices) smoke. Smoke is just smoke – a meaningless arrangement of particles. Because smoke is typically caused by fire, we can interpret it as a sign of fire; but in that case the meaning is all in us, not in the smoke. That it's caused by fire explains why smoke "means" fire to us – that is, why it means fire rather than, say, water. But that it "means" anything at all has nothing to do with its causal connection to the fire and everything to do with our powers of interpretation and evaluation of evidence. In so far as the intuitive plausibility of causal theories of meaning rests on appeal to such examples as "smoke means fire," it thereby seems to rest on little more than a pun. The sense of "means" in that case just isn't the same sense as that in which your thought about fire means fire. The latter is a case of what Searle calls *intrinsic* intentionality, while the former is, when not a case of mere *as-if* intentionality, at best a case of *derived* intentionality.

There is a third, and perhaps even deeper, objection to any possible causal theory. The point derives from an argument presented by Karl Popper in the context of a critique of causal accounts of language, but it seems to be applicable to causal theories of intentionality as well. Any account such theories could give of the relevant causal relations holding between a particular mental state and a particular object in the external world will require picking out a particular beginning point of the causal series (call it A) as the thing represented and a particular end point (B) as the mental state doing the representing. So suppose A is a particular cat you are looking at and B a particular brain state that the causal theorist wants to identify with the perceptual mental state representing the cat. The problem is this: in the external physical world as it is in itself, apart from human purposes and interests, there seems to be nothing more than an ongoing causal flux, comprising an unimaginably complex sequence of events. Nothing in this flux is objectively either the determinate starting point of a particular sequence of events or the determinate ending point. It is we who pick out certain events and count them as beginnings and endings; their status as beginnings and endings is relative to certain purposes and interests of ours. This is as true of A and B as of anything else: there is no *objective* reason why A should be the cat rather than the cat's fur or a particular photon in the stream leading from the cat to our retinas, and no *objective* reason why B should be this particular brain state rather than the one immediately before or after it in the causal sequence of brain processes. So the "fact" that the causal chain purportedly explaining your perceptual experience of the cat begins with A and ends with B would appear to be a *mind-dependent* fact, determined by human purposes and interests – that is to say, it appears to presuppose intentionality. But then, the characterization of all such causal chains would presuppose intentionality – in which case, no appeal to such causal chains could truly explain it after all.

3. Biological theories

Materialist philosophers of mind sensitive to the difficulties inherent in deriving meaning from brute causation have suggested that a more plausible candidate for a purely physical property capable of grounding intentionality might be found in the notion of biological function. Fins perform the function of allowing the organism having them to move through the water. Wings perform the function of allowing winged creatures to fly. Hearts perform the function of pumping blood. These organs serve these functions because natural selection formed them to do so. Might this sort of function underlie the meaningfulness of mental states? It is, after all, surely the function of a *desire to drink water* to get a creature that has that desire actually to drink water, which a creature needs to do in order to survive and reproduce; that is plausibly why natural selection put such desires into creatures. And perhaps that's all it is for the desire to have the particular meaning or intentional content it has: its *representing* water is nothing more than its serving the *function* of getting the creature to drink water. Meaning, on this view, is identical to biological function – hence it is sometimes called a *biosemantic* theory of meaning (a label associated with Ruth Millikan, one of its main proponents).

An advantage of this theory is that it seems to provide a way of dealing with the misrepresentation problem. If the meaning or intentional content of a mental state derives from the biological function it serves, it will have that same meaning even if on some occasions it is caused by something other than what it is normally caused by. There thus need be no mystery about how a mental state could be about something other than what happens to cause it on some particular occasion, and thereby misrepresent what happens then to cause it. For example, if the desire to avoid snakes has the meaning it does because it serves the function of causing the creature having it to flee when snakes are present, it will still have this meaning even when a particular instance of it is caused, not by the presence of a snake, but by the presence of a rope or a hose that, due to odd lighting, looks like a snake.

Nevertheless, there are several serious objections to the biological theory. An obvious initial objection is that at best, it seems dubious that it could account for such sophisticated mental states as, say, one's belief that Wittgenstein was a more important philosopher than Russell: surely natural selection never hard-wired such a belief into anyone, for beliefs about the relative importance of Wittgenstein and Russell could not only not have occurred to anyone in the period of history in which natural selection formed human nature, but wouldn't have served any evident biological function even if they had occurred to anyone then.

Biosemantics advocates hold that such highly complex mental states might, nevertheless, derive a secondary functionality by virtue of their relationship to mental states – like the desire for water – that are more clearly functional. But however such a suggestion might be developed, there may be deeper problems. One of them is that the theory appears to entail that nothing that didn't evolve could possibly have intentionality, for, not having evolved, it wouldn't have states that serve any particular function. But this seems false: we can certainly at least imagine cases where creatures come into existence other than by evolution, and yet have intentionality. If a freak occurrence in a swamp were spontaneously to generate out of the muck a molecule for molecule living duplicate of you – "swampman," as philosophers who have discussed this sort of example have affectionately dubbed it – then this duplicate would surely have thoughts, experiences, and other intentional mental states, despite not having come about through evolution.

Another difficulty is that the biological theory seems unable to deal with the disjunction problem: if, for example, a desire to avoid cheetahs happened to be hard-wired into our ancestors as a result of their interactions with both cheetahs and tigers-in-certain-circumstances (for example, at night time when tigers might be hard to distinguish from cheetahs), then it would seem to follow that the biological function of this desire is to get us to avoid both cheetahs and tigers-in-certain-circumstances – and thus it would follow too that the desire represents, not *cheetahs* uniquely, but rather *cheetahs OR tigers-in-certain-circumstances.*

In reply to this, Daniel Dennett has suggested that if such examples indicate that meaning must be indeterminate on a biological theory of intentionality, this does not serve as an objection to the theory, for such indeterminacy is common throughout the biological realm. A certain organ may have evolved originally to serve one function, and then at a later stage in evolution taken on another: one creature might have evolved feathers because they served the function of attracting mates; while its descendants, having migrated to a colder environment, found that the feathers served to keep their bodies warm, a function the feathers might retain even if the mating function disappears. Which function the feathers really serve might, at some stage in this long evolutionary process, simply be indeterminate. But in that case, why couldn't the meaning of a desire to avoid cheetahs also be indeterminate (that is, not clearly about *cheetahs* uniquely as opposed to *cheetahs OR tigers-in-certain-circumstances*)? Why assume this is a problem for the biological theory, rather than just a further instance of the ambiguity evident in many biological phenomena?

One possible objection to this reply is that it fails to explain how the biological theory can deal with cases of mental states whose meaning or intentional content is determinate and unambiguous (the case for holding that there are indeed such mental states being something we'll examine shortly). Another objection is that even if all our mental states were indeterminate or ambiguous in their meaning or content, this would not save the theory; for even if the theory could explain why they have ambiguous meanings, it would not explain why they have any meaning at all. While a heart serves the function of pumping blood, the heart nevertheless doesn't mean or represent pumping blood – for it doesn't mean or represent anything at all. It's just a muscle. Words, sentences, and pictures mean things, but muscles surely don't, any more than gall stones or hangnails do. But if having evolved to serve a certain function doesn't suffice to give the heart meaning or intentional content, why would this suffice to give a belief or desire meaning or intentional content? Wouldn't mental states exhibiting intentionality already have to exist in the first place in order for natural selection to select some of them as having survival value? If so, then even if a mental state's serving a particular biological function could account for its having the specific meaning that it has (ambiguously or otherwise), it couldn't account for its having any meaning at all. Natural selection's purported ability to shape meaning would presuppose that there is meaning there to be shaped – in which case biological function couldn't possibly provide a full explanation of meaning.

This is, of course, an application to the biological theory of an objection already considered when discussing the conceptual role and causal theories – namely, that the operation of the mechanism the theory appeals to in order to explain intentionality itself presupposes intentionality. That this criticism seems to apply to the biological theory as much as to the causal theory is even more evident when one considers that ultimately, there may be no substantive difference between them. For, as Searle has argued, the trouble with appeals to biological function in this context is that all talk about biological function must, from a Darwinian point of view anyway, be regarded as nothing more than a shorthand for talk about causation. To say that the heart was selected by evolution to serve the function of pumping blood is, strictly speaking, to say something false; for evolution doesn't literally "select" anything, nor does the heart literally serve any purpose or function at all, at least not on a Darwinian view. Indeed, *the whole point* of Darwin's account of evolution by natural selection is to get rid of the need to appeal to literal purposes and functions in nature – to explain the appearance of purpose and function in terms that make reference only to purposeless, meaningless causal processes. The right thing to say about the heart is, in a Darwinian view, just this: it causes blood to flow, and it was in turn caused by a series of successive genetic mutations that allowed the creatures exhibiting them to survive and reproduce in greater numbers than those which lacked them. And that's it. If talk about the "purpose" or "function" for which the heart was "selected" has any application at all, it is only as a way of noting how what in reality are the purposeless, functionless, and meaningless results of unthinking causal processes can seem to be purposive, functional, and meaningful.

Talk about purposes and functions, if taken literally, seems to presuppose intentionality; in particular, it seems to presuppose the agency of an intelligence who designs something for a particular purpose or to serve a particular function. But the aim of Darwinian evolutionary theory is to explain biological phenomena in a manner that involves no appeal to intelligent design. As we've had reason to note in earlier chapters, just as modern physics has tended to explain phenomena by carving off the subjective quali-tative appearances of things and relocating them into the mind, so too did the Darwinian revolution in biology push purpose and function out of the biological realm, making them out to be mind-dependent and devoid of objective reality. This is of a piece with the general materialistic tendency to regard genuine scientific explanation as requiring the stripping away of anything that smacks of the subjective, first-person, intentional point of view. It thus seems odd that materialist philosophers should think it a hopeful strategy to appeal to biological function in order to account for intentionality. As Searle argues, this move is simply not open to them, given what is entailed by a Darwinian account of the biological realm – an account materialists must necessarily be deeply committed to.

4. Instrumentalist theories

Though Dennett, as indicated, sympathizes with biological theories of intentionality, he has also developed a distinctive approach of his own. It begins by proposing that what we're trying to understand in explaining intentionality is the behavior of certain complex physical systems: human beings and, perhaps, other animals. In explaining the behavior of a physical system, Dennett says, we can take one of three different "stances" toward it. We can, first of all, take what he calls the *physical stance* toward it, accounting for its behavior in terms of the laws of physics and the other natural sciences. This is the stance we typically take toward simple physical phenomena, whether in everyday life or in science. If we're trying to predict the course of a billiard ball or the consequences of mixing certain chemicals, it usually suffices to think of these phenomena as governed by basic physical laws. Sometimes, however, the physical stance is unhelpful. If we're trying to understand the workings of a bodily organ – the heart, say – or of a machine – an automobile, perhaps – then we won't get very far by treating these things merely as physical systems governed by basic scientific laws. Confidently predicting and explaining the behavior of such systems is made possible by adopting instead the *design stance* toward them, which involves considering them as performing a certain function. To think of the heart as a collection of basic particles governed by the laws of physics isn't going to help you diagnose arrhythmia, but thinking of it instead as an organ whose function is to pump blood will. There are cases, however, where even the design stance is insufficient to allow us to explain and predict a system's behavior. The fact that a chess-playing computer was designed to serve the function of playing chess won't help us to guess what its strategy against Kasparov will be; that we take a mouse to be "designed" by natural selection to avoid predators won't tell us what path it will take in order to escape an oncoming cat. Here, Dennett says, we need to take the *intentional stance*, which involves regarding something as an "intentional system" – an entity having beliefs, desires, and other mental states and being capable of reasoning on the basis of them – and predicting and explaining its behavior accordingly. We say that the mouse *thinks there is a place to hide over there* or that the computer *intends to employ the French defense*, and are thereby enabled to understand what the mouse or computer does.

Which of these stances is the correct one to take in a particular situation? It depends. If you're trying to determine, not what moves the computer will make, but how many people it will take to lift it and carry it over to the room where the match will be held, the physical stance rather than the intentional stance will be most appropriate; if you're trying to figure out how to turn the computer on, the design stance will be the one to take. In each case, the right answer depends only in part on objective features of the system itself; it depends also, and ultimately, on our interests. Does a computer really have the intentionality we attribute to it in taking the intentional stance toward it? Dennett's answer is that if it is complex enough in its behavior that we cannot usefully explain and predict that behavior without taking the intentional stance, then it has all the intentionality a thing could possibly have. But its having it is, again, ultimately a function of our finding it useful to treat it as having it. And all intentionality is in Dennett's view like this, including our own: we regard ourselves as intentional systems because that is the most practical way of dealing with ourselves and each other, of explaining and predicting our behavior. There is nothing more to it than that.

Given that Dennett seems not to be a *realist* about intentionality (that is, someone who takes it to exist independently of our purposes and interests) nor even, as causal and biological theorists appear to be, a *reductionist* who wants to reduce intentionality to something more basic (causal relations or biological functions), he is often classified instead as an *instrumentalist* – as holding that talk about the intentionality of our minds is a useful instrument or tool for understanding our behavior, but doesn't describe anything that exists objectively, independently of our purposes and interests. Thus understood, his view seems open to an obvious and seemingly fatal objection: for us to take a stance toward something, including the intentional stance, is itself a manifestation of intentionality; so we can't coherently suppose that intentionality is a mere artefact of the stance we take toward ourselves.

Dennett's reply to such an objection would seem to lie in his influential strategy of *homuncular decomposition*. The idea is this. We can usefully regard our minds as comprised of a number of subsystems that perform various mental functions: visual processing, linguistic competence, and so on. Each subsystem can itself be metaphorically understood as a "homunculus" – a "little man" who performs some particular task. But the functions performed by each of these homunculi can, like our own minds, be thought of as comprised of yet more basic functions performed by smaller subsystems; in other words, each of the homunculi comprising our own minds can be thought of as comprising smaller homunculi of its own. At the level of our minds as a whole, we are dealing with what we have reason to treat as systems possessing a very high degree of intentionality. But the homunculi that comprise our minds, precisely because they perform more specific, less comprehensive functions, possess a lower degree of intentionality; and by the same token, the smaller homunculi that comprise them possess even less intentionality. If we keep decomposing each level of homunculi into ever smaller levels, eventually we will come to a basic level of homunculi who, because they perform functions as simple as possible, have as little intentionality as possible. Think of these as extremely stupid homunculi – homunculi whose task is no more complicated than flipping a switch back and forth.

Such a task could, of course, be performed by a very simple machine. Yet it is not at all implausible to suppose that whatever intentionality was possessed by such a machine would be intentionality that existed only relative to the stance we might take toward it. But then it shouldn't be implausible to suppose that the intentionality possessed by the very stupid homunculi that comprise the most elementary level of the subsystems comprising our minds should be explicable in terms of the intentional stance – in which case the intentionality possessed by our minds as a whole, which is just a composite of the intentionality possessed by its various subsystems, is also so explicable.

This strategy is not without ingenuity, but that it fails genuinely to answer the objection at hand seems to follow if we accept Searle's distinction between intrinsic intentionality on the one hand, and derived and as-if intentionality on the other. Machines, of course, have whatever intentionality they have only in either a derived or an as-if way. But our intentionality is intrinsic. So if there really are basic homunculi comprising our minds, their intentionality too must be intrinsic – in which case they are not comparable to machines, which do not have intrinsic intentionality. The intuitive force of Dennett's argument seems to rest on his comparison of the stupidity of the basic homunculi and the stupidity of a machine. But the two are not "stupid" in the same sense. The homunculi are stupid because they have *extremely low* intelligence; the machine is stupid because it has *no intelligence at all*. Strictly speaking, the machine isn't really even stupid in the first place, because one has to have at least a very minimal level of intelligence even to count as stupid (by comparison, that is, with those with higher intelligence). The machine doesn't even rise to the level of stupidity, while the homunculi have at least that much going for them.

If their intentionality is intrinsic, then it isn't merely an artefact of our taking the intentional stance toward ourselves. Dennett might deny that it really is intrinsic – he might hold that the homunculi, no less than the machine, have at most derived or as-if intentionality. But if he says that the intentionality of the homunculi – and thus of our minds as a whole – is derived, he's back in the incoherent position of saying that we have intentionality only because we take ourselves to have it (where "taking ourselves to have it" is itself a manifestation of intentionality). And if instead he says that our intentionality is only "as-if," then he's saying something even more radical: that our intentionality doesn't *really* exist at all. But that brings us to another theory.

Eliminativism again

If the upshot of our discussion thus far seems to be that no naturalistic account of intentionality has yet succeeded, there are a number of materialists who would nevertheless deny that this has any tendency to cast serious doubt on the truth of materialism. What it really casts doubt on, they suggest, is the reality of intentionality itself. Recall from chapter 5 that some materialists have proposed that the way to deal with the problem posed by qualia is simply to deny that qualia exist in the first place. Many of them would apply the same strategy to the problem of intentionality: if intentional mental states turn out to be irreducible to purely material states of the brain, so much the worse for intentional mental states. We ought to stop looking for a way to reduce them, and instead consider eliminating them from our ontology altogether. Maybe they don't really exist at all, in which case there's no need to explain them.

This is the view known as *eliminative materialism*, most famously associated with Patricia and Paul Churchland, and if it doesn't sound utterly bizarre, you haven't understood it. Nor is this a biased description of the theory: eliminativists are under no illusions about how counter-intuitive and contrary to common sense their position is. They are willing frankly to deny what the average person would consider undeniable, namely that we have thoughts, experiences, beliefs, desires and all the rest – in short, that we have minds. The eliminative materialist view is, not that mental states are identical to brain states or that minds are identical to brains, but rather that *there are no mental states, and in short no minds, at all*. There is only the brain, and whatever a completed neuroscience will eventually tell us about it. The correct description of human nature will, at the end of the day, make no reference to what we think, feel, hope, fear, or believe, but instead only to physiological structure, neuronal firing patterns, chemical secretions and the like. It's not that your belief that it's raining is the same thing as such-and-such a neural process, as the identity theory would have it; it's rather that neither you nor anyone else has ever had any beliefs, nor any other mental states at all, and that the neural process is all there is and all there ever has been.

Why would anyone take such a proposal seriously? Part of the answer has to do with the notion, discussed in chapter 3, that our commonsense description of ourselves as having beliefs, desires, and other mental states constitutes a kind of theory: "folk psychology." There we noted that the identity theory can be understood as suggesting that this theory can be reduced to some neuroscientific theory, in just the way that the theory that made reference to genes was shown to be reducible to a theory making reference to DNA. But, as the Churchlands are fond of noting, there are cases in the history of science where a theory turns out not to be reducible to some deeper theory, but instead to have been utterly mistaken and thus in need of elimination. The pre-Copernican picture of the universe, according to which the earth was at the center of the solar system and surrounded by a series of heavenly spheres, was just wrong: it was not *reduced to* modern astronomy, but eliminated and *replaced by* modern astronomy. And if folk psychology is a theory, then it too might turn out to be mistaken. Moreover, since, unlike other scientific theories, it seems not to be reducible to some more basic theory that makes reference to nothing but purely physical laws and entities, this is itself a reason to think it might be false. We are better off just getting rid of it, and reconceiving of human nature entirely in terms of the purely materialistic categories of neuroscience. This might not be possible immediately – we still have much to learn about the brain and nervous system – but, at least in principle, and at some future date, we ought to be able to substitute a wholly neuroscientific description of ourselves for our current mentalistic idiom. Perhaps the citizens of eliminative materialist societies of the future will no longer say things like "Boy, this pain is really getting to me," but rather "there's a particularly high level of activity in my C-fibers and reticular formation." Someone getting off an amusement park ride will no longer report feeling dizzy, but instead note that "there's a residual circulation of the inertial fluid in the semi-circular canals of my inner ear." Romance novelists will eschew talk of love and longing in favor of neuronal action potentials and behavioral dispositions.

All this may seem pretty fanciful, but that doesn't prove it is false. As eliminativists never tire of pointing out, they all laughed at Jules Verne too, until Neil Armstrong set foot on the moon. But there may be much deeper problems for eliminativists than merely being ahead of their time. First, the notion that folk psychology is a kind of theory seems much less plausible than the view that regards it instead as a description of the *data* that any theory worth our attention must be consistent with. (And if the indirect realist view discussed in chapter 1 is correct, then it is precisely our direct awareness of mental phenomena that forms the starting point of all our theorizing about the mind and its relationship to the physical world, so that it can hardly make sense to suggest that such phenomena do not exist.)

There seems to be an even more basic, and more obvious, difficulty with the theory, however. In so far as eliminative materialism asks us to *reconceive* human nature, to *learn* more about the nervous system, and indeed to *believe* the theory itself, doesn't it presuppose the validity of the very concepts it proposes eliminating? Doesn't the theory ultimately contradict itself?

Eliminativists are, of course, well aware of this objection, but think it can be easily answered. The Churchlands propose that to accuse the eliminativist of self-contradiction is like accusing modern biologists of contradicting themselves in denying the pseudo-scientific concept of "vital spirit." It would obviously be foolish for vitalists to argue that people who disbelieve in vital spirit must be alive in order even to express their disbelief, in which case they must possess vital spirit after all and have thereby refuted themselves. Vitalists would, in this case, be begging the question, since their argument would presuppose that the only way to explain life is in terms of vital spirit, which is exactly what the anti-vitalist denies. Similarly, the reply goes, the critic of eliminative materialism is begging the question in assuming that eliminativists must "believe" their own theory, etc., since the existence of beliefs is exactly what eliminativists reject.

One reason to suspect that this reply will not work is that here again the eliminativist seems, unavoidably, to make use of concepts – "begging the question," "assuming," and the like – that are just the kind of mentalistic notions eliminative materialism denies the legitimacy of. This suggests that the analogy with vitalism may not be a good one. Anti-vitalists don't deny the existence of life, after all; they only deny a certain theory about how to explain life. That's why they aren't contradicting themselves, which they would be doing if they denied the existence, not only of vital spirit, but of living things (including themselves). But eliminativists don't just deny a certain theory about how to explain believing, assuming, thinking, etc.; they deny the very existence of these phenomena. Yet "denying" is itself an instance of the sort of phenomena whose existence is denied. In short, any attempt either to propose or reject a theory – eliminative materialism, folk psychology, or whatever – is to represent the world as being a certain way, and thereby to manifest intentionality. But in that case one cannot coherently propose a theory that denies the existence of representing or of intentionality.

Some eliminativists would acknowledge that their position has a real difficulty here, but suggest that it may be that we just don't yet have the conceptual resources to imagine how theories might be proposed, accepted, and rejected without using mentalistic and intentional language. We might be in a position similar to someone in ancient Greece trying to imagine quantum mechanics: the theoretical groundwork necessary even to conceive of the radically novel conceptual scheme eventually to be developed just hasn't been laid yet. Again, though, even to frame this suggestion the eliminative materialist has to use language – "imagine," "conceive," "conceptual resources," even "theory," "propose," and "reject" – which seems irreducibly mentalistic and intentional. Anything that could ever count as a "theory," or even as something relevantly analogous to a theory – no matter to how far off in the future it is put forward – would seem unavoidably to be something that involved representation and intentionality, in which case it could not coherently be used to express eliminative materialism. It is as if the eliminativist were suggesting that $2 + 2 = 23$ and that the only reason we can't make sense of this is that we don't yet have the conceptual resources to see what addition might look like in the future. The right thing to say about this is that whatever the people of the future might be doing if they go around asserting that $2 + 2 = 23$, it won't be addition of any sort. Similarly, eliminative materialists seem ultimately to be proposing a theory which is by their own admission currently unintelligible, with a promissory note that someday we might be able to make it intelligible. But the promise can in principle never be kept, since the possibility of intelligibility – which requires that we be able to *understand* or *make sense* of something, and thus involves intentionality – is something the theory itself appears to rule out as impossible. Eliminativists seem in effect to be inviting us not to believe them or their theory, now or ever. So how can they blame anyone who takes them up on their offer?

The indeterminacy of the physical

So far we have seen that all extant materialist attempts to deal with intentionality appear to face serious difficulties. The intuitive anti-materialist argument from intentionality with which we began this chapter remains, as yet, undefeated. But things are, in the view of some critics of materialism, even worse for the materialist than so far indicated. In their view there is, in addition to the fact that nothing material would seem capable of having any intrinsic meaning, a further problem: even if something physical could have intrinsic meaning, it could not by itself have the *determinate* meaning that (at least many) mental states have. The argument is, in short: at least some intentional mental states and processes are determinate in their meaning; no physical state or process could possibly be determinate in meaning; so intentional mental states cannot be identified with or reduced to physical states and processes.

We've already seen a number of ways in which physical processes can be inherently indeterminate: for instance, we noted in the previous chapter that it is indeterminate from its physical properties alone what interpretation is to be assigned to the algorithmic rules governing a computer, and it was suggested earlier in this chapter that it is indeterminate from the physical facts alone what counts as the beginning or end of a given causal chain. It is to a generalization of considerations like these that some critics of materialism have appealed in developing not just an objection to this or that specific materialist theory, but a comprehensive anti-materialist argument from the determinacy of meaning. If such an argument were to succeed, it would have the effect of buttressing Searle's suggestion, considered at the end of the previous chapter, that it is indeterminate from the third-person behavioral and neurophysiological facts alone what meaning is to be assigned to a person's utterances. The upshot of Searle's argument was that meaning must inevitably be determined from the subjective first-person point of view, and this, together with the considerations we want now to examine, arguably tends to reinforce the suggestion, considered over the course of the previous few chapters, that first-person, subjective facts are inexplicable in terms of third-person objective physical facts. These considerations will also suggest a way of responding to the possible objection to Searle considered at the end of the previous chapter, to the effect that mental states themselves may not be any more determinate than are physical processes.

The considerations in question concern three inter-related manifestations of intentionality: our use of *representations*, our grasp of *concepts*, and our capacity for *formal reasoning*. Let us consider each of these.

1. Representations:

We've already taken note of the concept of "mental representa-tions," and sentences of Mentalese as possible candidates of what form mental representations might take. But let us now consider for a moment a much more pedestrian example of a representation – a drawing you might make of your mother. When you draw your mother, you are creating a kind of representation of her. But notice that it is not the particular physical features of the drawing itself – the form of the lines you make, the chemicals in the ink you use, and so forth – which make it a representation of her. The reason is not merely the one noted at the beginning of the chapter, namely, that nothing physical seems capable of having any intrinsic inten-tionality; the reason is rather one that would apply even if the argu-ment of the beginning of the chapter were to be rejected. Someone looking over your shoulder as you draw might later on produce an exact copy of the drawing you were making. Perhaps the person admires your craftsmanship and wants to see if he or she can do as well. But in doing so the person would not, strictly speaking, be drawing a representation of your mother – he or she may have no idea, nor any interest in, who it was that you were drawing – but rather a representation *of your representation*. And, in general, the very same image could count either as a drawing of an X, or as a drawing of a drawing of an X – or indeed (supposing there's someone looking over the shoulder of the second artist and copying what he or she was drawing) as a drawing of a drawing of a drawing of an X, and so on *ad infinitum*.

Even if we count something as a drawing, and therefore as possessing some intentionality or other, exactly *what* it is a drawing *of* is still indeterminate from its physical properties alone. The same is true not just of drawings, but also of written and spoken words (for to say or write "cat" could be to represent cats, but it could also be to represent the word "cat") and indeed of *any* material representation, including purported representations encoded in neural firing patterns in the brain. There seems in general to be nothing about the physical properties of a material representation that make it a material representation of an X as opposed to a material representation of a material representation of an X.

Sometimes, however, you are determinately thinking about a particular thing or person, such as your mother. Your thought about your mother is about your mother – it represents your mother, and doesn't represent a representation of your mother (representations, pictures, and the like might be the furthest thing from your mind). But then your thought, whatever it is, cannot be entirely material. Given that there's nothing about a material representation *per se* that could make it a representation of an X as opposed to a representation of a representation of an X, if your thought was entirely material then there would be no fact of the matter about whether your thought represented your mother as opposed to a representation of your mother. Your thought is determinate; purely material representations are not; so your thought is not purely material.

The materialist might reply that we shouldn't look at a material representation in isolation to determine what it represents, but ought also to consider factors such as its conceptual relationships to other representations, its causal relations to the world, and the behavioral dispositions of, or rules followed by, the thinker having the representation. But as we've seen, such appeals to conceptual role, causation, behavioral dispositions and rules have serious problems of their own, some of which also concern indeterminacy. In particular, if the suggestion is that some system of material representations, of causal relations, behavioral dispositions, rules, or whatever, determines meaning, the problem is that the same difficulties which arise when we consider a single representation in isolation just recur at a higher level. Any such system of material elements or principles is indeterminate between alternative interpretations; but our representations seem, at least sometimes, not to be indeterminate in this way.

2. Concepts

In thinking about something, we bring it under a concept: we think of it as a cat or as a mother. And of course, we can also bring it under more than one concept – we might think of the same creature as both a cat and a mother. Either way, there is typically some determinate concept or concepts under which we bring whatever we are thinking about. We think of something as a cat or as a cat and a mother, say, and not as a dog or a father.

What is it that determines that our thoughts involve bringing something under exactly this particular concept or set of concepts rather than some other one? It seems it cannot be material facts alone. For instance, it cannot be some sort of physical relation (for example, a causal relation) of ours to all actual cats that makes our thoughts about cats involve applying the concept cat to them. For, to borrow an example from John Haldane, it could be that all actual cats also fall under a concept we can call *maxifourn*, where maxifourns are the most-common-four-legged-animals-whose-average-weight-is-W. Any physical relation of ours to cats will therefore also be a relation to maxifourns. But our thoughts about cats nevertheless involve applying the concept cat, and do not involve the concept maxifourn. In that case, it cannot be the physical relation alone that determines what concept we're applying.

As Haldane notes, the point is even clearer with examples like *triangle* and *trilateral*, which are concepts applying to exactly the same objects in every possible world (unlike *cat* and *maxifourn*, since these concepts will not apply to the same things in possible worlds where it is dogs rather than cats who are maxifourns). No physical relations between us and such objects can be sufficient to determine that we are thinking of them as triangular rather than trilateral. In general, there are always more ways to conceive of the objects of our thoughts than the physical facts can determine.

Related to this point is the consideration that concepts are inherently abstract and universal, whereas material phenomena are concrete and particular. Accordingly, a concept cannot be identified with anything concrete, particular, or material; and thus it cannot be identified with any physical symbol in the brain or nervous system. Nor can it plausibly be identified with a set of behavioral dispositions, as is sometimes suggested, since, as noted above, behavioral dispositions are susceptible of various interpretations and are thus indeterminate in a way that (at least many) concepts are not. For similar reasons, the propositions we grasp, assent to, and deny – and of which concepts are the constituents – cannot be identified with "sentences in the head" or with any other material entities. Propositions are necessarily abstract. Had there been no human beings, the proposition *there are no human beings* would have been true, even though there would then have been no "sentence in the head" for that proposition to be identical to. Had there been no physical world at all, the proposition *there is no physical world* would have been true, even though there would then have been no physical entity of any sort for that proposition to be identical to. Some propositions are necessarily true, that is, true in all possible worlds, but no physical entity exists in all possible worlds (for example, there are possible worlds where there are no brains, and thus no "sentences in the head"). And so on.

This obviously poses a further problem for the Mentalese hypothesis, and for any theory which takes thought to consist of nothing but material processes. In the view of some critics of materialism, it also suggests a further general anti-materialist argument: when the mind grasps a concept or proposition, there is clearly a sense in which that concept or proposition is in the mind; but if these things are in the mind and yet (for the reasons given above) cannot be in the brain, it would seem to follow that the mind cannot be identified with the brain, or for that matter with anything material.

3. Formal reasoning

Whatever one thinks of such an argument (and it surely stands in need of further development), the topic of abstract thought brings us to one last respect in which mental states, especially thoughts concerning necessary truths, can be determinate in a way material processes are not. When we make judgments of a mathematical or logical sort, our judgments have a certain determinate form: the form of addition or squaring, for instance, or of *modus ponens*, conjunction, or disjunction. Nothing that does not have exactly the form of $2 + 2 = 4$ counts as adding 2 and 2 to get 4; nothing that does not have exactly the form that *If Socrates is a man, then Socrates is mortal; Socrates is a man; so Socrates is mortal* has counts as an instance of reasoning via *modus ponens*. But, as James F. Ross has argued, no physical process can have the determinate form had by such formal thought processes. Just as a paper plate or a Frisbee can approximate a "perfect" circle but can never truly realize one – that is, paper plates, Frisbees and all other "circular" physical objects are never really circles at all, strictly speaking (every true circle is already a "perfect" circle) – neither can any physical process ever do more than approximate formal reasoning.

When one considers the circle analogy, the intuitive plausibility of this claim already becomes evident. But Ross appeals to a number of results in recent philosophy to bolster the argument. One of them is Quine's argument for the indeterminacy of translation, already considered in the previous chapter. Quine argues that if the physical facts about us are all the facts there are, then there is no fact of the matter about what any of our utterances mean: meaning will be indeterminate. This would entail that our reasoning processes would also be indeterminate; there would be no fact of the matter about whether we are applying *modus ponens* or only some approximation to it. Another relevant example is Saul Kripke's distinction (which Ross adapts for his own purposes) between addition and what he calls "quaddition," where addition has the form "$x + y$," but quaddition has the form "$x + y$, if x, $y < 57$, $= 5$ otherwise." A calculating machine doing addition and a machine doing quaddition will give the same results when the numbers they are computing are less than 57, but when the one doing addition computes 58 and 100 it will get 158, whereas the one doing quaddition will instead get 5. Because they'll get the same results in the first case, there is no fact about their behavior that can then determine whether they are doing addition or quaddition. But suppose the difference in the results would manifest itself, not at 57 but instead at some much higher number – indeed, at a number that is higher than the highest number either calculator is capable of displaying. Then there would be, not only no way of knowing which of either of the machines was doing quaddition instead of addition, but *no fact of the matter at all* about which was performing which. The physical facts about the calculators are equally consistent with either addition or quaddition, and thus indeterminate between them. But if, as with calculating machines, the physical facts about us were all the facts there are, then it would be indeterminate with us too whether we are performing addition or quaddition. But it *isn't* indeterminate: we do addition, period. Our doing so thus cannot be a purely material process.

Some materialists – Quine, and perhaps Dennett – might reply that the right conclusion to draw from all this is that since (they claim) we are purely material beings, we just don't in fact add, or do *modus ponens*, or carry out any other piece of formal reasoning after all; it only seems like we do because we approximate doing so. In fact, they might say, all thought is as indeterminate as physical processes are. However, this move is not only highly counter-intuitive – it entails that you've never once added 2 and 2 to get 4, for example, but only think you have – but it threatens every argument that anyone has ever given, including every argument anyone has ever given for materialism. For if none of us ever really reasons via *modus ponens* or any other valid argument form, then we never reason validly. Every single argument anyone has ever given will have been invalid! This materialist response would thus undermine itself.

This shows just how extreme and costly is the suggested reply to Searle considered at the end of the previous chapter. It also indicates that such a reply cannot succeed, for the claim that none of our thoughts is determinate seems demonstrably false. As Ross notes, even to deny that we really have determinate thoughts, certainly where the thoughts in question concern addition, *modus ponens*, and the like, presupposes that we have determinate thoughts; for even to deny that we ever add or do *modus ponens* requires that we grasp these operations, and to grasp them is to have a thought of a form as determinate as that which is grasped.

Materialism, meaning, and metaphysics

Arguments of the sort considered in the previous section go back as far as Plato and Aristotle; indeed, their contemporary proponents typically present them as merely reformulations in modern guise of essentially Platonic or Aristotelian lines of thought. In so far as these arguments tend, in essence, to expand some of the objections made to specific recent materialist theories of intentionality into comprehensive critiques of materialism, they illustrate the point I made in chapter 3 that many of the criticisms directed at materialism today are but variations on the same objections that have been made for two and a half millennia. This point is further bolstered if we accept the intentionalist thesis that to be a subject of conscious experience is just to be a subject of certain intentional states, so that the problems of consciousness and qualia – often thought to constitute distinctively modern challenges to materialism – really boil down at the end of the day to the ancient problem of intentionality.

In summary, the difficulty intentionality seems to pose for the materialist is this: if Searle is right, intrinsic meaning or intentionality and the first-person point of view of the conscious, thinking subject are inextricably bound up together; and if the arguments of the preceding section are right, meaning or intentionality, and thus the first-person point of view of the conscious, thinking subject, are irreducible to and inexplicable in terms of anything material, including the brain. Dualism would seem to be vindicated.

Materialists might, nevertheless, suggest that we shouldn't be too quick to draw such a conclusion. For is the dualist really in any better a position than the materialist where meaning or intentionality is concerned? How, after all, does appeal to the existence of a non-physical subject or non-physical properties *explain* intentionality? Hasn't the dualist really just supplemented one mystery – the mystery of intentionality – with another, namely the mystery of the nature and operation of non-physical minds? And doesn't the interaction problem that has plagued the dualist since Descartes's time indicate that this second mystery is itself unlikely to be solved?

As we've seen when considering the argument from reason and the problem of mental causation, it isn't quite right to say that the interaction problem poses a challenge to the dualist alone, but the questions just raised are fair. The dualist might respond that the point of arguments of the sort considered in the last section isn't to explain intentionality in the first place but rather to demonstrate that whatever intentionality is, it isn't physical. And if it isn't, to try to find some physical explanation of it will be a waste of time. Of course, the materialist might complain that non-physical processes are not the kind that can possibly be studied via the methods of physical science. But to this the dualist could reply that it is a mistake to think that physical science is the only legitimate avenue of inquiry. The proper approach to the study of the mind, in the dualist's view, is via metaphysics rather than physics, and philosophy rather than natural science. For since, in the dualist's view, the arguments for dualism show that the mind is non-physical, they thereby show also that it is only via inquiry other than scientific inquiry that we are going to understand its nature, if we are going to understand it at all. For the materialist to reject the possibility of such inquiry, a priori, would simply be to beg the question against the dualist.

But can metaphysics really say anything to clarify the nature of non-physical minds that hasn't been said already by Descartes and his successors? That brings us to the topic of our final chapter, where we will see that, as with some of the arguments we've considered in this chapter, dualists may be well advised to look to their ancient rather than modern forebears to find the most promising means of defending their position.

Further reading

Brentano's famous analysis of intentionality is to be found in his *Psychology from an Empirical Standpoint* (London: Routledge and Kegan Paul, 1973). Interest in the topic was renewed among analytic philosophers by a famous exchange between Wilfrid Sellars and Roderick Chisholm entitled "Intentionality and the Mental," in Herbert Feigl, Michael Scriven, and Grover Maxwell, eds., *Minnesota Studies in the Philosophy of Science, Vol. II: Concepts, Theories, and the Mind-Body Problem* (Minneapolis: University of Minnesota Press, 1958). John Searle's distinction between kinds of intentionality and critique of the appeal by naturalistic theories of intentionality to the notion of biological function are to be found in his *The Rediscovery of the Mind* (Cambridge, MA: The MIT Press, 1992). His own account of intentionality, including the role of the Network and the Background, is developed in his *Intentionality: An Essay in the Philosophy of Mind* (Cambridge: Cambridge University Press, 1983).

An excellent source of articles representing all the main naturalistic theories of intentionality is Stephen P. Stich and Ted A. Warfield, eds., *Mental Representation: A Reader* (Oxford: Blackwell, 1994). Some of the more influential full-length studies are: Fred Dretske's *Knowledge and the Flow of Information* (Cambridge, MA: The MIT Press, 1981), Jerry Fodor's *Psychosemantics: The Problem of Meaning in the Philosophy of Mind* (Cambridge, MA: The MIT Press, 1987), and Fodor's *A Theory of Content and Other Essays* (Cambridge, MA: The MIT Press, 1990), all of which defend versions of the causal theory; Ruth Millikan's *Language, Thought, and Other Biological Categories* (Cambridge, MA: The MIT Press, 1986) and David Papineau's *Philosophical Naturalism* (Oxford: Blackwell, 1993), which defend versions of the biological theory; Daniel Dennett's *Brainstorms* (Cambridge, MA: The MIT Press, 1981) and *The Intentional Stance* (Cambridge, MA: The MIT Press, 1987), which contain essays developing his own unique approach to the problem; and Robert Cummins' *Meaning and Mental Representation* (Cambridge, MA: The MIT Press, 1989), which critically surveys the various naturalistic theories. Popper's critique of causal accounts of meaning is developed in "Language and the Body-Mind Problem," in *Conjectures and Refutations: the Growth of Scientific Knowledge* (New York: Harper and Row, 1968) and at greater length in Karl Popper and John C. Eccles, *The Self and Its Brain* (London: Routledge and Kegan Paul, 1977).

Different versions of eliminative materialism are articulated and defended by Paul Churchland in "Eliminative Materialism and the Propositional Attitudes," available in the Chalmers and Rosenthal anthologies cited at the end of earlier chapters, and at length in his *Scientific Realism and the Plasticity of Mind* (Cambridge: Cambridge University Press, 1979), and by Stephen Stich in *From Folk Psychology to Cognitive Science: The Case Against Belief* (Cambridge, MA: The MIT Press, 1983). The objection that eliminativism is ultimately self-refuting is developed by Lynne Rudder Baker in *Saving Belief: A Critique of Physicalism* (Princeton, NJ: Princeton University Press, 1987).

The argument about the indeterminacy of material representations was inspired by some remarks made by Herbert McCabe in his "The Immortality of the Soul: The Traditional Argument," in Anthony Kenny, ed., *Aquinas: A Collection of Critical Essays* (Garden City, NY: Anchor Books, 1969). Haldane develops his argument about concepts in several places, most accessibly in J. J. C. Smart and J. J. Haldane, *Atheism and Theism*, second edition (Oxford: Blackwell, 2003), which also contains a criticism of Dennett's strategy of homuncular decomposition along the lines suggested in the text.

That propositions cannot be identified with anything material is elegantly demonstrated by Alvin Plantinga in chapter 6 of his *Warrant and Proper Function* (New York: Oxford University Press, 1993). That the abstract and universal character of the objects of thought – concepts and propositions – entails that thinking cannot be a material operation is an idea as old as Plato and Aristotle. A popular contemporary version of the argument is to be found in Mortimer Adler's *Intellect: Mind Over Matter* (New York: Collier Books, 1990). A more rigorous presentation is given by David Oderberg in "Hylomorphic Dualism," forthcoming in *Social Philosophy and Policy*, vol. 22, no. 2 (June 2005). James Ross's argument is developed at length in "Immaterial Aspects of Thought," *The Journal of Philosophy* 89: 136–50 (1992). Kripke explains "quaddition" in *Wittgenstein on Rules and Private Language* (Cambridge, MA: Harvard University Press, 1982).

8
Persons

Our examination of the various mental phenomena philosophers have found problematic – qualia and consciousness, thought and intentionality – indicates that Descartes's basic contention that the mind is irreducible to the brain or body has not been refuted. At any rate, no materialist attempt to show that these various features of the mind are really just physical features of the brain has yet succeeded. But the central materialist argument – the argument from causation – is one that the dualist still seems not to have answered satisfactorily. Recall that, as Descartes characterizes the mind, it is difficult to see how it could possibly get in causal contact with the body. This is the *interaction problem*, and while it is not an outright refutation of dualism, it would nevertheless be deeply unsatisfying if the dualist could not answer it convincingly (that is, without resorting to occasionalism, parallelism, or epiphenomenalism). But is there a satisfying answer?

Some dualists have suggested that there is, but that the answer, and the very existence of the problem, show that Descartes and dualists influenced by him have given a seriously inadequate characterization of the metaphysics of dualism. As it turns out, this inadequacy lies, in their view, precisely where Cartesian dualism has something in common with materialism: a mechanistic concept of the material world in general, and of the human body in particular. To see just how far-reaching are the consequences of this concept, and to set the stage for considering an alternative construal of dualism, it will be helpful to look briefly at a metaphysical issue closely related to the mind-body problem: the problem of *personal identity*.

Personal identity

The problem of personal identity is the problem of explaining what it is that accounts for the fact that a person remains the same person over time despite dramatic changes in his or her bodily and psychological characteristics. Ethel starts out as a fertilized ovum; she develops into a zygote, then an embryo, then a fetus; she's born, goes through infancy, childhood, adolescence, young adulthood, middle age, and old age; and then she dies. On some views she might continue to exist after death – as a disembodied soul, say, or perhaps in a cloned body into which her memories have been transplanted. Her bodily traits change significantly throughout her life, and may even disappear altogether in some post-mortem state of existence. Her psychological traits change no less significantly, and may also disappear as a result of amnesia or a lapse into a coma. And yet in some sense it seems to be one and the same person who undergoes all these changes. So what makes her the same person throughout?

Cartesian dualism provides one possible answer: what remains the same is a person's immaterial substance, the *res cogitans* with which Descartes identified the mind. But there is a serious problem with this answer: it seems to make it impossible in principle ever to know that one is dealing with the same person from day to day, or even from moment to moment. A Cartesian immaterial substance is unobservable, devoid as it is of any physical properties. In dealing with other people, all you ever observe are their bodily and behavioral traits, not their immaterial substances. But then, how do you know that the immaterial substance interacting with someone's body today isn't different from the one that was interacting with it yesterday? Even appeal to a person's psychological traits – memories, behavioral tendencies, or personality quirks – won't help, since perhaps these have "jumped" from one immaterial substance to another since yesterday. Maybe the old body and the old personality traits are now associated with a new immaterial substance – in which case, since it is sameness of immaterial substance which makes for sameness of person, it would follow that you are dealing with a different person today, however much this person might look and act the same as the person you dealt with yesterday.

It is important to see that the problem here is not merely that this consequence is highly counter-intuitive – it entails that you can never know whether you're really dealing with your spouse or best friend, since you can never know whether their immaterial substances are present – though that would be bad enough. This would be merely one instance of a famous puzzle in the philosophy of mind known as the "problem of other minds": given that all I can ever observe is your bodily characteristics and behavior, how do I know they are associated with a mind? How do I know you're not a zombie? And the other minds problem is not a special difficulty for Cartesian dualism; in principle it poses a challenge to other views as well (since there seems to be an epistemic gap between knowledge of the physical states of a person's body or brain and knowledge of the person's mental states). The deeper problem for a Cartesian dualist theory of personal identity is that our inability to reidentify immaterial substances over time poses a challenge to the very coherence of the idea of an immaterial substance. For if there is no way in principle to re-identify such a substance – if the same substance may or may not be present whatever physical or even psychological traits might be associated with it – then it becomes difficult to see what it could mean to speak of the same immaterial substance existing over time. In that case, however, it becomes difficult to see what it could mean to speak of an immaterial substance existing at all.

This sort of difficulty has led most contemporary philosophers to adopt an approach to personal identity that involves reducing it to some kind of bodily and/or psychological continuity. Theories that stress bodily continuity hold that what makes a person the same over time is ultimately a matter of maintaining continuity of physical features – being associated with the same body, or at least the same brain. The problem with such theories is that they seem to emphasize our physical features at the expense of our psychological ones. It is often objected that it seems, at least conceptually, possible that a person could come to exist in a totally new body – perhaps as a result of having the data scanned from his or her brain just before death and then put into the brain of another person's body (where that other person's memories and psychological traits have been "erased" beforehand). Surely it would be plausible to say that the person who exists in the new body, since he or she arguably has all the memories and other psychological features of the person who existed in the old body, is *the same person* as the person who was in the old body. Yet the bodily continuity theory would seem to deny this, since there is no bodily continuity from the original person to the person in the new body. Other versions of the bodily continuity approach seem to have similar problems. The "animalist" approach, which holds that persons are identical to human beings considered merely as living organisms, appears to entail that if your cerebrum were taken from your body and transplanted into someone else's, then you would, nevertheless, continue to exist in your now mindless but still living body (since that body would still constitute the same *animal* that existed before the cerebrum was taken from it, now just missing an organ) even though your thoughts, memories, and personality traits would now exist in the body of the person who got the transplant.

To avoid these problems, psychological continuity theories stress the centrality of psychological characteristics – memories, personality traits, and behavioral dispositions – to personal identity (though since most psychological continuity theorists are materialists of one kind or another, they would identify psychological characteristics with certain kinds of physical characteristics, for example, the having of certain kinds of brain states). The problem with these theories is that it seems conceptually possible that more than one person could be psychologically continuous with some earlier person. To appeal to a famous illustration, it seems, at least conceptually, possible that people could one day travel to another planet via "teletransportation": Ethel could step into a machine on Earth, have her body and brain scanned by the machine and then destroyed, and then the scanned information could be beamed to Mars, where a similar machine reconstructs an exact duplicate of the original body, who walks out and says "Wow! I got here in no time at all!" Arguably, the person who walks out of the machine on Mars, being psychologically continuous with Ethel, would just be Ethel. But if this is possible, it also seems possible that, due to a glitch in the machine's programming or the machine operator's playful mood, two new bodies are made on Mars and walk out of the machine, both of which have Ethel's memories and psychological characteristics. These two people can't be identical with each other – they're in different points in space, will soon develop different memories, and might go out of existence at different times (for example, if one kills the other in a fit of jealousy after catching her with Ethel's husband Fred). In that case, though, how can either be identical with the original Ethel (since it is a law of logic that if A = B and B = C then A = C)?

Some philosophers suggest that the solution to this sort of problem is to hold that it is not just psychological continuity that is necessary for personal identity, but *non-branching* continuity: the person who walks out of the machine on Mars will really be Ethel only if she is the only one who walks out (that is, if there aren't two or more duplicates made by the machine). One problem with this is that it seems *ad hoc*. Another is that it makes your personal identity depend in part on completely external factors: whether you continue as the same person tomorrow depends on whether someone makes an exact psychological duplicate of you tonight. If someone does, you will no longer exist as the same person – in a sense, you will die – even if absolutely nothing happens to your body and even if your thoughts will continue just as they would have anyway (because you never found out about the duplicate). This hardly seems plausible.

Other philosophers would maintain that an appeal to some mix of bodily and psychological continuity is necessary to avoid such problems, though it is not clear that even this will do the trick: what if your brain is divided exactly evenly and put into two new bodies, so that each resulting person has exactly the same degree of physical and psychological continuity? Yet others would respond that whoever has the highest degree of continuity with the original person counts as the original person. But, as Derek Parfit has argued, whatever version of a reductionist theory one adopts, it seems clear that one will be committed to abandoning any robust concept of personal identity; indeed, one will really be abandoning the concept of the person as it has traditionally been understood. All one can truly say given such theories is that there exists in some later person (or persons) some greater or lesser degree of psychological and bodily continuity with some earlier person – and that's it. There is no "further fact" about the person, over and above the facts concerning physical and psychological continuity. The degrees of psychological and bodily continuity are all that objectively exist, and they might exist in more than one later body (as in the teletransportation case).

Consequences of mechanism

The upshot of both Cartesian and reductionist theories of personal identity seems to be the complete disappearance of persons as such, and for similar reasons: in the case of Cartesian dualism, there appears to be no way, in principle, to identify anything as an immaterial substance, and thus (in this view) as a person, since no appeal to the only plausible criteria for making such an identification – bodily and psychological characteristics – can suffice; in the case of reductionist theories, such characteristics are all that really exist in the first place, so that talk about the persons who have the characteristics comes to seem otiose or even empty. The reason for this consequence, some would suggest, is identical to the reason why there is an interaction problem: the mechanistic conception of the human body that Cartesian dualism shares with materialism.

You will recall from chapter 3 that modern science has tended to explain phenomena by carving off from them any aspects tied to the subjective first-person point of view of the conscious subject: the feeling of heat, for example, gets pushed into the mind, leaving only molecular motion as the objective physical phenomenon with which heat is to be identified; the apparent functions served by bodily organs come to be regarded as mere projections of our minds, the objective reality being merely that certain organs have survived because those organisms which lacked them tended to die out, and so on. Materialists and Cartesian dualists alike have tended to draw the conclusion that matter must be inherently devoid of anything irreducibly mental. Indeed, this seems to be the essence of the materialist concept of matter. As we also saw in chapter 3, the materialist position is difficult to define with precision. Even the older concept of mechanism as essentially involving contact between physical components is inadequate, given that modern physical theory – from Newton's concept of gravitation, to Maxwell's theory of electromagnetism, to quantum mechanics – has gotten progressively farther from this model. As William Hasker has noted, the materialist's working conception of material processes has thus come instead to involve seeing them as mechanistic in the different sense of being utterly devoid of intrinsic purpose, meaning, or consciousness. Matter comes to be defined precisely in terms that contrast it to mind; indeed, by definition, it comes to be seen as devoid of anything inherently mental. Cartesian dualists have essentially endorsed this definition, and conclude from it that what is irreducibly mental must therefore inhere in a non-physical substance; while materialists conclude that there is nothing irreducibly mental – what seems to be so are really just complex material processes.

One result of this is that materialists have, in the view of their critics, a tendency to give accounts of mental phenomena that leave out everything essential to them: qualia, consciousness, thought and intentionality get redefined in physicalistic terms, with the consequence that materialist analyses convey the impression that the materialist has changed the subject, and failed genuinely to explain the phenomenon the analysis was supposed to account for. This is arguably the deep source of the difficulties that have perennially plagued materialist philosophies of mind. If the materialist conception of explanation entails always stripping away from the phenomena to be accounted for anything that smacks of subjectivity, meaning, or mind-dependence, then a materialist "explanation" of the mind itself will naturally seem to strip away the very essence of the phenomenon to be explained. Being, at bottom, attempts to explain the mental in terms that are intrinsically non-mental, such would-be explanations appear implicitly to deny the mental; that is to say, they seem to end up being disguised forms of eliminative materialism. Some professedly non-eliminativist philosophers of mind come close to admitting this: Fodor, for instance, has famously written that "if aboutness [that is, intentionality] is real, it must be really something else."

For the Cartesian, an inevitable result of the mechanical view of the human body is, again, the interaction problem. If matter is absolutely devoid of anything inherently mental, then mind and matter come to seem so different in their natures that it is difficult to see how they can possibly get in causal contact with each other. It is important to remember, though, that materialism seems left with much the same consequence, and for the same reason. As we saw in chapter 6, when discussing the argument from reason and the problem of mental causation, materialistic theories appear to have the implication that mental properties have no causal efficacy, so that materialism no less than dualism is threatened by epiphenomenalism.

If such interaction becomes mysterious for Cartesian dualists and materialists alike, so too does personal identity. The human body is, on both accounts, intrinsically devoid of the mental characteristics essential to persons. Being only contingently related to persons on the Cartesian account, the body thus cannot be used to identify the immaterial substances that the Cartesian view says constitute persons; being devoid of anything essentially mental on the materialist account, no robust subject of conscious experience and intentionality – no person – can possibly be found in it.

The only way to avoid these dire consequences would seem to be to find a more adequate conception of matter – in particular, a conception in which matter isn't utterly devoid of mental properties. At first glance, the Russellian position we considered earlier might seem to provide such a way. But as we saw, in its metaphysical aspects – the aspects relevant to the question at hand – that position arguably has serious problems (even if its epistemological aspects are arguably sound). Russellian metaphysics seems, for one thing, to entail panpsychism – which would seem a rather high price to pay to get a view of matter more congenial to mind. More to the present point, it seems also to be no less immune to epiphenomenalism than are Cartesian dualism and materialism.

Hylomorphism

Russellianism is not the only option, though. Another possibility lies in the conception of the material world in general and of the human body in particular that Descartes, along with his materialist contemporaries, rejected in favor of mechanism: the *hylomorphism* associated with Aristotle (384–322 BC), St. Thomas Aquinas (1225–1274), and the schools of thought deriving from them.

The term "hylomorphism" derives from the Greek words *hyle*, meaning "matter," and *morphe*, meaning "form," and the central idea of the view is that a concrete substance is a composite of matter and form, and cannot properly be understood except as such. The form of a substance is its organizational structure; the matter is that which is given organizational structure by the form. (If a chair has a round seat, for example, the roundness is an aspect of the chair's form, and the wood or plastic or whatever it is made of would constitute its matter.) *Substantial* form is that specific aspect of a substance's organizational structure by virtue of which it is the kind of substance it is. (A seat's roundness isn't part of the substantial form of a chair – a chair could have a square seat instead, for instance, and still be a chair – but having some kind of seat would be.) Form on this view is understood in a decidedly realist way: it is abstract and universal, irreducible either to any particular material thing or to some aspect of our classificatory practices. Form exists in some sense out there, independent of our minds. Hylomorphists are generally Aristotelian rather than Platonic realists, that is, their view is that form generally exists in the substances it informs (rather than subsisting in a kind of Platonic "third realm" of the sort briefly described in chapter 3). Because a piece of matter wouldn't be the particular thing it is without its specific form, however, hylomorphism entails that no material thing can be said to be "nothing but" a collection of particles (or whatever), after the fashion of materialistic reductionism. If form generally does not exist apart from matter, neither does matter exist without form; and thus, without grasping a material object's form, we cannot understand it.

The fact that understanding a thing entails, in the hylomorphic view, understanding the form that makes it what it is indicates how different the view's concept of explanation is from those of contemporary materialism and Cartesian dualism. In the classical hylomorphism of Aristotle and Aquinas, a full explanation of a material substance involves identifying at least four irreducible causal components: its *material cause*, its *formal cause*, its *final cause*, and its *efficient cause*. A heart, for example, cannot be understood except as being an organ having a certain material constitution (its material cause), as possessing a certain form or principle of organization (its formal cause), as serving a certain function – to pump blood (its final cause) – and as having been brought about by antecedents such as the genetic programming inherent in certain cells that led them to develop into a heart rather than a kidney or liver (its efficient cause). Materialism and Cartesian dualism alike eliminate formal and final causes from the explanation of material things, replacing the classical hylomorphic conception of material substances as inherently purposive composites of matter and form with a conception of them as collections of particles or the like devoid of either intrinsic purpose or objective, irreducible form, and explicable entirely in terms of efficient causation.

Living things have form no less than chairs and the like, and the form of a living thing is precisely what a hylomorphist means by the *soul*. There is a sense in which plants and non-human animals have souls just as human beings do (though as we'll see, this by no means entails that they can think or continue to exist after death). The *nutritive soul* is the sort which informs the matter of which plants are composed, and imparts to them powers of nutrition, growth, and reproduction. The *sensory soul* is the kind of soul possessed by animals, and includes the powers of the nutritive soul as well as its own distinctive powers of perception, appetite, and locomotion or movement. Finally, the *rational soul* is the kind of soul possessed by human beings. Incorporating the powers included within the nutritive and sensory souls, it also imparts the further characteristics of intellect, will, and memory. The rational soul is the substantial form of the human body, in virtue of which human beings are what they are: rational animals. This is a very different concept of the soul from that of the Cartesian dualist, who regards it not as a substantial form – which is, in the hylomorphic view, only one aspect of a complete substance – but rather as a complete substance in its own right, devoid of material properties but nevertheless (somehow) capable of efficient causation.

There is a tendency in Cartesian thinking – though Descartes himself, contrary to popular belief, did not take this view – to regard the Cartesian *res cogitans* as the person, with the body being an inessential excrescence. Materialists, by contrast, often identify a person with the body, or some aspect of the body. But in the hylomorphic view, just as the form of a chair is not a chair, neither is the soul of a person a person; and just as the matter of a chair is, apart from the form a chair, not a chair, neither is a person's body *qua* body a person. A person is, rather, essentially a composite of soul and body.

One consequence of this is that the disappearance of the person that seems entailed by Cartesian and reductionist accounts of personal identity is not entailed by hylomorphism. Since the soul is the substantial form of the body – of, that is, a certain material thing – there seems to be no difficulty in determining when a person's soul is present. Just as you know that a certain object has the form of a chair just by virtue of its being a chair at all, so too you know that a person's body is associated with the person's soul just by virtue of its being that person's body. The soul is present as long as the person's body is present, for that body just wouldn't be the body it is without the person's soul informing it. And, contrary to reductionist views, the person isn't reducible to some bundle of psychological or bodily characteristics. *Contra* Parfit in particular, there is indeed a "further fact," over and above one's having certain bodily and psychological traits, that constitutes being a person, just as there is a further fact over and above the existence of chair legs, a seat, and a back that constitutes a chair being a chair. It is that these various bodily and psychological traits are organized in just the way they are – that they involve a substantial form informing a certain kind of matter – that makes them a person, just as it is a chair's various components being organized in just the precise way they are that makes them into a chair.

Another consequence of the hylomorphic view is, arguably, that there is no mystery about how soul and body get into causal contact with one another, for the soul-body relationship is just one instance of a more general relationship existing everywhere in the natural world, namely, the relationship between forms – the form of a chair, the form of a tree, the form of an animal – and the matter they organize. If this general relationship is not particularly mysterious, neither is the specific case of the relationship between soul and body. The mistake of Cartesian dualists and materialists alike, according to the hylomorphist, is to think of all causation as efficient causation. When it is allowed that there are other irreducible modes of explanation – in particular, explanation in terms of formal causation – the interaction problem disappears.

Thomistic dualism

Aristotelians and Thomists (those philosophers whose views are derived from St. Thomas Aquinas) sometimes suggest that their hylomorphic position is no more a version of dualism than it is of materialism. But though their view is not a Cartesian form of dualism, it is clear from a consideration of how the human soul differs from the souls of plants and animals (at least on the Thomistic variation of hylomorphism) that the view does amount to a kind of dualism: *Thomistic dualism* or *hylomorphic dualism*, as it has variously been called.

For something to go out of existence is, in the hylomorphic view, for its matter to lose its form. The matter of a chair continues to exist when the chair is chopped into bits, but the chair itself doesn't, since its matter is no longer organized by the form of a chair. Since perishing involves such a separation of matter and form, forms themselves are not susceptible of perishing: a particular chair goes out of existence, but the form of a chair does not. Nevertheless, as noted already, hylomorphism, associated as it is with an Aristotelian-Thomistic conception of form, takes forms to exist in some sense "in" the material objects that instantiate them. As a corollary of this, the view holds that forms in general do not exist as concrete particular things; apart from their instantiation in matter, their reality is purely abstract. You can, after all, sit in a chair, but you can't sit in the form of a chair. While forms are, in a sense, imperishable by nature, the sort of imperishability they have just by virtue of being forms isn't very interesting. In particular, it isn't the sort that would justify believing that the souls of plants and animals are immortal. True, since the soul of a living thing is a kind of form, and forms are imperishable, there is a sense in which the souls of your favorite plant and of your loyal canine companion do not perish when these living things themselves perish. But they continue on only in the uninteresting sense in which the form of your favorite chair does not perish when the chair itself does. The form of the chair may continue to exist in an abstract way, but that particular chair itself is gone forever; similarly, the form of a fern or of Fido may continue on abstractly, but the fern and Fido themselves – that particular plant and that particular dog – are gone for good.

Things are very different where the rational soul – the substantial form of a human being – is concerned, at least according to the version of hylomorphism associated with Aquinas. (The proper interpretation of Aristotle's version is more controversial.) The forms of all other material things are utterly dependent on the matter that instantiates them for their operation: again, you cannot sit in the form of a chair, for a chair cannot function as a chair at all without there being matter to serve as its legs, seat, and back; or, to take an example involving the forms of living things, the digestion of a cheeseburger cannot occur without there being matter to constitute the stomach, chemical processes, and other elements involved in digestion. But the rational soul, uniquely in all of nature, does not fully depend on the matter that it informs for its operation. The evidence the Thomistic dualist would give for this claim would be arguments for the irreducibility of thought and intentionality to material processes of the sort considered in chapters 6 and 7. Thought, even when the rational soul is conjoined to a body so as to constitute a human person, does not depend entirely on that body or its processes, for the reasons examined in those chapters; it is, in Aquinas's view, not strictly speaking a bodily operation at all, but an immaterial one. But if the rational soul operates independently of the body, it cannot depend for its continued existence on the continued existence of the body. In short, the human soul, unlike the souls of plants and animals and unlike any form of any other kind, is a *subsistent* form: it is capable, in principle anyway, of continuing in existence as a particular thing after its separation from the body in death, and even after the destruction of that body.

It is important to emphasize that the human soul does not, in this view, continue on as a complete *person*, for a person exists only as a union of soul and body; it survives only as a kind of incomplete substance, incapable of performing all its functions, and in particular those associated with matter. If the person whose soul it is the soul of is ever to exist again as a whole person, the soul must be reunited with its body. This is the rationale for the traditional theological doctrine of the resurrection of the body, though the truth of such a doctrine is not something Aquinas would claim to be able to establish via purely philosophical argument: philosophy, in his view, can demonstrate at most the immateriality and immortality of the soul, and thus the possibility of resurrection; the actuality of resurrection presupposes the existence of God and the truth of an alleged divine revelation of God's intent to bring it about, and thus requires not only further philosophical argument, but the defense of a particular theological doctrine.

Those are matters beyond the scope of this book. Suffice it to note that, since the Thomistic hylomorphist takes the human soul to be something that operates independently of the body, and something which is capable in principle of surviving the destruction of the body, there is an obvious sense in which the doctrine is a form of dualism, however different from the Cartesian form, over which it seems to have a number of significant advantages. We have already noted two of them:

1. It suggests a possible solution to the interaction problem, thus undermining the most important objection to dualism.
2. It arguably solves the re-identification problem, since the connection between soul and body is so close that a body just wouldn't be the body it is without the presence of its soul. (By the same token, the soul wouldn't be the soul it is without having been conjoined to its body; for a soul is, in the hylomorphic view, necessarily always the soul of *the particular body* that it is, or was, the soul of.)

Related to these advantages are two others:

3. The view seems more consonant with the close dependence modern neuroscience has revealed many mental states to have on states of the brain. Cartesian dualism seems open to the objection, that, if the mind were as independent of the brain as the theory implies, then we shouldn't expect that brain damage could so severely impair mental functioning. But on the Thomistic view, the soul is (almost) as close to the body as the form of a chair is to the matter of the chair. Just as the form of a chair cannot function apart from the chair's matter, neither can the soul, for the most part anyway, function apart from the matter of the brain and body. So we should expect, on the Thomistic version of dualism, that damage to the body and brain would impair mental functioning. This is especially so given that, on the Thomistic form of dualism, sensation and perception are, unlike the higher intellectual mental operations, purely material processes which cannot exist or function independently of the body.
4. The Thomistic view also suggests a solution to the problem of other minds: since someone's body, according to hylomorphism, wouldn't be a body at all if it had no soul, and wouldn't be that

person's body in particular if it didn't have that person's soul, there is arguably no mystery about how we can know that a mind is present, even a specific mind, when a body is present. (For the same reason, the Thomistic view entails that zombies are not possible – though this wouldn't help the materialist, since zombies would be impossible on this view only because any creatures with bodies like ours would necessarily have to have immaterial souls like ours.)

There are other apparent advantages too. They are:

5. Thomistic dualism, if true, would undermine the materialist "duplication argument" discussed in chapter 3. If a person's living body was duplicated molecule for molecule, this wouldn't show that a person had no non-material components, for the duplicate wouldn't count as a living human body at all (much less as a human body capable of meaningful speech and the like) if it lacked a rational soul.

6. Thomistic dualism also seems immune to the materialist's argument that whatever is in time must also be in space, which poses a challenge to Descartes's claim that the soul is outside space but not time. For, in the hylomorphic view, forms – and thus souls – are in a sense "in" the matter they inform, so that a soul cannot be said to be utterly outside space after the manner of Cartesian immaterial substances.

7. Finally, Thomistic dualism seems better placed than Cartesian dualism to explain how the self could persist when unconscious. For Descartes, consciousness is of the essence of an immaterial substance; it thus becomes mysterious how such a substance, and the self it is identical with, could ever become unconscious (as we surely sometimes do). But in the Thomistic view, a soul, being the form of the body, doesn't cease to exist when the person it is the soul of becomes unconscious.

Given that some of the arguments discussed in this book seem to provide (at least significant) support for dualism, and that the foregoing considerations suggest that framing dualism in hylo-morphic terms has significant advantages over framing it in stand-ard Cartesian terms, it seems clear that a strong case could be made for Thomistic dualism. When we consider also that some kind of realism about form (whether Aristotelian or Platonic) is, as I sug-gested in chapter 3, as philosophically defensible today as it ever was, and in particular at least as defensible as any nominalist alter-native, it is clear that Thomistic dualism is well worth the con-sideration of contemporary philosophers of mind. Indeed, just as Aristotelian and Thomistic concepts in ethics have in recent years enjoyed a revival, so too does there appear to be a revival of serious attention to Aristotelian and Thomistic conceptions in meta-physics, as evidenced especially by the work of philosophers repre-sentative of the school of thought known as "analytical Thomism," some of whom – Elizabeth Anscombe, John Haldane, and James F. Ross – have been mentioned in the course of the last several chapters.

Philosophy of mind and the rest of philosophy

The obvious response the materialist could make to such a Thomistic approach is that it constitutes a very radical departure from the metaphysical assumptions made by most contemporary philosophers and informing the standard interpretation of modern science – a departure that raises as many questions as it answers. In order to defend it, one would need to present a detailed case for the general realism about form that, despite its long and distinguished history in Platonic and Aristotelian thinking, is rejected by many contemporary philosophers. One would also need to examine more carefully the contentious, and uniquely Thomistic idea, of a subsistent substantial form – the kind of substantial form which can somehow exist apart from the matter it typically informs, and which Aquinas takes the human soul to be. And one would need to show how modern science, whose founders rejected the notion of substantial form and allied concepts, could be reinterpreted along neo-Thomistic lines.

Without a doubt, this can only be regarded as a very ambitious and controversial approach to solving the mind-body problem. Nor would advocates of Thomistic dualism deny it. They would suggest, however, that *some* such ambitious departure from current assumptions is necessary if the mind-body problem is finally to be solved – and this sort of suggestion has, in the light of the difficulties facing the usual approaches to the problem, become very widespread in recent philosophy of mind (and not only among dualists and Thomists).

Philosophers who favor such a departure from current mainstream assumptions differ over the precise nature it ought to take. It is, from the point of view of Thomistic dualists, going to require not only a return to hylomorphism, but also to the incorporation of theism into our metaphysical picture of the world, for only an appeal to God's intervention can in their view adequately explain the origin of immaterial rational souls within the world of material beings. Some non-Thomistic dualists, such as the Cartesian dualist Richard Swinburne, would also endorse this appeal to theism. Atheistically inclined dualists like Karl Popper and David Chalmers would suggest instead that a revision of our concept of scientific method and/or of the basic laws of physics might be sufficient to account for the relationship between physical and non-physical reality. Still other philosophers advocate a reconsideration of idealism. And as we've seen, materialists have not been without radical proposals of their own – eliminative materialism being the most obvious example.

And yet, more mainstream materialists would reject all such proposals. They continue to insist that a more thorough application of current assumptions and methods will eventually vindicate their position. Clearly, the dispute between materialists and dualists over the nature of the mind ultimately cannot be settled conclusively without attention to broader issues – issues in metaphysics and epistemology, and perhaps even in philosophy of religion and philosophy of science.

These reflections reinforce a theme that was raised in chapter 3, and has recurred throughout the course of this book: that controversies in the philosophy of mind cannot be isolated from controversies in other areas of philosophy. Wilfrid Sellars famously wrote that "the traditional mind-body problem is … a veritable tangle of tangles. At first sight but one of the 'problems of philosophy,' it soon turns out, as one picks at it, to be nothing more nor less than the philosophical enterprise as a whole." If this book accomplishes nothing else, I trust that it will at least have established the truth, and the wisdom, of Sellars' observation.

Further reading

The most useful and up-to-date anthology of readings on the problem of personal identity is Raymond Martin and John Barresi, eds., *Personal Identity* (Oxford: Blackwell, 2003). Another recent anthology, emphasizing the relevance of the problem of personal identity to the possibility of life after death, is Kevin Corcoran, ed., *Soul, Body, and Survival: Essays on the Metaphysics of Human Persons* (Ithaca, NY: Cornell University Press, 2001). Parfit's position is developed at length in his influential *Reasons and Persons* (Oxford: Clarendon Press, 1984).

Hasker's reflections on the content of mechanism can be found in chapter 3 of *The Emergent Self*, which I have cited several times in earlier chapters. Fodor's famous remark is from p. 97 of *Psychosemantics*, which I cited in chapter 7. That the materialist's working conception of what is "physical" is ultimately determined by contrast with the mental is made evident in Levine's helpful discussion of the content of materialism in chapter 1 of *Purple Haze*, also cited earlier in this book. For further discussion of the difficulty of giving a useful definition of "materialism" or "physicalism," see Tim Crane and Hugh Mellor, "There Is No Question of Physicalism," in Paul K. Moser and J. D. Trout, eds. *Contemporary Materialism: A Reader* (London: Routledge, 1995).

A useful anthology of readings from Aquinas relevant to the philosophy of mind is Thomas Aquinas, *On Human Nature*, edited by Thomas S. Hibbs (Indianapolis: Hackett, 1999). Recent book-length studies include Anthony Kenny, *Aquinas on Mind* (London: Routledge, 1993) and Robert Pasnau, *Thomas Aquinas on Human Nature* (Cambridge: Cambridge University Press, 2002). Some useful short introductions are Norman Kretzmann, "Philosophy of mind" in Norman Kretzmann and Eleonore Stump, eds., *The Cambridge Companion to Aquinas* (Cambridge: Cambridge University Press, 1993), and the articles in part III of Anthony Kenny, ed., *Aquinas: A Collection of Critical Essays* (Garden City, NY: Anchor Books, 1969).

Two collections of articles representative of "analytical Thomism" are available: John Haldane, ed., *Mind, Metaphysics, and Value in the Thomistic and Analytical Traditions* (Notre Dame: University of Notre Dame Press, 2002); and *The Monist*, vol. 80, No. 4 (October 1997), a special issue on *Analytical Thomism* edited by Haldane. Articles exploring the application of Thomistic ideas to contemporary issues in the philosophy of mind include Haldane's "The Breakdown of Contemporary Philosophy of Mind," in the *Mind, Metaphysics, and Value* anthology; Haldane's "A Return to Form in the Philosophy of Mind," in David S. Oderberg, ed. *Form and Matter: Themes in Contemporary Metaphysics* (Oxford: Blackwell, 1999); Brian Leftow's "Souls Dipped in Dust" in the Corcoran anthology cited above; and David S. Oderberg's "Hylomorphic Dualism," cited at the end of the previous chapter. Book-length treatments include David Braine's *The Human Person: Animal and Spirit* (Notre Dame: University of

Notre Dame Press, 1992); Ric Machuga, *In Defense of the Soul* (Grand Rapids. MI: Brazos Press, 2002); and J. P. Moreland and Scott B. Rae, *Body and Soul* (Downers Grove, IL: InterVarsity Press, 2000).

Sellars' remark is from his introduction to his exchange with Chisholm in "Intentionality and the Mental," cited in chapter 7.

9
Postscript (2006)

The response to the first edition of *Philosophy of Mind* has been very gratifying. One of the features of the book that readers have appreciated most is its positive and detailed treatment of various non-materialist approaches to the mind–body problem, especially dualism and hylomorphism. I thought I would take the opportunity of this reissue of the book to add some further remarks intended to dispel certain misunderstandings of these views that the first edition perhaps did not adequately address.

Dualism versus materialism

There are several respects in which the dispute between dualism and materialism is widely misunderstood, certainly among non-philosophers but sometimes even among philosophers too.

One mistake philosophers seldom make, but which is very common among students and even educated laymen and researchers in academic fields outside philosophy, is to assume that the debate fundamentally hinges on the question of whether there is some aspect of our mental lives for which neuroscientists will never discover a correlated brain process. It is then assumed that the materialist side has the better of the argument, since neuroscience seems to be discovering more and more correlations between neural processes and mental phenomena every day. Discovering a neural correlate for every aspect of the mind thus seems to be merely a matter of time.

The fallacy here is to confuse *causal correlation* for either *identity* or *supervenience*. The mind-body problem has never fundamentally been about the former. Modern dualists have always acknowledged that there is a close correlation between neural processes and mental ones, and even when they have denied that the correlation is a causal one (as in occasionalism or parallelism) the reasons have had to do with certain philosophical theories about the nature of causation, not ignorance of neuroscience. The debate is rather about whether mental processes can plausibly be said to be either *identical* with neural processes or metaphysically *supervenient* upon them. Further discoveries in neuroscience are largely irrelevant to this question, for it is ultimately a philosophical one that requires philosophical analysis. To note that there is a causal correlation between smoke and fire does not show that smoke is identical with fire, or even that smoke metaphysically supervenes on fire or vice versa (since it is possible for one to exist without the other). By the same token, however close are the causal connections neuroscientists might find to hold between the mind and the brain, such correlations cannot, by themselves, establish identity or supervenience.

A related misunderstanding – and this time, one that even many philosophers are prone to – is to assume that dualism is to be understood as a kind of quasi-scientific "explanatory hypothesis," presented as an ostensibly more plausible way of accounting for the same data that materialist theories try to explain. It is then objected that qualia and intentionality are still problematic even if they are said to inhere in an immaterial rather than material substance, that "postulating" immaterial substances thus needlessly complicates our ontology, and so forth. Given Occam's razor, materialism is held to be the more scientifically respectable view.

I briefly touched on this misunderstanding in chapter 7, but I find that it is so widespread that I now think I should have said more. The problem with this characterization of the debate is that it fundamentally misconceives the nature of the key arguments for dualism, and subtly begs the question in favor of a scientistic conception of philosophy that is itself part of what is at issue in the dispute between materialists and their critics.

Descartes' arguments for immaterial substance, for example, are intended to be straightforward *demonstrations* of its existence. He is not "postulating" its existence as merely the most plausible way among others of "explaining" the "data" that both dualists and materialists seek to "account for." If anything, the existence of immaterial substance is for Descartes itself part of the data that any truly scientific picture of the world has to take into consideration. Something similar could be said of arguments purporting to show that qualia, rationality, and intentionality cannot be accounted for in materialistic terms. The aim of such arguments is *not* to suggest that dualism is a "better explanation" of such phenomena than materialism is. Their aim is rather to establish decisively that such phenomena *cannot possibly* be identical with or supervenient upon material properties, so that we must simply recognize immaterial properties as among the data with which any scientific picture of the world must deal. In short, dualistic arguments are more like (though of course not exactly like) the proofs of geometry than they are like the probabilistic hypotheses put forward in empirical science. One could, of course, try to show that they fail as proofs; but it is as proofs that they need to be evaluated, rather than as second-rate quasi-scientific hypotheses.

In general, dualists tend to reject the idea that empirical science is the paradigm of rational inquiry, so that philosophy, to be intellectually respectable, ought to model its methods of analysis and argumentation on those of empirical science. Such scientism, most famously associated with W. V. Quine, has become very widespread in contemporary philosophy, so widespread that many philosophers who are committed to it seem unaware of how deeply it has influenced their understanding of many traditional philosophical problems. Hence, they reflexively interpret rival philosophical positions (like dualism) as if they were attempts to formulate scientific hypotheses; or, if it is understood that they are not intended to be "scientific," it is assumed that this must mean that they are somehow irrational or indefensible. What such philosophers too often fail seriously to consider is the possibility that empirical science is simply not the only form of rational inquiry. Mathematics, of course, would be the paradigm of a form of inquiry that is both clearly rational and not plausibly empirical (as at least some philosophers otherwise committed to scientism would concede). For the dualist, metaphysics is another example, a form of inquiry that is every bit as rational as empirical science, but non-empirical. Dualistic arguments themselves could be appealed to in defense of this claim, for if they succeed, they provide genuine knowledge of a level of reality that is not material, and do so without resting on empirical observation or theory-construction of the sort familiar in science. Of course, one could try to refute this claim, but the point is that to do so one would also have to defend scientism, rather than simply presuppose it.

There is a useful analogy to be drawn here between the debate over the mind-body problem and the debate over the existence of God. The traditional arguments for God's existence are often assumed to be arguments for what has been called a "God of the gaps" – that is, a God whose role is to fill a current gap in our scientific knowledge by providing an explanation for some specific empirical phenomenon that empirical science has so far not yet explained. The objection is then made that such arguments are useless because it is only a matter of time before science provides some perfectly adequate naturalistic account of the phenomenon in question. But in fact the classical theistic arguments, and certainly the arguments of such major philosophical theologians as Anselm, Aquinas, and Leibniz, are not properly interpreted as "God of the gaps" arguments at all. They are not "hypotheses" or attempts to "postulate" a quasi-scientific explanation for particular phenomena that science has not yet accounted for, but which it could in principle account for someday. They are rather attempts conclusively to demonstrate the existence of a Necessary Being or First Cause of the world on the basis of premises (concerning the metaphysics of causation, say, or the contingency of the material world, or the concept of a greatest possible being) about which empirical science has nothing to tell us. The question of whether they succeed or fail as proofs is thus independent of the current state of our scientific knowledge.

Similarly, it seems that many of dualism's critics erroneously interpret it as positing a kind of "soul of the gaps," an ontologically extravagant means of remedying what are surely only temporary deficiencies in our understanding of the brain. Again, this is a mis-interpretation, and dualism stands or falls more or less independently of the current state of our scientific knowledge. In the final analysis, the debate between materialists and dualists, like the debate between atheists and theists, isn't a scientific debate, but a philosophical one. Indeed, it is if anything a debate over which overarching metaphysical framework the results of empirical science ought to be interpreted in light of. To be sure, it is a debate in which rational analysis and argumentation can and ought to be applied, but most of that analysis and argumentation must of necessity be philosophical rather than empirical in character.

It should also be noted, however, that notwithstanding the con-fusion of philosophical and scientific modes of argument that many criticisms of dualism rest on, there is at least one method that scientific and metaphysical inquiry have in common, namely the resort to (often fantastic) thought experiments. Yet for some reason many critics of dualism seem implicitly to want to deny the dualist precisely this one common methodological tool. No materialist would dream of criticizing Einstein for his bizarre "twin paradox," or scruple over Stephen Hawking's talk about what someone might see if he or she could watch a black hole being formed, despite the fact that in reality such a person would in that circumstance be torn apart and thus unable to see any-thing. Materialists would judge, quite rightly, that the practical impossibility of such scientific thought experiments is irrelevant, because their point is to teach us certain conceptual truths about the theories in question. But when a dualist philosopher appeals to the notion of a zombie, or a Cartesian demon, or whatever, some of the same materialists react as if odd thought experiments are out of bounds in respectable intellectual debate. It is hard to see what rational justification there could be for this double standard.

Functionalism and hylomorphism

What has been said about dualism applies also to hylomorphism, which is another metaphysical alternative to materialism rather than a kind of empirical hypothesis. Here too current scientific knowledge is less relevant than philosophical analysis and argumentation, since what the hylomorphist disagrees with the materialist about is not so much any empirical evidence or theory but rather what metaphysical interpretation to put on all empirical evidence and theories.

Oddly enough, though, I have found that while some people are hostile to hylomorphism because of its incompatibility with the naturalistic spirit of the times, others, in stark contrast, see in it little more than one more version of the most popular of naturalistic philosophies of mind, namely functionalism. The hylomorphist regards the soul as the form of the human body; the functionalist identifies the mind with the organizational structure of the brain. Aren't these mere variations on the same theme? Aren't the similarities more significant than the differences (such as the hylomorphist's emphasis on the entire body rather than just the brain – which is, as it happens, an emphasis even many contemporary functionalists have recently come to adopt)?

In fact the two theories couldn't be more dissimilar. It must be remembered that hylomorphism is part of a broadly Aristotelian metaphysics, which includes a commitment to the reality of formal and final causes as irreducible components of the natural world. This contrasts with the modern tendency to think only in terms of what Aristotle would call material and efficient causes (and even then in senses of these terms somewhat different from the Aristotelian ones). This is a tendency shared by contemporary functionalism. For the functionalist, the "organizational structure" of a thing is essentially just the pattern of efficient-causal relations its components bear to one another. But for the hylomorphist, the "form" of a thing is something very different, and entails a commitment to realism about universals (Aristotelian if not Platonic) that is no part of functionalism (and indeed would probably be rejected by most functionalists). In particular, a thing's form includes the specific set of properties (not just efficient-causal ones) that make it the thing it is. And in the case of a substantial form – the specific kind of form the hylomorphist identifies the soul with – it comprises an immutable essence that the thing having the form instantiates.

Aristotelian final causes are another key element of this picture. For the hylomorphist, there are objective purposes, goals, or ends in nature that cannot be reduced to patterns of efficient causation. This constitutes a flat rejection of the mechanistic model of the natural world that functionalists share with other materialists. Perhaps most crucially, functionalists would generally try to reduce intentionality to some pattern of efficient causal relations, whereas hylomorphists would regard intentionality as but one irreducible instance of finality or "goal-directedness" among others.

Finally, the specifically Thomistic version of hylomorphism I have described in this book is dualistic insofar as it regards the soul as a *subsistent* form, something which does not entirely depend on matter for its operations and which is capable of persisting in being beyond the death of the body of which it is the form. Obviously, this is something no contemporary functionalist would accept.

As acknowledged earlier in this book, a rejection of the modern mechanistic conception of the natural world in favor of a return to a broadly Aristotelian conception would be a fairly radical philosophical move. Any evaluation of such a move would have to consider carefully the reasons why early modern thinkers like Descartes, Locke, and their scientific contemporaries opted to abandon Aristotelianism for mechanism, and determine how philosophically sound those reasons were and are all things considered. These are matters dealt with to some extent in my forthcoming book *Locke*.

In any event (and as this book has also shown) the idea that a solution to the mind-body problem might call for a fairly radical overhaul of our general metaphysical picture of the world is by no means uncommon today. Dualistic and hylomorphist views in particular are attracting an increasing amount of attention, as evidenced by some of the citations in the "Further reading" sections of this book. In closing, I want to draw the reader's attention to several further important works. Peter Unger's *All the Power in the World* (Oxford: Oxford University Press, 2005), a rigorous defense of dualism, appeared after the first edition of the present work went to press, as did Joel B. Green and Stuart L. Palmer, eds., *In Search of the Soul* (Downers Grove, IL: InterVarsity Press, 2005). Geoffrey Madell's *Mind and Materialism* (Edinburgh: Edinburgh University Press, 1988) and John R. Smythies and John Beloff, eds., *The Case for Dualism* (Charlottesville, VA: University of Virginia Press, 1989) are two important pro-dualism works I neglected to mention in the first edition. Another book I should have mentioned is Edward Pols, *Mind Regained* (Ithaca: Cornell University Press, 1998), a work sympathetic to the Aristotelian view described above. A broadly Aristotelian-Thomistic metaphysical picture of the world is also endorsed by many of the contributors to Craig Paterson and Matthew S. Pugh, eds., *Analytical Thomism: Traditions in Dialogue* (Aldershot: Ashgate, 2006).

Glossary

Analytical Thomism

A philosophical school of thought devoted to applying the methods of contemporary analytic philosophy to problems and concepts derived from **Thomism** in particular and medieval philosophy in general, and to applying concepts and arguments derived from Thomism and medieval philosophy to issues in contemporary analytic philosophy.

Anomalous monism

Anomalous monism holds that all events, including mental events, are identical to physical events, but that there are no scientific laws correlating mental events and physical events, so that a type-type reduction of mental events to brain events is impossible. It is also sometimes referred to as the **token identity theory**.

Aristotelian realism

Aristotelian realism, like **Platonic realism**, takes **forms** (for example, the forms of tables, chairs, and animal and human bodies) to be in some sense real and irreducible to physical properties, but unlike Platonic realism it also holds that in general, forms exist in some sense only "in" the physical substances they inform.

Attribute

See **property**.

Background

Searle's technical term for the set of non-**intentional** capacities and ways of acting that in his view underlie all manifestations of **intentionality**.

Behaviorism

A philosophical theory which holds that for a creature to exhibit mental states or capacities is just for it to have certain behavioral dispositions. The theory is sometimes called "logical behaviorism" or "philosophical behaviorism" to distinguish it from behaviorism in psychology, which is the view that a scientific approach to the study of the mind ought to eschew inner states and processes and focus on outward behavior.

Biological naturalism

Searle's term for his view that mental phenomena are not ontologically reducible to physical processes in the brain but are nevertheless caused by and "realized in" the brain. It is often suggested that the view is essentially a variety of **property dualism**, though Searle himself regards it as an alternative to both dualism and materialism.

Biological/biosemantic theories

A biological or "biosemantic" theory of intentionality is one that attempts to explain the **intentional** content of a mental state in terms of the biological function served by that mental state.

Bodily continuity theory

A bodily continuity theory of **personal identity** holds that what makes a person A existing at one time identical with a person B existing at another time is that A and B are associated with the same **body**.

Body

According to both **Cartesian dualism** and classical **materialism**, the human body is a mechanical system no different in its essential nature and principles of operation from any other **physical** system. According to **hylomorphism** and **Thomistic dualism**, the body is an irreducible composite of **form** and **matter** inherently distinct in its nature from non-living physical systems, and its operations cannot ultimately be explained in entirely mechanical terms.

Cartesian dualism

The version of **dualism** associated with the philosopher René Descartes, namely a form of **substance dualism**.

Causal theories

A causal theory of mind is one that tries to explain some aspect of the mind by showing that it is reducible to or **supervenient** upon a certain kind of causal relation. For example, causal theories of **intentionality** attempt to show that a **mental** state's possessing intentionality amounts to its having certain causal relations to other mental states and/or to features of the external world.

Computational/representational theory of thought (CRTT)

The view that thoughts are best understood on the model of linguistic representations (for example, sentences) and that the transition from one thought to another is best understood on the model of the computational processes instantiated in modern digital computers. The CRTT is usually regarded as one possible way of developing **functionalism**.

Conceptual role theories

Conceptual role theories of **intentionality** attempt to show that the **intentional** content of any particular mental state can be explained in terms of its conceptual relations to other mental states.

Direct realism

Direct realism holds that in perceptual experience we are directly or immediately aware of an external world of **physical** objects existing independently of us. It is also sometimes known as "naïve realism" and is usually contrasted with **indirect realism**.

Dualism

Dualism holds that **mind** and **matter** are equally fundamental aspects of reality, neither reducible to the other. Two main versions are usually distinguished: *substance* dualism, which holds that there are two fundamental kinds of **substance**, namely **mental** substance and **physical** substance; and *property* dualism, which allows that there is only one fundamental kind of substance, namely physical substance, but holds that physical substance nevertheless has two fundamental kinds of **property**, namely, physical properties and mental properties. But **Thomistic dualism** would seem to be yet a third variety.

Eliminativism

A version of **materialism** according to which at least some, and maybe all, **mental** states and properties are, appearances notwithstanding, non-existent and ought to be eliminated entirely from a completed scientific account of human nature. This view is also sometimes referred to as "eliminative materialism."

Epiphenomenalism

The view that **physical** processes in the brain cause **mental** processes, but are not causally influenced in turn by those mental processes. It is usually classified as a form of **dualism**, though some versions of **materialism** also seem to entail it, given the **mental causation problem**.

Epistemology
The philosophical study of the nature, grounds, and scope of knowledge.

Folk psychology
A term philosophers and psychologists use to refer to our ordinary ways of describing and explaining human behavior in terms of beliefs, desires, thoughts, experiences, and the like. The idea is that this everyday way of speaking constitutes a kind of rudimentary quasi-scientific theory.

Form
The form of a thing is its organizational structure; something irreducible to the sum of its parts. **Platonic realism** about form holds it to exist completely independently of either the **mind** or the **material** world. **Aristotelian realism** takes it generally to exist in some sense only "in" the things it informs.

Functionalism
Functionalism holds that **mental** states and processes can be analyzed in terms of the causal relations they bear to those environmental influences on the body that typically generate them, to the behavioral tendencies they in turn tend to generate, and to the other mental states they are typically associated with. The specific set of causal relations a particular mental state bears to these other elements is commonly said to constitute its "functional role." (See also **multiple realizability** and **Universal Turing Machine**.)

Higher-order theory
A higher-order theory of consciousness is a theory that holds that what makes a **mental** state conscious is that it is the object of some other, higher-order mental state.

Hylomorphic dualism

See **Thomistic dualism**.

Hylomorphism

Hylomorphism holds that all **physical** substances are composites of **matter** and **form**, and that in the case of a living thing, its **soul** is to be identified with the form of its **body**.

Idealism

Idealism holds that all reality is fundamentally **mental** in nature, and in particular that the purportedly **physical** phenomena that seem, to common sense, to exist independently of any mind are, appearances notwithstanding, in some way reducible to mental phenomena.

Identity theory

The identity theory holds that **mental** states and processes are identical with states and processes of the brain and central nervous system – in short, that the mind is identical to the brain. It is usually regarded as a version of **materialism**, and thus is sometimes called "central state materialism." But it can also be interpreted instead in terms of **neutral monism**, and the version of the theory that results in this case is sometimes called the **Russellian identity theory**. A further distinction between versions of the theory is that between the **type identity theory** and the **token identity theory**.

Indirect realism

Indirect realism holds that in perceptual experience we are aware of an external world of **physical** objects existing independently of us, but only indirectly, via our direct awareness of perceptual representations of those external objects. It is also sometimes known as "causal realism" or "representative realism," and is usually contrasted with **direct realism**.

Instrumentalism

In the philosophy of mind, an instrumentalist theory is one that takes **mental** phenomena to be convenient fictions: like **eliminativism**, it holds that such phenomena do not really exist objectively, but unlike eliminativism it nevertheless regards them as indispensable parts of a useful vocabulary for explaining and predicting everyday human behavior.

Intentional

An intentional mental state is one that manifests **intentionality**.

Intentionalism

Intentionalism is the view that all **mental** states are ultimately intentional, in the philosophical sense of being manifestations of **intentionality**. (See also **representationalism**.)

Intentionality

Intentionality is that feature of mental states like beliefs, desires, and thoughts by virtue of which they are about, directed at, mean, or represent, something beyond themselves. (In the typical case anyway, though sometimes a mental state could be about, directed at, mean, or represent itself.)

Material

Material things are those composed of **matter**.

Materialism

Materialism holds that all reality is fundamentally **material** or **physical** in nature, and in particular that all **mental** phenomena are reducible to, or at least **supervenient** upon, physical phenomena. (See **naturalism** and **physicalism**.)

Matter

There is, perhaps surprisingly, no general agreement on the precise meaning of this term, crucial though it is to science and philosophy in general and to the **mind-body problem** in particular. For **hylomorphism**, matter is defined essentially in terms of its contrast with **form**, where form is just what gives matter its organizational structure. For some versions of **dualism** and **materialism**, matter tends to be defined instead in terms of its contrast with **mind**, where mind is understood as essentially involving consciousness and/or **intentionality** and matter as essentially involving neither. For other versions of these doctrines, matter is defined as whatever is characterized by the basic properties to be posited in a completed physics, though this definition seems unhelpful if it is allowed that a "completed physics" could take **mental** phenomena like consciousness and intentionality to be among the basic physical properties. Yet for some advocates of **structural realism**, such as certain defenders of the **Russellian identity theory**, the intrinsic nature of matter just is mental; while for other advocates of structural realism, we cannot know the intrinsic nature of matter. Given this variety of uses of "matter" and "material," the content and status of **materialism** seem far less clear than is usually assumed.

Mental

What is **mental** is just whatever is characteristic of the **mind**. The term is also commonly defined by way of contrast with what is **physical**, though it is controversial whether the mental and the physical are mutually exclusive categories.

Mental causation problem

The problem of explaining how the **intentionality** of **mental** states can possibly play any causal role in generating other mental states and behavior if mental states are, as **materialism** claims, reducible to or **supervenient** upon purely **physical** phenomena.

Metaphysical possibility/impossibility

What is metaphysically possible is just what is possible in at least one **possible world**. For example, a human being running a mile in ten seconds, while not physically possible, is metaphysically possible in the sense that there is a possible world where the laws of nature are different enough from the ones in the actual world that human beings are capable of such a feat. What is metaphysically impossible is what is not possible in any possible world. For example, drawing a round square is metaphysically impossible because it involves a contradiction, so that there is no coherently describable possible world wherein round squares exist. Metaphysical possibility/impossibility is often contrasted with **physical possibility/impossibility**.

Metaphysics
The philosophical study of the ultimate constitution and fundamental structure of reality.

Mind
On the most uncontroversial characterization, the **mind** is just the seat of such phenomena as thoughts and conscious experiences. Disagreement begins as soon as one tries to give a more precise definition. Some theorists take consciousness to be the feature most fundamental to mind, while others regard **intentionality** as more basic. **Dualism** takes mind to be essentially non-**physical**, and **substance dualism** takes it to constitute a distinct kind of **substance**, while **materialism** rejects both claims. Some theorists deny that the mind is any kind of substance at all, and take it instead to be nothing more than a bundle of mental **properties**. For **Cartesian dualism**, the mind is identical to the **soul**, while for **hylomorphism, mental** properties are only one aspect of the human soul, alongside such non-mental properties as the capacity for growth, digestion, reproduction, etc. Given the variety of ways in which the term "mind" is used (and the variety of ways the term "**matter**" is used), the **mind–body problem** can be very difficult to formulate in a clear, concise, and uncontroversial way.

Mind-body problem

The mind-body problem is the problem of explaining what the metaphysical relationship is between **mental** phenomena and **physical** phenomena. It is difficult to state the problem in a more precise way without seeming to beg the question in favor of some specific theory or other: for instance, to characterize it as the problem of explaining how immaterial mental substances can interact with the **body** seems to presuppose the truth of **dualism**; while to characterize it as the problem of explaining how mental processes are produced by physical processes in the brain seems to assume the truth of **materialism**.

Multiple realizability

Minds are claimed by **functionalism** to be "multiply realizable" in the sense that the causal relations associated with the having of **mental** states could be instantiated not only in the neural structure of the brain, but also in, for example, the very different biological make-up of an alien life form or the circuits of the artificial brain of a sophisticated enough robot.

Mysterianism

The view associated with McGinn, according to which there is a true and complete **naturalistic** explanation of consciousness and other **mental** phenomena, but one which the human **mind** is constitutionally incapable of grasping.

Naturalism/naturalistic

The term "naturalism" is sometimes used to refer to the view that the natural world is all that exists, and in particular that there is no supernatural reality of divine beings, **souls**, and the like (in which case it is roughly equivalent to "materialism"), and sometimes used to refer, somewhat less vaguely, to the view that only what can be understood via the methods of natural science can be said to exist. (See **materialism** and **physicalism**.)

Network

Searle's technical term for the complex set of interconnected **mental** states and processes in which our **intentionality** is primarily manifested.

Neutral monism

Neutral monism holds that there is (contrary to **dualism**) only one fundamental kind of reality, but also that that kind is (contrary to **idealism** and **materialism**) inherently neither **mental** nor **physical** in nature.

Nominalism

Adherents of nominalism, in opposition to both **Platonic realism** and **Aristotelian realism**, deny that there are any genuine universals, and also usually hold that there are no abstract objects of any sort (**forms**, numbers, propositions, etc.).

Occam's razor

A principle of scientific and philosophical reasoning according to which, all things being equal, a more parsimonious explanation is to be preferred to a more complex one.

Occasionalism

A version of **dualism** in which **mind** and **body** do not interact with one another, but appear to do so because God intervenes from moment to moment to ensure that a given **mental** event is followed by an appropriate bodily event, and vice versa.

Ontology

The ontology of a philosophical or scientific theory is the class of entities it recognizes as existing. For example, non-**physical** substances are part of the ontology of **Cartesian dualism**, but are excluded from the ontology of **materialism**.

Other minds problem

The problem of explaining how, based only on our observation of another person's **physical** attributes and behavior, we can be justified in believing that he or she has thoughts, experiences, and **mental** states in general.

Panpsychism

Panpsychism is the view that all of **physical** reality is in some way associated with **mental** properties like consciousness and/or **intentionality**. Some versions of panpsychism seem more or less identical to **idealism**, though other versions seem closer to **property dualism** or the **Russellian identity theory**.

Parallelism

A version of **dualism** in which **minds** and **bodies** do not interact with one another, but appear to do so because the operations of each have been pre-established by God to run in parallel.

Personal identity

The relation by virtue of which a person A existing at one time and a person B existing at another time are one and the same person.

Physical

Used sometimes as a synonym for **material**, and sometimes to refer to whatever is posited by, or governed by the laws of, physical science. Whether "material" should also be regarded as a synonym for "whatever is posited by, or governed by the laws of, physical science" is unclear. (See **matter**.)

Physical possibility/impossibility

What is physically possible is just what is possible given the laws of nature (of physics, chemistry, and the like) operative in the actual world, while that which is physically impossible is what is not possible, given those laws. It is physically possible for a human being to run a mile in ten minutes, for example, but physically impossible for a human being to run the same distance in ten seconds. Physical possibility/impossibility is often contrasted with **metaphysical possibility/impossibility**.

Physicalism

The term "physicalism" is sometimes used as a synonym for **materialism**, and sometimes used instead to refer to a specific version of materialism that holds that everything that exists is ultimately reducible to, or at least **supervenient** upon, the fundamental entities and properties postulated by physics. (See **materialism** and **naturalism**.)

Platonic realism

Platonic realism holds that abstract entities like propositions, numbers, universals and **forms** exist completely independently of either the **physical** world or the **mind**. It is usually contrasted with **Aristotelian realism** and **nominalism**.

Possible world

A possible world, in the philosophical sense, is a comprehensive and coherent description of some way that the world as a whole might have been. For example, in the actual world you are reading this book, but there is another possible world exactly like it except that you decided to take a nap instead. The idea of possible worlds provides one way of explaining the distinction between **physical possibility/impossibility** and **metaphysical possibility/impossibility**.

Property

A property is an attribute, quality, feature, or characteristic of a **substance**. For example, the redness and roundness of a red ball are properties of the ball.

Property dualism
See **dualism**.

Propositional attitudes
A propositional attitude is a **mental** state which involves taking a certain sort of stance toward a proposition. Believing, desiring, hoping, and fearing are the standard examples. In believing that Smith will win the election, for example, one takes a certain sort of stance toward the proposition that Smith will win the election, which is different from the sort of stance one takes when one merely hopes that Smith will win it, and different in still another way from the stance one takes when one fears that Smith will win it. Propositional attitudes are paradigm instances of mental states involving **intentionality**.

Psychological continuity theory
A psychological continuity theory of **personal identity** holds that what makes a person A existing at one time identical with a person B existing at another time is that A and B are linked by such psychological characteristics as memory and personality traits.

Qualia
Qualia are those aspects of a conscious experience in virtue of which there is something it is like to have the experience (for example, the smell of a rose or the way pain feels). They are commonly held to be directly accessible only from the first person point of view of the conscious subject, and also often held to be intrinsic in the sense of not being analyzable into more basic elements or relations. "Qualia" is the plural form of the singular "quale."

Representationalism
Representationalism is the view that **mental** states involving **qualia** are ultimately entirely representational in nature, in the sense that their possessing qualia is said to be reducible to their

being representations of a certain sort, where being a representation is understood to involve nothing more than having **intentionality**. Representationalism is thus a variety of **intentionalism**.

Rigid designator
A rigid designator is a linguistic expression that refers to the same thing in every **possible world**.

Russellian identity theory
A version of the **identity theory** associated with Bertrand Russell, which rejects the materialist metaphysics usually coupled with the mind-brain identity thesis and substitutes for it a variety of **neutral monism** (or, in some versions, a variety of **panpsychism**).

Skepticism
Skepticism, in the philosophical sense of the term, is the view that knowledge about some domain that common sense takes to be unproblematic is in fact impossible. For example, common sense holds that we know that there is a **physical** world existing outside our **minds**, but the philosophical skeptic holds that we do not, and cannot, really know this.

Solipsism
A solipsist is someone who believes that he or she is literally the only thing that exists, so that things that seem to exist independently (everyday **physical** objects, for example) are really just elements in the private world of his or her experience (like the objects one encounters in dreams or hallucinations).

Soul
In **Cartesian dualism**, the soul is a non-**physical** substance whose essence is to think, and which causally interacts with the

body, from which it is utterly distinct. On **Thomistic dualism**, a soul is the form of a living body, whether plant, animal, or human being; and in the case of the human soul (and it alone) it is associated with the powers of intellect and will, and has the capacity to continue to exist beyond the death of the body.

Structural realism

Structural realism is the view that natural science does not reveal to us the intrinsic or inner nature of the external **physical** world, but only its abstract causal structure.

Substance

A substance, in the metaphysical sense, is an independently existing thing, and is usually contrasted with a **property**, which typically exists as an attribute or characteristic of a substance. For example, a red ball is a substance, but the redness of it is a property.

Substance dualism

See **dualism**.

Substantial form

A substantial form, according to **hylomorphism**, is a **form** that makes a **substance** the distinct kind of substance that it is.

Supervenience/supervenient

One thing is said to supervene on (or be supervenient upon) another when there could not be a difference in the first without there being a corresponding difference in the second.

Thomism

A philosophical school of thought which derives its main doctrines, concepts, and methods from the work of St. Thomas Aquinas.

Thomistic dualism

A version of **dualism** derived from St. Thomas Aquinas, which regards the human **soul** neither as a distinct **substance**, à la **substance dualism**, nor as a bundle of non-**physical** properties, à la **property dualism**, but rather as the **substantial form** of the human **body**, à la **hylomorphism**. It also regards the human soul as being unique among the **forms** of **material** bodies in being subsistent, that is, capable of continuing in existence beyond the death of the body. The view is also sometimes known as "hylomorphic dualism."

Token identity theory

A version of the mind-brain **identity theory** which holds that it is not possible to identify each **mental** state type with a brain state type, and that the most the identity theorist can hope for is an identification of each particular mental state token (for example, the specific thought about the weather I'm having right now) with some particular brain state token or other (for example, the specific neural event occurring right now in a certain region of my brain). The theory is also known as **anomalous monism**, and is usually contrasted with the **type identity theory**.

Type identity theory

A version of the mind-brain **identity theory** which holds that it is possible to correlate and identify each type of **mental** event (for example, thinking about the weather) with a type of brain event (for example, neural activity of such-and-such a kind). It is usually contrasted with the **token identity theory**.

Universal Turing machine

A Turing machine is, to oversimplify, an abstract specification of a mechanical device capable of instantiating any algorithm and thereby carrying out any computation. The variety of **functionalism** that takes the **mind** to be a kind of Turing machine is sometimes referred to as "Turing machine functionalism."

Zombie

A "zombie," in the philosophical sense, is a creature behaviorally, organizationally, and physically identical to a normal human being down to the last particle, but which is nevertheless devoid of any conscious experiences whatsoever.

Index

Note: subheadings are listed in page order to help coherence of argument.